First World War
and Army of Occupation
War Diary
France, Belgium and Germany

37 DIVISION
112 Infantry Brigade
Royal Warwickshire Regiment
11th Battalion
30 July 1915 - 21 February 1918

WO95/2538/2

The Naval & Military Press Ltd
www.nmarchive.com
Published in association with The National Archives

Published by

The Naval & Military Press Ltd

Unit 10 Ridgewood Industrial Park,

Uckfield, East Sussex,

TN22 5QE England

Tel: +44 (0) 1825 749494

www.naval-military-press.com

www.nmarchive.com

This diary has been reprinted in facsimile from the original. Any imperfections are inevitably reproduced and the quality may fall short of modern type and cartographic standards.

© **Crown Copyright**
Images reproduced by permission of The National Archives, London, England, 2015.

Contents

Document type	Place/Title	Date From	Date To
Heading	WO95/2538/2		
Heading	37th Division 112th Infy Bde 11th Bn Roy. Warwicks. Aug 1915-Feb 1918		
Heading	11th Battn. The Royal Warwickshire Regiment. August (30.7.15 to 31.8.15) 1915		
Heading	War Diary Of 11th (Ser) Battalion Royal Warwickshire Regt. From July 30th 1915 To August 31st 1915		
War Diary	Windmill Hill	30/07/1915	30/07/1915
War Diary	Boulogne	01/08/1915	01/08/1915
War Diary	Zutkerque	01/08/1915	04/08/1915
War Diary	Arques	05/08/1915	05/08/1915
War Diary	Hazebrouck	06/08/1915	24/08/1915
War Diary	Godewaersvelde	25/08/1915	25/08/1915
War Diary	Amplier	26/08/1915	27/08/1915
War Diary	Hebuterne	28/08/1915	31/08/1915
Heading	112th Inf. Bde. 37th Div. 11th Battn. The Royal Warwickshire Regiment. September 1915		
Heading	War Diary Of 11th Service Battalion Royal Warwickshire Regt. From Sept 1st 1915 To Sept 30th 1915 Volume I No 2		
War Diary	Hebuterne	01/09/1915	04/09/1915
War Diary	St Amand	05/09/1915	05/09/1915
War Diary	Humbercamp	06/09/1915	08/09/1915
War Diary	Berles Au Bois	09/09/1915	12/09/1915
War Diary	Humbercamps	13/09/1915	15/09/1915
War Diary	Hannescamps	16/09/1915	27/09/1915
War Diary	Humbercamps	28/09/1915	30/09/1915
Miscellaneous	Appendix III		
Miscellaneous	11th (Service) Battalion Royal Warwickshire Regiment.	07/09/1915	07/09/1915
Heading	112th Inf. Bde. 37th Div. 11th Battn. The Royal Warwickshire Regiment. October 1915		
Heading	War Diary of 11th (Ser) Battalion Royal Warwickshire Regt. October 1st 1915 To October 31st 1915 Volume I No 3		
War Diary	Humbercamps	01/10/1915	09/10/1915
War Diary	Hannescamps	10/10/1915	21/10/1915
War Diary	St Amand	22/10/1915	28/10/1915
War Diary	Bienvillers	29/10/1915	31/10/1915
Heading	112th Inf. Bde. 37th Div. 11th Battn. The Royal Warwickshire Regiment. November 1915		
Heading	War Diary Of 11th (Ser) Bn. Royal Warwickshire Regiment From November 1st 1915 To November 30th 1915 Volume No 4		
War Diary	Bienvillers	01/11/1915	02/11/1915
War Diary	Hannescamps	03/11/1915	14/11/1915
War Diary	St Amand	15/11/1915	26/11/1915
War Diary	Hannescamps	27/11/1915	30/11/1915
Heading	112th Inf. Bde. 37th Div. 11th Battn. The Royal Warwickshire Regiment. December 1915		

Heading	War Diary Of 11th (Ser). Bn. Royal Warwickshire Regt. From 1st December 1915 To 31st December 1915 Volume I No V		
War Diary	Hannescamps	01/12/1915	08/12/1915
War Diary	St Amand	09/12/1915	20/12/1915
War Diary	Hannescamps	21/12/1915	31/12/1915
Heading	112th Brigade. 37th Division. 11th Battalion Royal Warwickshire Regiment January 1916		
Heading	11th Warwickshire Vol 6 Jan 16		
Heading	War Diary Of 11th (Ser) Bn Royal Warwickshire Regiment From 1st January 1916 To 31st January 1916 Volume 2 No. 1		
War Diary	Hannescamps	01/01/1916	01/01/1916
War Diary	St Amand	02/01/1916	13/01/1916
War Diary	Hannescamps	14/01/1916	25/01/1916
War Diary	St Amand	26/01/1916	31/01/1916
Heading	112th Brigade. 37th Division. 1/11th Royal Warwickshire Regiment February 1916		
Heading	11th Warwicks Vol 7		
Heading	War Diary Of 11th (S) Bn. Royal Warwickshire Regt. From 1st February 1916 To 29th February 1916 Volume II No 2		
War Diary	St Amand	01/02/1916	06/02/1916
War Diary	Hannescamps	07/02/1916	13/02/1916
War Diary	Humbercamps	14/02/1916	16/02/1916
War Diary	Berles Au Bois	17/02/1916	22/02/1916
War Diary	Humbercamps	23/02/1916	29/02/1916
Heading	112th Brigade. 37th Division. 1/11th Royal Warwickshire Regiment March 1916		
Heading	War Diary Of 11th (S) Bn. Royal Warwickshire Regiment From 1st March 1916 To 31st March 1916 Volume II No 3		
War Diary	Hannescamps	01/03/1916	06/03/1916
War Diary	Pommier	07/03/1916	08/03/1916
War Diary	Pommier	09/03/1916	09/03/1916
War Diary	Pommier	10/03/1916	12/03/1916
War Diary	Hannescamps	13/03/1916	18/03/1916
War Diary	St Amand	19/03/1916	26/03/1916
War Diary	Mondicourt	27/03/1916	31/03/1916
Heading	112th Brigade. 37th Division. 1/11th Royal Warwickshire Regiment April 1916		
Heading	War Diary Of 11th (S) Bn. Royal Warwickshire Rgt. From 1st April 1916 To 30th April 1916 Volume II No 4		
War Diary	Mondicourt	01/04/1916	09/04/1916
War Diary	Le Souich	10/04/1916	30/04/1916
Heading	112th Brigade. 37th Division. 1/11th Royal Warwickshire Regiment May 1916		
Heading	War Diary Of 11th (S) Bn. Royal Warwickshire Regt. From 1st May 1916 To 31st May 1916 Volume II No 5		
War Diary	Le Souich	01/05/1916	01/05/1916
War Diary	Humbercamps	02/05/1916	02/05/1916
War Diary	Hannescamps	03/05/1916	14/05/1916
War Diary	La Cauchie	15/05/1916	26/05/1916
War Diary	Hannescamps	26/05/1916	31/05/1916
Heading	1/11th Royal Warwickshire Regiment June 1916		

Heading	War Diary Of 11th (S) Battalion Royal Warwickshire Regiment From 1st June 1916 To 30th June 1916 Volume II No 6		
War Diary	Hannescamps	01/06/1916	06/06/1916
War Diary	La Cauchie	07/06/1916	18/06/1916
War Diary	Hannescamps	19/06/1916	30/06/1916
Heading	1/11th Battalion Royal Warwickshire Regiment July 1916		
War Diary	Hannescamps	01/07/1916	03/07/1916
War Diary	Bienvillers	04/07/1916	04/07/1916
War Diary	Halloy	04/07/1916	06/07/1916
War Diary	Mellincourt	06/07/1916	06/07/1916
War Diary	Albert	07/07/1916	08/07/1916
War Diary	Albert (Battle Of The Somme)	08/07/1916	09/07/1916
War Diary	Battle Of The Somme	09/07/1916	15/07/1916
War Diary	Puzieres		
War Diary	Battle Of The Somme	16/07/1916	16/07/1916
War Diary	Albert	17/07/1916	18/07/1916
War Diary	Bresle	19/07/1916	19/07/1916
War Diary	La Houssoye	20/07/1916	31/07/1916
Heading	112th Brigade. 34th Division Till 22nd. 37th Division From 22nd Aug. 1/11th Battalion The Royal Warwickshire Regiment August 1916		
War Diary	Becourt Wood	01/08/1916	06/08/1916
War Diary	Bazentin-Le-Pitit	07/08/1916	14/08/1916
War Diary	Mametz Wood	15/08/1916	15/08/1916
War Diary	Becourt Wood	16/08/1916	16/08/1916
War Diary	La Houssoye	17/08/1916	18/08/1916
War Diary	Longpre	18/08/1916	20/08/1916
War Diary	Neuf Berquin	21/08/1916	22/08/1916
War Diary	Bruay	23/08/1916	24/08/1916
War Diary	Mazin-Garbe	25/08/1916	25/08/1916
War Diary	14th BIS Loos	25/08/1916	31/08/1916
War Diary	Battle Of The Somme	07/07/1916	16/08/1916
Miscellaneous	A Form. Messages And Signals.	11/08/1916	11/08/1916
Miscellaneous	A Form. Messages And Signals.		
Miscellaneous	A Form. Messages And Signals.	11/08/1916	11/08/1916
Miscellaneous	11th Coy Warwick Regt.	12/08/1916	12/08/1916
Miscellaneous	Not To Be Taken Beyond Present Front Trenches	12/08/1916	12/08/1916
Miscellaneous	Headquarters 112th Inf Bde.	13/08/1916	13/08/1916
Miscellaneous	Action N. Of Bazentin Le Petit	13/08/1916	13/08/1916
Miscellaneous	Headquarters 112th Inf. Bde.	13/08/1916	13/08/1916
Heading	112th Brigade. 37th Division. 1/11th Royal Warwickshire Regiment September 1916		
Heading	War Diary Of 11th (S) Bn. Royal Warwickshire Regiment From 1st September 1916 To 30th September 1916 Volume II No 9		
War Diary	14 BIS Loos	01/09/1916	01/09/1916
War Diary	Mazingan	02/09/1916	02/09/1916
War Diary	La Comte	03/09/1916	18/09/1916
War Diary	Coupigny	19/09/1916	19/09/1916
War Diary	Bully Grenay	20/09/1916	24/09/1916
War Diary	Angres II Sector	25/09/1916	27/09/1916
War Diary	Angres II	27/09/1916	30/09/1916
Heading	112th Brigade. 37th Division. 1/11th Royal Warwickshire Regiment October 1916		

Heading	War Diary Of 11th (S) Bn Royal Warwickshire Regiment From 1st October 1916 To 31st October 1916 Volume II No 10			
War Diary	Angres II		01/10/1916	01/10/1916
War Diary	Fosse 10		02/10/1916	06/10/1916
War Diary	Angres II		07/10/1916	15/10/1916
War Diary	Fresnicourt		16/10/1916	16/10/1916
War Diary	Basus		17/10/1916	18/10/1916
War Diary	Neuville Au Cornet		19/10/1916	20/10/1916
War Diary	Bouret		21/10/1916	21/10/1916
War Diary	Longvevillette		22/10/1916	22/10/1916
War Diary	Sarton		23/10/1916	23/10/1916
War Diary	Mailly-Maillet		24/10/1916	25/10/1916
War Diary	Acheux		26/10/1916	30/10/1916
War Diary	Amplier		31/10/1916	31/10/1916
Heading	112th Brigade. 37th Division. 1/11th Battalion Royal Warwickshire Regiment November 1916			
Heading	War Diary Of 11th (S) Bn. Royal Warwickshire Regiment. From 1st November 1916 To 30th November 1916 Volume II No 11			
War Diary	Doullens		01/11/1916	12/11/1916
War Diary	Louvencourt		13/11/1916	13/11/1916
War Diary	Mailley-Mallet		14/11/1916	14/11/1916
War Diary	White City		14/11/1916	14/11/1916
War Diary	Minde Tx		15/11/1916	15/11/1916
War Diary	Beaucourt Tr		16/11/1916	17/11/1916
War Diary	Englebelmer		18/11/1916	18/11/1916
War Diary	Station Rd		18/11/1916	20/11/1916
War Diary	Redoubt Alley		21/11/1916	23/11/1916
War Diary	Station Rd		24/11/1916	24/11/1916
War Diary	Redoubt Alley		25/11/1916	26/11/1916
War Diary	Mailly-Maillet		27/11/1916	27/11/1916
War Diary	Louvencourt		28/11/1916	30/11/1916
Heading	112th Brigade 37th Division. 1/11th Royal Warwickshire Regiment December 1916			
Heading	War Diary Of 11th (Service) Battalion Royal Warwickshire Regiment. From 1st December 1916 To 31st December 1916 Volume II No XII			
War Diary	La Vicogne		01/12/1916	13/12/1916
War Diary	Beauval		14/12/1916	14/12/1916
War Diary	Fortel		15/12/1916	15/12/1916
War Diary	Blangerval		16/12/1916	16/12/1916
War Diary	Boyoval		17/12/1916	17/12/1916
War Diary	Westrehem		18/12/1916	20/12/1916
War Diary	Bethune		21/12/1916	22/12/1916
War Diary	Le Touret		23/12/1916	28/12/1916
War Diary	Ferme Du Bois Section (Right Sub-Section)			
War Diary	Ferme Du Bois (Right Sub-Section)		29/12/1916	31/12/1916
Heading	War Diary Of 11th (Service) Battalion. Royal Warwickshire Regiment From 1st January 1917 To 31st January 1917 Volume No. 1			
War Diary	Ferme Du Bois Right Sub Section		01/01/1917	03/01/1917
War Diary	Le Touret		04/01/1917	09/01/1917
War Diary	Ferme Du Bois Right Sub Section		10/01/1917	15/01/1917
War Diary	Le Touret		16/01/1917	21/01/1917
War Diary	Ferme Du Bois Right Sub-Section		22/01/1917	26/01/1917

War Diary	Le Touret	27/01/1917	27/01/1917
War Diary	'B' Area	28/01/1917	31/01/1917
Heading	War Diary Of 11th (Service) Battalion Royal Warwickshire Regiment From 1st February 1917 To 28th February 1917 Volume III No 2		
Miscellaneous	War Diary Febr 1917 Headquarters 112th Inf Brigade.	28/02/1917	28/02/1917
War Diary	B Area	01/02/1917	09/02/1917
War Diary	Petit Sains	10/02/1917	11/02/1917
War Diary	Maroc	12/02/1917	17/02/1917
War Diary	Loos (Rt Sub-Section)	18/02/1917	23/02/1917
War Diary	Les Brebis	24/02/1917	26/02/1917
War Diary	Loos (Rt Sub Section)	27/02/1917	28/02/1917
Heading	War Diary Of 11th (S) Bn. Royal Warwickshire Regiment From 1st March 1917 To 31st March 1917 Volume 20		
War Diary	Loos (Rt. Sub-Section)	01/03/1917	02/03/1917
War Diary	Les Brebis	03/03/1917	03/03/1917
War Diary	Bethune	04/03/1917	04/03/1917
War Diary	Robecq	05/03/1917	05/03/1917
War Diary	Allouagne	06/03/1917	06/03/1917
War Diary	Febvin Palfart	07/03/1917	08/03/1917
War Diary	Hestrus	09/03/1917	09/03/1917
War Diary	Canettemont	10/03/1917	31/03/1917
Heading	War Diary Of 11th (Service) Bn. Royal Warwickshire Regiment. From 1st April 1917 To 30th April 1917 Volume III No IV		
War Diary	Cannettemont	01/04/1917	04/04/1917
War Diary	Noyellette	05/04/1917	06/04/1917
War Diary	Montenescourt	07/04/1917	07/04/1917
War Diary	Warlus	08/04/1917	30/04/1917
Map			
Heading	War Diary Of 11th (S) Bn. Royal Warwickshire Regiment From 1st May 1917 To 31st May 1917 Volume III No V		
War Diary	Denier	01/05/1917	18/05/1917
War Diary	Goures	19/05/1917	19/05/1917
War Diary	Tilloy	20/05/1917	20/05/1917
War Diary	Trenches	21/05/1917	21/05/1917
War Diary	N.E.guemappe	21/05/1917	28/05/1917
War Diary	Achicourt	29/05/1917	31/05/1917
Heading	War Diary Of 11th (Service) Battalion Royal Warwickshire Regiment. From 1st June 1917 To 30th June 1917 Volume 3 No. 6		
War Diary	Duisans	01/06/1916	03/06/1916
War Diary	Izel-le-Hameau	04/06/1917	08/07/1917
War Diary	Coyecque	09/06/1917	25/06/1917
War Diary	Locre	26/06/1917	30/06/1917
Heading	War Diary Of 11th (Service) Battalion Royal Warwickshire Regiment. From 1st July 1917 To 31st July 1917 Volume 3 No 7		
War Diary		01/07/1917	01/07/1917
War Diary	Dranoutre	02/07/1917	11/07/1917
War Diary	Kemmel	12/07/1917	25/07/1917
War Diary	Kemmel Hill Camp	26/07/1917	26/07/1917
War Diary	Dranoutre	27/07/1917	31/07/1917
Miscellaneous	11th (Service) Battalion Royal Warwickshire Regiment.	06/07/1917	06/07/1917

Heading	War Diary 11th Warwicks Aug 1917 Vol 25		
Heading	War Diary Of 11th (Service) Battalion Royal Warwickshire Regt. From 1st August 1917 To 31st August 1917 Volume 3 No 8		
War Diary	Dranoutre	01/08/1917	02/08/1917
War Diary	Beaver Hall	03/08/1917	12/08/1917
War Diary	Onrret	12/08/1917	17/08/1917
War Diary	Rossignol Camp	18/08/1917	22/08/1917
War Diary	Field Line	23/08/1917	24/08/1917
War Diary	Support Line	25/08/1917	29/08/1917
War Diary	Rossignol Wood	30/08/1917	31/08/1917
Heading	War Diary Of 11th (S) Bn. Royal Warwickshire Regiment. From 1st September 1917 To 30th September 1917 Volume 3 No 9		
Heading	Rossignol Wood	01/09/1917	01/09/1917
War Diary	Bois Carre	02/09/1917	02/09/1917
War Diary	Trenches	03/09/1917	10/09/1917
War Diary	Mont Noir	11/09/1917	22/09/1917
War Diary	Trenches		
War Diary	Bulgar Wood	23/09/1917	23/09/1917
War Diary	Bulgar Wood Trenches	24/09/1917	29/09/1917
War Diary	Rosignal Wood	28/09/1917	28/09/1917
War Diary	N 9 b 2.9	29/09/1917	30/09/1917
Heading	War Diary Of 11th (Service) Battalion Royal Warwickshire Regiment From 1st October 1917 To 31st October 1917 Volume 3 No 10		
War Diary	N 9.b.2.9 Near Swan Seolor	01/10/1917	05/10/1917
War Diary	Tower Hamlets	06/10/1917	10/10/1917
War Diary	N 9.b.2.9 (Swan & Edgar) Noir	11/10/1917	12/10/1917
War Diary	Mont Noir	14/10/1917	16/10/1917
War Diary	N E Of Ypres	17/10/1917	22/10/1917
War Diary	Mont Noir	22/10/1917	26/10/1917
War Diary	Dranoutre	26/10/1917	31/10/1917
Heading	War Diary Of 11th (S) Bn. Royal Warwickshire Regiment From 1st November 1917 To 30th November 1917 Volume 3 No 11		
War Diary	Dranoutre	01/11/1917	30/11/1917
Heading	War Diary Of 11th (Service) Bn. Royal Warwickshire Regiment From 1st December 1917 To 31st December 1917 Vol 29		
War Diary	Curragh Camp	01/12/1917	04/12/1917
War Diary	Trenches White Chateau Sector	05/12/1917	14/12/1917
War Diary	Parrat Camp	15/12/1917	29/12/1917
War Diary	Bulgar & Bitter Wood		
War Diary	J 26.b.2.5 to J 32.a.3.3	30/12/1917	30/12/1917
War Diary	Trenches Bulgar-botter Wood Section	31/12/1917	31/12/1917
War Diary	Trenches	01/01/1918	01/01/1918
War Diary	Bulgar-bitter Wood Sector	01/01/1918	04/01/1918
War Diary	Spoil Bank	05/01/1918	10/01/1918
War Diary	Lynde	11/01/1918	20/01/1918
War Diary	Micmac Camp	21/01/1918	31/01/1918
Heading	War Diary Of 11th (S) Battalion Royal Warwickshire Regiment. From 1st February 1918 To 21st February 1918 Volume 4 No 2		
Miscellaneous	D A G G H Q 3rd Echelon	21/02/1918	21/02/1918
War Diary	Micmac Camp	01/02/1918	01/02/1918

War Diary	Dickebusch	02/02/1918	21/02/1918
Miscellaneous	Not For Visitors. Extracts From The Diary Of Brevet-Colonel C.S. Collison D.S.O. 11th Royal Warwickshire Regiment.		
Heading	Col Collision D S O 11th R Warwick 1915		
Miscellaneous			
Miscellaneous	Chapter VII (Extract). Hannescamps, Nov 7th 1915.	07/11/1915	07/11/1915
Miscellaneous	Appendices. Continuation Of Notes On Trench Warfare.	16/09/1915	16/09/1915
Miscellaneous	Trench Notes. (Part III).	18/09/1915	18/09/1915
Miscellaneous	Orders In The Event Of An Advance.		
Miscellaneous	Appendix IV. Normal Form Of Attack Of The Division On The Enemy Trenches On A Front Of 1,200 Yards		

W9QS/2538/2

37TH DIVISION
112TH INFY BDE

11TH BN ROY. WARWICKS.
AUG 1915 - FEB 1918

DISBANDED

112th Inf. Bde.
37th Div.

Battn. disembarked
Boulogne from
England 30.7.15.

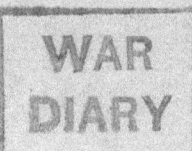

11th BATTN. THE ROYAL WARWICKSHIRE REGIMENT.

A U G U S T

(30.7.15 to 31.8.15)

1 9 1 5

Feb '18

Confidential.

War Diary

of

11th (Ser) Battalion, Royal Warwickshire Regt.

From July 30th 1915
To August 31st 1915.

Volume I.

Army Form C. 2118.

WAR DIARY
or
INTELLIGENCE SUMMARY.
(Erase heading not required.)

Regt 1   11th Service Battn Royal Warwickshire Regt

Instructions regarding War Diaries and Intelligence Summaries are contained in F. S. Regs., Part II. and the Staff Manual respectively. Title pages will be prepared in manuscript.

Place	Date	Hour	Summary of Events and Information	Remarks and references to Appendices
	1915			Appendix I Advance
WINDMILL HILL	July 30	1.30 AM	Advance party 3 officers 109 rank and file under Major C.P. ROOKE left LUDGERSHALL at 1.30 AM with orders from 112th B'de to proceed to HAVRE via SOUTHAMPTON.	Major C.P. ROOKE 2 Lt A.H. BOWDEN 2 Lt E.H. DAVIE
WINDMILL HILL	July 30	3.35 PM	Headquarters and A, B, C, D Coys under Lt Col C.S. COLLISON left LUDGERSHALL in two trains leaving LUDGERSHALL at 3.35 PM and 4.25 PM with orders to proceed to BOULOGNE via FOLKESTONE. 1st trainload consisting of 15 officers and 428 men and second trainload consisting of 12 officers and 418 men (see appendix I for list of officers). 1st train arrived FOLKESTONE at 8.45 PM and 2nd train at 9 PM. Both trainloads were embarked on S.S. ONWARD leaving FOLKESTONE at 9.30 PM and arriving at BOULOGNE at 11 PM. On arriving at BOULOGNE the battalion less the advance party marched to OSTEROVE rest camp where tents were supplied.	Appendix II Lt Col C.S. COLLISON Maj A.M. JONES 2ndy in comd Capt T.H. LLOYD Capt & Adjt J. FALVEY-BEYTS Capt E.H. BROCKSOPP Capt F.G. FLUX Capt W.T. HART Capt W.H. LOWE Capt E.L. ROUTH Lt A.V. MILLARD Lt A.H. BUNTING Lt F.R. REPTON Lt H.W.E. BARWELL Lt S.W.G. CHAMBERS 2 Lt A.C. HANDS 2 Lt A.A. GROSS 2 Lt A.H. BOWDEN 2 Lt J.K. JONES 2 Lt V.S. THAIN 2 Lt W.J. LITTLE 2 Lt D.J. ODELL 2 Lt E.E. JENKINS 2 Lt G. BROOKE 2 Lt N.F. GRAHAM 2 Lt A.E. BOUCHER & 5 SHEWRING Lt & Qr Mr A. HERBERT.
BOULOGNE	Aug 1	10.30 AM	The Battn less advanced party proceeded to PONT DE BRIQUES railway station where it entrained for an unknown destination. The advanced party was already on the train having been brought up from HAVRE the previous night. One casualty Pte	112 B
ZUTKERQUE	Aug 1	2.15 PM	At the station of AUDRUICQ the train was met by the Staff Captain 112th Brigade and the battn was ordered to detrain and march to ZUTKERQUE	

Army Form C. 2118.

WAR DIARY
or
INTELLIGENCE SUMMARY.

(Erase heading not required.)

Sheet 2   11th Service Battn Royal Warwickshire Regt

Place	Date 1915	Hour	Summary of Events and Information	Remarks and references to Appendices
ZUTKERQUE	Aug 1		On arrival at ZUTKERQUE the battalion was billeted.	933B
ZUTKERQUE	Aug 2		The battalion started out on a route march but owing to the incessant heavy rain returned to billets and the rest of day was spent under company arrangements.	933B
ZUTKERQUE	Aug 3		Battalion route march but again owing to incessant rain battalion returned to billets early	938B
ZUTKERQUE	Aug 4	1:15AM	Orders received to march on HAZEBROUCK. Battalion left ZUTKERQUE at 7:30AM reaching ARQUES at 5PM where it went into billets for the night	948B
ARQUES	Aug 5"		Battalion continued march leaving ARQUES at 7:30AM reaching HAZEBROUCK at 2.30 PM. The day was very hot and 25 men fell out on the march and were unable to march into HAZEBROUCK with the battalion. Twelve of these men rejoined later. Battalion went into billets at New Hospital HAZEBROUCK	948B
HAZEBROUCK	Aug 6"		Battalion rested, company commanders carried out inspection of kits, rifles, ammunition, smoke helmets etc.	937B
HAZEBROUCK	Aug 7"		Battalion Route march during morning, afternoon under company arrangements	950B

T2134. Wt. W708—776. 500000. 4/15. Sir J. C. & S.

Army Form C. 2118.

WAR DIARY
or
INTELLIGENCE SUMMARY.

Xeuie Botter
11th Royal Warwickshire Regt

Sheet 3

(Erase heading not required.)

Instructions regarding War Diaries and Intelligence Summaries are contained in F. S. Regs., Part II. and the Staff Manual respectively. Title pages will be prepared in manuscript.

Place	Date	Hour	Summary of Events and Information	Remarks and references to Appendices
	1915			
HAZEBROUCK	Aug 8		Battalion under company arrangements	
HAZEBROUCK	Aug 9		Battalion route march under Major Rooke to canal in BOIS CLEBER	9'B
HAZEBROUCK	Aug 10		Orders received to send a detachment to DRANOUTRE for digging parties. Accordingly A & C coys and no 8 Platoon B coy no 15 Platoon D coy, Medical Officer, Transport Officer and a proportion of the transport left HAZEBROUCK under the command of Major ROOKE at 6.55 AM and marched to DRANOUTRE where they encamped. The day was very hot and a number of men fell out on the march. They all rejoined later at	9'B 9.7-B 9.8-B
			DRANOUTRE.	
HAZEBROUCK	Aug 11		Work under company arrangements at Hd. qrs. Detachment report that work of improving trenches at S.E foot of KEMMEL HILL has been started	9.9.B
HAZEBROUCK	Aug 12		Detachment report enemy shell fire in no way affected the digging parties and the work on trenches continued	9.9.B
HAZEBROUCK	Aug 13		All available officers NCOs and men at headquarters attended a demonstration of the employment of Poisonous gas and the use of the smoke helmet. A trench 7 foot deep 18 wide and 80 feet long	9.7-B

Army Form C. 2118.

WAR DIARY
or
INTELLIGENCE SUMMARY.
(Erase heading not required.)

Sheet 4   11th Service Batt Royal

Place	Date	Hour	Summary of Events and Information	Remarks and references to Appendices
HAZEBROUCK	Aug 13		was filled with chlorine gas and smoke helmets having been adjusted all ranks walked through the trench, no ill effects being felt and the helmets proving a perfect protection against the gas.	9.7.15
HAZEBROUCK	Aug 14		OC detachment at DRANOUTRE reports that digging was interrupted by enemy shell fire but that there were no casualties. OC detachment ordered by 112th Brigade that in future all digging was to be done at night.	9.3.15
HAZEBROUCK	Aug 15		Nothing special to report.	9.7.15
HAZEBROUCK	Aug 16		Nothing worthy of report.	9.7.15
HAZEBROUCK	Aug 17		OC detachment reports the accidental discharge of a revolver, taken the bullet from which struck CSM STYLES in the forearm. CSM STYLES was removed to hospital, the medical officer reporting that the wound would incapacitate him for about 7 weeks.	
HAZEBROUCK	Aug 18		Nothing worthy of report.	9.7.15
HAZEBROUCK	Aug 19		2 Lt THAIN and Sgt HAMMOND proceed to CAESTRE to undergo a three days course of the employment of grenades.	9.8.5

Army Form C. 2118.

WAR DIARY
or
INTELLIGENCE SUMMARY.

(Erase heading not required.) 11th Service Battn Royal Warwickshire Regt

Abert 5

Place	Date	Hour	Summary of Events and Information	Remarks and references to Appendices
HAZEBROUCK	Aug 20		O.C. detachment at DRANOUTRE reports that no 8744 Pte RICHARDS has been wounded in the right shoulder by a shrapnel bullet. This is the first casualty in the Battalion caused by the enemy 1/RSR. Nothing worthy of report. 1/RSR	
HAZEBROUCK	Aug 21			
HAZEBROUCK	Aug 22		O.C. detachment at DRANOUTRE report no 2559 Pte CLARKE wounded in back by a splinter from shrapnel. A draft composed of 45 n.co.s & men from 12th Reserve battn 15 n.cos & men from 12th reserve battn and 4 men from 9th Battn arrived at HAZEBROUCK at 4PM and was taken on the strength of the Battn. 1/RSR	
HAZEBROUCK	Aug 23		Nothing worthy of report. 1/RSR	
HAZEBROUCK	Aug 24		Battn receives orders to march to GODEWAERSVELDE and remain there the night. The battn left HAZEBROUCK at 1.30 P.M and arrived at GODEWAERSVELDE at 3.30 Mand was met there by the DRANOUTRE detachment. Both bivouaced for the night on SE side of GODESVELDE near MONT DES CATS. 1/RSR	
GODEWAERSVELDE	Aug 25		Battn entrained at 7.53 P.M orders having been received that it was intended to proceed to MONDICOURT and that the train would arrive at 1.55 A.M. 1/RSR	

Army Form C. 2118.

WAR DIARY
or
INTELLIGENCE SUMMARY.

(Erase heading not required.)

Sheet 6   11th Service Battn Royal (1) Cumberland Regt

Place	Date	Hour	Summary of Events and Information	Remarks and references to Appendices
AMPLIER	Aug 26		On train arriving at DOULLENS battn was ordered to detrain and moved to AMPLIER and bivouac for the night.	A.F. B-53
AMPLIER	Aug 27		Orders received that battn is to proceed to HEBUTERNE leaving AMPLIER at 7AM Aug 27th.	A.F.B-53
AMPLIER	Aug 27		Battn left AMPLIER at 7AM at COIGNEUX ± 10AM the battn was met by DAAG 48th Divn (to which the battn is attached for instructions) and ordered to bivouac for the day and move on in the evening and attached to HEBUTERNE when the battn is to be split up and attached to the 145th Brigade for trench instruction. In the evening at 6.30 PM battn moved to HEBUTERNE and was met at SAILLY AU BOIS by guides from the battalions to which it is to be attached. Headquarters being attached to Headquarters 1st BUCK'S Battn. A coy and 13·14 platoons attached to 1st BUCK'S battn. B coy and 15 and 16 platoons attached to 1/4th BERKS battn and C coy attached to 1/5th GLOUCESTER Battn. Machine gun section placed under orders of 145th Brigade machine gun officer. Transport attached 4/36	

Army Form C. 2118.

WAR DIARY
or
INTELLIGENCE SUMMARY.
(Erase heading not required.) 11th Service Bn. Royal Warwickshire Regt

Sheet 7

Place	Date	Hour	Summary of Events and Information	Remarks and references to Appendices
HEBUTERNE	Aug 28		to transport of 1/1 BUCKS bttn and left at COIGNEUX. Companies receive instruction in trench work from the companies of the battalions to which they are attached.	App.
HEBUTERNE	Aug 29		Companies continue their instruction the men taking great interest in their work and working well at everything they are set to do.	App.
HEBUTERNE	Aug 30		Instruction in trench work continued. No 8603 Pte CHILES was hit in leg by shrapnel bullet while drawing water in HEBUTERNE village	App.
HEBUTERNE	Aug 31		Instruction in trench work continued	App.

J. Olney-Beets
CAPTAIN.
ADJ. 11th SERVICE BN. R. WARWICKSHIRE REGT.

112th Inf.Bde.
37th Div.

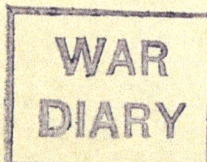

11th BATTN. THE ROYAL WARWICKSHIRE REGIMENT.

S E P T E M B E R

1 9 1 5

Attached:
Appendix III.

Confidential

War Diary
of
11th (Service) Battalion, Royal Warwickshire Regt.

From Sept. 1st 1915
To Sept. 30th 1915

Volume I.   No. 2.

Army Form 2118.

WAR DIARY
or
INTELLIGENCE SUMMARY.

(Erase heading not required.) 11th Service Battn Royal Warwickshire Regt

Sheet 8

Instructions regarding War Diaries and Intelligence Summaries are contained in F.S. Regs., Part II. and the Staff Manual respectively. Title pages will be prepared in manuscript.

Place	Date 1910	Hour	Summary of Events and Information	Remarks and references to Appendices
HEBUTERNE	Sept 1		Trench Instruction with 1st BUCKS Battn continued.	
HEBUTERNE	Sept 2		Trench Instruction continued	
HEBUTERNE.	Sept 3		Trench Instruction continued. Capt FLUX detailed to proceed to ROUEN BASE on Sept 4th. Sgt BILSON D Coy to accompany him. Orders received that they are to do one months duty training reinforcements. At 5.5 AM No. Pte LIVESAY M.G. machine gunner accidentally discharged his rifle and blew off his left thumb. G.J.B.	
HEBUTERNE	Sept 4		B. attached continued trench instruction until 6 PM. At 7 PM on orders received from 145th Brigade, Battn marched out of HEBUTERNE by platoons, assembled at SAILLY AU BOIS and marched to ST AMAND when it was bivouaced for the night, receiving orders to march to HUMBERCAMP under battn arrangements and to clear the village of ST AMAND by 10.30 AM. Sept 5th	
ST AMAND.	Sept 5		Battn marched out of ST AMAND at 10 AM and arrived at HUMBERCAMP at 10.40 AM where battn was billeted,	
HUMBERCAMP	Sept 6		A conference of all officers was held at 9 AM with a view to discussing	

WAR DIARY
or
INTELLIGENCE SUMMARY.

(Erase heading not required.) 11th Service Battalion Royal Warwickshire Regiment

Army Form C. 2118.

Sheet 9

Place	Date	Hour	Summary of Events and Information	Remarks and references to Appendices
	1915			
HUMBERCAMP	Sept 6		The experiences and suggestions of officers as to the organisation of the Battn, companies, platoons, sections etc for trench warfare. As a result of this conference a number of Battalion standing orders for trench work were formulated, a copy of these are attached (see appendix III).	Appendix III (attached)
			The day was employed by the men in the cleaning of kits, rifles etc etc.	f J B.
HUMBERCAMP	Sept 7		Battn (as strong as possible) made a circular route march of 10 miles via GUDIEMPRE – HENU – COUIN – SOUASTRE – ST AMAND.	f J B. Appendix IV
HUMBERCAMP	Sept 8		Battn ordered to proceed to BERLES AU BOIS for digging duties with 110th Infy Brigade. Details (see Appendix IV) being left at HUMBERCAMP under command of Major C.P. ROOKE. Battn arrived at BERLES AU BOIS at 4.30 PM, was placed in the billets of 6th LEICESTERSHIRE REGT (at that time in the trenches) and at 8 PM marched off 600 strong as a digging party. Work on a new communication trench was carried out until 3 AM. The work was carried out at a distance of	f J B. A signaller Transport Machine gun section Reserve Machine gun section 2nd Reserve Machine gun section & grenadiers
	Sept 5		300 yards from the enemy, who maintained an intermittent fire rifle fire all night. This was the first time that the Battn as a whole was under	
	Sept 4		rifle fire in the open and the behaviour of all ranks left nothing to be desired.	f J B.

Army Form C. 2118.

WAR DIARY
or
INTELLIGENCE SUMMARY.
(Erase heading not required.) 11th Service Battn Royal Warwickshire Regt.

Sheet 10

Place	Date	Hour	Summary of Events and Information	Remarks and references to Appendices
	1915			
BERLES AU BOIS	Sept 9		Battn rested in billets all day and at 8 PM marched off and worked until 2 AM on "fatters" to the communication trenches occupied by the 8th Leicester Regiment, after which it returned to billets in BERLES AU BOIS	J 7-13
BERLES AU BOIS	Sept 10		Battn rested in billets and continued the work on the trenches at the same hours as on Sept 9th	J 7-13
BERLES AU BOIS	Sept 11		Battn rested by day and worked on the trenches at night from 8th 9th and 10th	J 7-13
BERLES AU BOIS	Sept 12		Battn rested by day at BERLES AU BOIS and at 6 PM returned to HUMBERCAMP	J 7-13
HUMBERCAMPS	Sept 13		Battn rested day being spent in cleaning huts etc.	J 7-13
HUMBERCAMPS	Sept 14		Battn worked under company arrangements on 15th Battn ordered to proceed to take over trenches occupied by 13 Royal Fusiliers at HANNES CAMP. Advance party sent to HANNESCAMP to learn geography of trenches	J 7-13
HUMBERCAMPS	Sept 15		at 6.15 PM Battn marched out of HUMBERCAMPS arriving at HANNESCAMPS at 8 PM. Owing to inadequate arrangements of guides being made by 13th Royal Fusiliers it was not until 1.15 AM that the battn was finally settled in the trenches supporting points and billets.	J 7-13
HANNESCAMPS	Sept 16		A number of shells from German batteries in LES ESSARTS wood	J 7-13

WAR DIARY or INTELLIGENCE SUMMARY

Army Form 2118.

(1st Service South Royal Warwickshire Regt. 8)
Sheet II

Place	Date	Hour	Summary of Events and Information	Remarks and references to Appendices
HANNESCAMPS	1915 Sept 16		wood fell in HANNESCAMPS village. Major C.P. ROOKE was wounded by one of those and had to be taken away. Lg. Corp Woodward 1715 was accidentally killed by a rifle shot	g.7-13
HANNESCAMPS	Sept 17		Ambulance fire from a man, more or less taken over in a dirty condition and all available men were put on to clean up and bury all refuse. 2nd Lt BARWELL made a reconnaissance of the german line opposite trench 77.	g.30
HANNESCAMPS	Sept 18		Situation normal.	g.3B
HANNESCAMPS	Sept 19		Situation normal. 2nd Lt JENKINS accidentally wounded, seeming to be slipping and falling on to a sentry's bayonet when returning to the fire trench after examining the wire.	g.7-13
HANNESCAMPS	Sept 20		From 3PM to 5PM trenches 75-77 were shelled intermittently by german from direction of ESSARTS – no damage done. 2nd Lt THAIN made a useful reconnaissance of german trenches on the south of the MONCHY ROAD.	g.7-13
HANNESCAMPS	Sept 21		Situation normal. A and D coys were relieved by B and C coys respectively.	g.7-13
HANNESCAMPS	Sept 22		Situation normal.	g.7-13
HANNESCAMPS	Sept 23		Enemy aeroplanes active between 7 and 8 AM. 5 german shells burst to the rear of trenches 76-77 held by C coy. No damage done.	g.30

Army Form C. 2118.

WAR DIARY
or
INTELLIGENCE SUMMARY.

(Erase heading not required.) 11th Service Battalion Royal Warwickshire Regt

Sheet 12

Place	Date	Hour	Summary of Events and Information	Remarks and references to Appendices
	1915			
HANNESCAMPS	Sept 24		German howitzers dropped a number of shells in trenches 71-73 between 5 and 6 PM at 11914 St Hedges was killed and 8 men were wounded. The damage to trenches was not considerable, most of the casualties occurring owing to a shell penetrating one of the machine gun section's dug-outs. Our Artillery opened a very heavy fire on enemy's wire near E 55 A 47 5 and caused considerable damage. We were ordered to keep up an intermittent rifle fire in order to prevent the Germans from repairing the gaps made in their wire.	
HANNESCAMPS	Sept 25		Our artillery active and a great number of shells could be seen bursting over ADINFER WOOD. Reports received that our 1st Army had attacked the Germans in the north and made considerable progress.	J.3.3
HANNESCAMPS	Sept 26		A number of German Howitzer shells fell to the rear of trench 77 about 8.15 A.M. A considerable amount of rifle fire by LEICESTER BATTN on our left about 11:30PM several rifle grenades were fired from German trenches on the route of MONCHY ROAD and landed in trench 77.	J.3.63
HANNESCAMPS	Sept 27		Battn relieved by 13th Royal Fusiliers. Relief complete by 8 PM. Battn marched back to billets in HUMBERCAMPS by companies.	J.3.63

Army Form C. 2118.

WAR DIARY
or
INTELLIGENCE SUMMARY.
(Erase heading not required.) 11th Service Batt'n Royal Warwickshire Regt

Instructions regarding War Diaries and Intelligence Summaries are contained in F. S. Regs., Part II. and the Staff Manual respectively. Title pages will be prepared in manuscript. **Sheet 13**

Place	Date	Hour	Summary of Events and Information	Remarks and references to Appendices
	1915			
HUMBERCAMPS	Sept 28		Batt'n rested. Day spent in cleaning up kit equipment etc.	
HUMBERCAMPS	Sept 29		Batt'n found two digging parties of 100 men each for work on village defences of ST AMAND.	J3-8
HUMBERCAMPS	Sept 30		200 men again found for the ST AMAND defences. This batt'n had the use of the 37th Divisional Baths at PAS. The baths were found to be very good and were much appreciated by the men.	J3-9
			J. T. Alney - Bayet Captain. Adjutant	
			11th Service Batt'n Royal Warwickshire Regt	

APPENDIX III.

11th (Service) Battalion ROYAL WARWICKSHIRE REGIMENT.

NOTES on TRENCH WARFARE (PART I).

Should it be necessary to alter, or add to, these Notes, such alterations or additions will be notified to all concerned.

....

1. DISCIPLINE.

(a) The strictest discipline must be maintained, and this state of discipline will be shown by the cleanliness of the trenches, the care of arms, the alertness of the sentries and the general order and regularity prevailing.

(b) Whenever possible the men should SHAVE: the Company Commanders will use his discretion in giving orders to this effect.

(c) No salutes or compliments are to be paid by men on duty in the FIRE Trenches.

(d) Cap-comforters may be worn when off duty in the dug-outs. They are never to be worn in the fire-trenches, or when on duty (but see para:3(d)).

2. RELIEVING COMPANIES IN THE TRENCHES.

The procedure should be as follows:-

(a) THE RELIEVING COMPANY COMMANDER should proceed to the Company Headquarters of the Company to be relieved in sufficient time to enable him to make himself acquainted with the general lie of the trenches and of the duties to be taken over. In taking over a new line of trenches this time might be as much as 24 hours. A representative of each Platoon should accompany him.

(b) From this centre the Company Commander in consultation with the Company Commander whom he relieves issues written orders to his Platoon Commanders as to the route by which their Platoons are to arrive, and the route to be followed by the outgoing Platoons, after relief.

(c) THE RELIEVING PLATOON Commander will send a N.C.O. ahead to notify the Platoon Commander to be relieved of the time of his own Platoon's arrival in the trenches. (In order to avoid congestion in the trenches it is advisable that the PLATOON TO BE RELIEVED, except the Sentries on duty, should be in the Dug-outs when the Relieving Platoon arrives).

(d) THE RELIEVING PLATOON then lines the fire Trench and relieves the Sentries there posted. After which it proceeds to its Dug-outs, or to its pre-arranged Stations (but see para.7(b)).

(e) When the relief has been effected the Platoon Commanders concerned inform their respective Company Commanders of the fact, and the latter inform their Battalion Headquarters accordingly.

(f) So far as possible absolute SILENCE should be observed during this and on all other relieving duties.

3. SENTRIES.
(a) BY NIGHT Sentries will fix bayonets and will neither sling nor place their rifles on, or against, the parapets.
   BY DAY, bayonets will not be fixed (except by order), and the rifle may be slung over the shoulder, not round the back, when looking through the periscope.

(b) The rifles of SENTRY GROUPS may be placed in the slots made for them in the Bay, but should any man of the Group leave the Bay, for any purpose, he must take his rifle with him.

(c) Only an Officer or N.C.O. on duty is allowed to talk to a Sentry, and only then on matters connected with his (the Sentry's) duty. Sentries are not to take their eyes from their front, or from the periscope, whether spoken to, or not.

(d) SENTRIES WILL ALWAYS WEAR CAPS. Other men of the Group may wear Cap-comforters when resting in the Bay.

(e) On no account are Sentries to place their waterproof sheets over their heads, as a protection from rain, or for any other reason.

4. THE SENTRY GROUP SYSTEM.

(a) The Single Group system should be adopted wherever possible, but it it within the discretion of Company Commanders to adopt the double group system if they think it desirable.

(b) In a group of either three or six men the following duty roster should be adopted and in the following order of tours of duty:-
   (i) Sentry duty.
   (ii) Work, where necessary.
   (iii) Rest.

(c) N.C.Os in charge of Sentry Groups should carry Field Glasses.

5. PATROLS.

(a) Patrols are only to be sent out on an order from Battalion Headquarters and should always be given a definite object. Should a Company Commander wish to send out a Patrol he should notify Battalion Headquarters.

(b) The Strength of the Patrol, its hour of departure and probable hour of return will be notified to Companies.

(c) As the presence of a friendly patrol in front of the line may cause a total cessation of fire for a considerable time and so arouse the enemy's suspicions, occasional shots, at a safe elevation, may be fired at the discretion of Platoon Commanders on duty in the Fire Trench.

6. COMMUNICATION.

(a) Company Commanders are responsible for initiating and maintaining as efficient a means of communication as possible between the Fire Trench, Platoon Centres, and themselves. They must remember that the telephone system may fail at any moment and that reliance upon it, and upon anything but a well thought-out system of orderlies may be fatal.

(b) If a gap exists between two trenches bridged only by a Communication trench, Visiting Patrols must be used for keeping touch between them

7. ACTION IN CASE OF ATTACK.

(a) In case of attack the Company Commander will remain in his dug-out. It is only from there that he can properly control the action. Should he at any time leave his dug-out (either in case of attack or otherwise) he must leave a representative with information as to his position and his probable time of return.

(b) If there are no dug-outs in the Fire Trench, the First Line troops will occupy that Trench all night.

(c) If possible Dug-outs should have two entrances and should have short lengths of trenches communicating with the fire-trench. Both these means will greatly facilitate a rapid reinforcement of the latter.

8. RIFLES and EQUIPMENT.

(a) Arms must be examined at least twice a day. Too much attention cannot be given to this matter, and men who allow their rifles to remain in a dirty condition should invariably be brought before the Commanding Officer for disposal.

(b) Every Officer, N.C.O. or Man is to wear his equipment whilst on duty in the trenches and must be armed. Packs are not to be worn.

(c) Officers will wear the same equipment as the men but will carry revolvers and not rifles.

9. AMMUNITION.

(a) On taking over a line of trenches Platoons will be given ammunition from the Trench Stores, in bandoliers. The ammunition in the pouches must be considered as a reserve supply and is not to be used until the other is exhausted.

(b) Each Platoon will detail a N.C.O. to examine the ammunition in the BROKEN boxes and see that it is in good condition and oiled.

(c) The ammunition marked K, KL, and KN is the most suitable for rapid fire and should be ear-marked for use as a reserve, or in an emergency.

(d) Spare ammunition should be kept in at least every other Bay.

10. LISTENING POSTS.

(a) Two sentries should always be on duty in each sentry post, the remainder of the group lying down near them.

(b) The men in the adjacent Fire Trenches must be warned to be particularly careful to keep very quiet.

11. BOMBS.

Reserves of bombs and grenades should be kept on each Platoon front in charge of the Grenade N.C.O., under the Platoon Commander.

12. PARAPETS.

(a) It is very necessary to ensure that individual men are able to fire over that part of the parapet allotted to them. It is better to have a lower parapet throughout than to run the risk of small men not being able to direct an effective fire to their front. One or two sandbags can be kept in every Bay for use as steps for these men.

(b) Experience has shown that the crest of the parapet is better adapted for concealment if it is IRREGULAR in shape.

(c) When strengthening the parapet with Sandbags the seams of the bags should always be inside.

(d) The order recommended is 2 stretchers, then a header, and so on.

13. TRENCH STORES.

(a) Trench Stores should not, as a rule, be kept in one place. It is better to distribute them equally in Platoon Centres.

(b) "Very" pistols should be supplied in the proportion of 1 per Platoon.

14. WIRING PARTIES.

Company Commanders must be careful to warn the Companies on their right and left when they have parties repairing the wire in their front.

15. RATIONS.

(a) Ration Parties should be provided from the support or reserve trenches. They should also take back the empty dixies. On no account should these duties be performed by the men in the Fire trenches.

(b) The Rations should be taken to the dug-outs and there issued. Men must not be allowed to collect in a Communication or fire trench for this issue. The rations for the Sentries must be taken to them.

16. TRENCH DUTY ROSTER.

An ordered system of reliefs within the Trenches is being arranged and will be issued.

(Signed) C.S.Collison, Lieut.Colonel,
Commanding 11th (Service) Bn
Royal Warwickshire Regiment.

7th September 1915.

112th Inf.Bde.
37th Div.

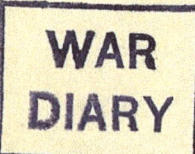

11th BATTN. THE ROYAL WARWICKSHIRE REGIMENT.

O C T O B E R

1 9 1 5

Confidential.

War Diary
of

11th (Ser) Battalion, Royal Warwickshire Regt.

From October 1st 1915 To October 31st 1915

(Volume I No 3.)

Army Form C. 2118.

WAR DIARY
or
INTELLIGENCE SUMMARY.
(Erase heading not required.) 11th Service Battalion Royal Warwickshire Regt

Instructions regarding War Diaries and Intelligence Summaries are contained in F.S. Regs., Part II. and the Staff Manual respectively. Title pages will be prepared in manuscript. Sheet 14

Place	Date	Hour	Summary of Events and Information	Remarks and references to Appendices
	1915			
HUMBERCAMPS	Oct 1		600 men of battalion working on Corps line at SOUASTRE.	AP
HUMBERCAMPS	Oct 2		Battn made a strong as possible march on following route LAHERLIERE – MONDICOURT – PAS – HENU – ST AMAND.	A-D
HUMBERCAMPS	Oct 3		Battn found 2 parties each of 200 men 1 for work on the village defences of ST AMAND.	A-B
HUMBERCAMPS	Oct 4		Battn found 2 parties each of 100 men for work on village defences ST AMAND	AB
HUMBERCAMPS	Oct 5		Battn found a working party of 600 men for work on the Corps line at SOUASTRE. This party were under the command of Major Anjona.	A-B
HUMBERCAMPS	Oct 6		Battn found 2 working parties each of 100 men for work on ST AMAND village defences.	AB
HUMBERCAMPS	Oct 7		Battn made a strong as possible route march under Major Anjona. route ST AMAND – SOUASTRE – COIGNEUX – COUIN – HENU – GAUDIEMPRE.	AB
HUMBERCAMPS	Oct 8		Battn found 2 working parties each of 50 men for work on ST AMAND village defences. The Divisional Adviser 3rd Army gave a lecture on a demonstration in the use of smoke helmets. Every man who had not already attended a demonstration in the use of gas, was marched through a trench 30 yards long, gas being a driver into the trench.	A-R

Army Form C. 2118.

WAR DIARY
or
INTELLIGENCE SUMMARY.
(Erase heading not required.) 11th Service Battalion Royal Warwickshire Regt

Sheet 15

Place	Date	Hour	Summary of Events and Information	Remarks and references to Appendices
	1915			
HUMBERCAMPS	Oct 8		as the men marched through.	¶ 3a.
HUMBERCAMPS	Oct 9		The Battn marched to HANNESCAMPS by companys and relieved the 13th Royal Fusiliers in the trenches. The relief being completed by 8 PM.	¶ 3-17
HANNESCAMPS	Oct 10		Companies in trenches report that the situation is very quiet	¶ 3a3
HANNESCAMPS	Oct 11		A german aeroplane flew over our line at 11 AM and at 11.20 three shells fell behind trench 77. The 88 Trench between reported that a ZEPPELIN was seen flying south from LENS. A return (german) reported by O.C. D coy to be actively employed on MONCHY ROAD. Cpl Mole wounded by a stray bullet. Coys in trenches report situation normal	¶ 3-03 ¶ 3-03 ¶ 3-B
HANNESCAMPS	Oct 12		Situation normal during the day. At 6.30 PM a very heavy rifle fire opened on our right in the direction of FONQUEVILLERS. Telephoned to	¶ 3-B
HANNESCAMPS	Oct 13	10th	LOYAL NORTH LANCASHIRE REGT on our right but they said that the firing was to their right. Two Platoons were sent to support trenches and garrison Company were ordered to hold themselves in readiness to move. After about half an hour, ie at 7 PM the firing ceased	¶ 3-B

Army Form C. 2118.

WAR DIARY
or
INTELLIGENCE SUMMARY.

(Erase heading not required.) 11th Service Batt. Royal Warwickshire Regt

Sheet 16

Place	Date	Hour	Summary of Events and Information	Remarks and references to Appendices
	1915			
HANNESCAMPS	Oct 14		Situation generally quiet. At 12.45 PM about 8 enemy field gun shells over trench 76. No damage.	1-3-0
HANNESCAMPS	Oct 15		Situation normal. B and C coy relieved A and D coys in the trenches. Relief completed at 5.40 PM.	1-3-5
HANNESCAMPS	Oct 16		Situation normal. At 3 PM a few German rifle grenades fell in front of trench 76. No casualties.	9-5-0
HANNESCAMPS	Oct 17		Weather very misty. Sentries posted in listening posts. Situation normal	9-3-5
HANNESCAMPS	Oct 18		Situation normal. At 2 PM 4 HE shell fell behind trench 75. No damage done.	1-7-0
HANNESCAMPS	Oct 19		Enemy working parties to our right front observed by our rifle fire at 9AM. At 3PM a heavy bombardment was heard to our north.	1-3-5
HANNESCAMPS	Oct 20		Situation quiet.	
HANNESCAMPS	Oct 21		Situation normal. Batt. was relieved by the 13th Royal Fusiliers and companies marched off to ST AMAND where the batt. went into billets.	4-3-5

WAR DIARY
or
INTELLIGENCE SUMMARY.

(Erase heading not required.) 11th Service Batt. Royal Warwickshire Regt

Army Form C. 2118.

Title pages April 17

Place	Date	Hour	Summary of Events and Information	Remarks and references to Appendices
	1915			
ST AMAND	Oct 22		Battn rested in billets, kits and equipment were cleaned.	J 3-9
ST AMAND	Oct 23		Battn found a working party of 600 men for work on the Corks line at SOUASTRE. Major A.H. Jones was in command of the party.	J 3-9
ST AMAND	Oct 24		Battn under Company arrangements	
ST AMAND	Oct 25		The Battn took part in a ceremonial parade at ACHEUX. Marching there and back. At ACHEUX the Battn in company with 3 other Battns of the regt. were inspected by His Majesty the King and the President of the French Republic	1 Edward 7th Regent Hythe A.S. Heffernan Public School 4th Oxford Battn J 36 J 30
ST AMAND	Oct 26		Battn found a working party of 500 men for work on the Corks line. Capt Lloyd was in command of the party.	J 30
ST AMAND	Oct 27		The Battn had the use of the Divisional Baths at PAS.	J 30
ST AMAND	Oct 28		The Battn marched to BIENVILLERS and took over billets from the 6th BEDFORDSHIRE REGT. At 5 P.M. the Battn furnished a working party for the 152nd Coy R.E.	J 30
BIENVILLERS	Oct 29		The Battn found working parties totalling 300 men for the 112th Brigade	J 30

Army Form C. 2118.

WAR DIARY
or
INTELLIGENCE SUMMARY.

(Erase heading not required.) 11th Service Batt. Royal Warwickshire Regt.

Sheet 18

Place	Date	Hour	Summary of Events and Information	Remarks and references to Appendices
BIENVILLERS	Oct 30		With the exception of 116 men rations carrying for 9th LEICESTERSHIRE REGT and 52 men guards the Batt. rested	J-147
BIENVILLERS	Oct 31		One batln found 400 men for work under 152nd Coy R.E. the work being for 110th Infantry Brigade	J-3-B

J. Falmey-Boyte Capt. a/Adjt
11th Service Batn. Royal Warwickshire Regt.

112th Inf.Bde.
37th Div.

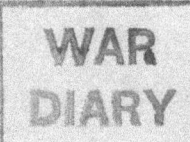

11th BATTN. THE ROYAL WARWICKSHIRE REGIMENT.

N O V E M B E R

1 9 1 5

Confidential

War Diary
of

11th (Serv) Bn. Royal Warwickshire Regiment

from November 1st 1915 to November 30th 1915.

(Volume 1. No. 4)

Army Form C. 2118.

WAR DIARY
or
INTELLIGENCE SUMMARY.
(Erase heading not required.)

14th Service Battalion Royal Warwickshire Regt

Sheet 19

Place	Date	Hour	Summary of Events and Information	Remarks and references to Appendices
	1915			
BIENVILLERS	Nov 1		Bn with the exception of 116 men carrying rations for 9th LEICESTER REGT and 52 men guards men were left at the disposal of Company Commanders.	1.50
BIENVILLERS	Nov 2		Bn. moved to HANNESCAMPS and took over trenches 69 to 77 from the 13th ROYAL FUSILIERS. The relief of trenches was completed satisfactorily but owing to the bad state of the roads the transport encountered considerable difficulties in bringing up the regimental baggage and stores. O.C. A & D coys who took over the trenches telephoned to say that the trenches are in very bad condition owing to the rain. O.C. A coy reports that 5 traverses collapsed and had to be rebuilt. The 10th LOYAL NORTH LANCASHIRE REGT are on our right and the 7th LEICESTERSHIRE REGT on our left.	9.7 n
HANNESCAMPS	Nov 3		Weather continues wet. G.O.C. 112th Brigade suspended the Working parties and all available men were sent to work on front trenches. A few shells came over HANNESCAMPS but no damage was done.	9.3 - 13

T2134. Wt. W708—776. 500000. 4/16. Sir J.C. & S.

Army Form C. 2118.

WAR DIARY
or
INTELLIGENCE SUMMARY.

(Erase heading not required.) 11th Service Battalion Royal Warwickshire Regt

Sheet 20

Place	Date.	Hour	Summary of Events and Information	Remarks and references to Appendices
	1915			
HANNESCAMPS	Nov 4		Heavy rain during morning. Trenches in a very bad state some of the support trenches being waterlogged, the condition of the lower part of LULU LANE communication trench being the same. 2nd Lt A.E. BOUCHER took out a battle patrol of 10 men with the object of surrounding and capturing a small German patrol which appeared to be in the habit of going out nightly from the German trench south of the MONCHY ROAD. Our patrol reached the German wire without seeing any of the enemy, and after patrolling along the wire without seeing anyone, they returned to our own lines.	J.3-13
HANNESCAMPS	Nov 5		Heavy mist in early morning. At 9.40 A.M. O.C. A Coy reported that Germans had sent between 30 and 40 Minenwerfer over Trenches 71-72 and 73. Reprisals were asked for by telephone and after 9 minutes 2 field guns shells were sent by Battery 153. We endeavoured to telephone to 112th & Battn Brigade but the wire was evidently cut and a cyclist orderly was sent asking for reprisals from heavy battery, as minenwerfer were	J.3-13.

T2134. Wt. W708—776. 500000. 4/15. Sir J. C. & S.

WAR DIARY
or
INTELLIGENCE SUMMARY.

(Erase heading not required.) 1/1st Service Battalion Royal Warwickshire Regt

Sheet 21

Army Form C. 2118.

Place	Date	Hour	Summary of Events and Information	Remarks and references to Appendices
	1915			
HANNESCAMPS	Nov 5		still coming over.	1.3.G
HANNESCAMPS	Nov 6		All available men were employed in the work of repair to the trenches caused by minenwerfer. At 2PM enemy minenwerfer again opened on our trenches. This time the trenches of the left flank company were badly damaged. Three dug outs were blown in and the eastern end of LULU LANE was blocked. Considerable damage was done to our wire. At 5.30 PM a party of some ten Germans was seen in front of our wire, a machine gun opened on them and grooving was heard. 2Lt THAIN accompanied by Privates 8177 TIMBRELL and 11056 BAGLEY went out with the intention of bringing in the wounded men, who they believed to be some 15 yards beyond our wire where there was a large hole caused by a minenwerfer. On reaching this point they found that the hole in question was occupied by 8 or 9 Germans who opened fire on them, wounding 2Lt THAIN and Pt TIMBRELL. Pt BAGLEY succeeded in driving off the Germans by throwing 3 grenades and firing a lot of cartridges into them, later Lt BARWELL made an examination of the shell	f.3.G.

Army Form C. 2118.

WAR DIARY
or
INTELLIGENCE SUMMARY.
(Erase heading not required.) 1st Service Battalion Royal Warwickshire Regt.

Sheet 22

Place	Date	Hour	Summary of Events and Information	Remarks and references to Appendices
	1915			
HANNESCAMPS	Nov 6th		Role and discovered 4 unexploded German grenades also a clip for mauser cartridges. Seven men were wounded during the day by splinters from mauser	J.3-13.
HANNESCAMPS	Nov 7		Situation normal. All available men working on the damaged trenches. Sergt Gilbert and 11 grenadiers went out to ambush a german patrol. They left LYCEUM sap at 3.30 AM. At dawn the mist lifted very rapidly and it would appear that Sgt Gilbert did not consider it advisable to return to the trenches in daylight. At 9 PM Sgt Gilbert's party not having returned A/Sgt HOLLYOAK and PTE JONES (A coy) went out in search of them. At 10 PM they returned not having found any trace of the party and it is feared that they must have been captured.	
HANNESCAMPS	Nov 8		Situation normal. No further news of Sgt GILBERT's patrol. A and B coys were relieved by B and C coys.	J.7-9.
HANNESCAMPS	Nov 9		Situation normal. "Lt SHEWRING while out with a party of grenadiers as a screen to the party that was repairing the wire, found a loaded mauser rifle and a live german hand grenade	J.3-9.

Army Form C. 2118.

WAR DIARY
or
INTELLIGENCE SUMMARY.
(Erase heading not required.) 11th Service Batt. Royal Warwickshire Regt.

Place	Date	Hour	Summary of Events and Information	Remarks and references to Appendices
	1915			
HANNESCAMPS	Nov 10		Situation normal. Much rain causing many parts of the trenches to fall in. Companies report that the night was exceptionally quiet	9.33
HANNESCAMPS	Nov 11		at 10 AM a number of minenwerfer were heard to burst to the south near FONQUEVILLERS.	9.73
HANNESCAMPS	Nov 12		Situation normal	9.7-G.
HANNESCAMPS	Nov 13		Situation normal	9.7-G.
HANNESCAMPS	Nov 14		The battalion was relieved by the 13th Royal Fusiliers and on relief marched to ST AMAND by companies, and there took over the billets of the 13th Kings Royal Rifle Corps	9.7-G.
ST AMAND	Nov 15		Day spent in resting as far as possible after kits rifles etc had been cleaned	9.7-G.
ST AMAND	Nov 16		Working party of 450 found by batt. for work at BIENVILLERS on HANNESCAMPS. Training of reserve grenadiers and machine gunners continues	9.7-G.
ST AMAND	Nov 17		100 men working parties remainder of batt. under company arrangements	9.7-G.
ST AMAND	Nov 18		Working party of 450 found for work at BIENVILLERS and HANNESCAMPS	9.7-G.
ST AMAND	Nov 19		Batt. had use of 37th D memorial Baths at PAS	9.7-G.

WAR DIARY or INTELLIGENCE SUMMARY

(Erase heading not required.) 11th Service Battn Royal Warwickshire Regt

Army Form C. 2118.

Sheet 24

Place	Date	Hour	Summary of Events and Information	Remarks and references to Appendices
	1915			
ST AMAND	Nov 20		Working party of 450 men at BIENVILLERS and HANNESCAMPS.	9.7-13.
ST AMAND	Nov 21		100 men working parties. Remainder of Battn at disposal of O.C. coys after church parade at 11.30 AM.	9.7-03.
ST AMAND	Nov 22		450 men working at BIENVILLERS and HANNESCAMPS.	9.7-03.
ST AMAND	Nov 23		Genrl ALLENBY inspected the grenadiers at practice, Br Gen SNOW Count GLEICHEN and Brigadier General ROBINSON were also present. Battalion did a route march to GAUDIEMPÉ and practiced the attack on the high ground between ST AMAND and GAUDIEMPRE.	9.7-12.
ST AMAND	Nov 24		450 men working parties at BIENVILLERS and HANNESCAMPS	9.7-09.
ST AMAND	Nov 25		100 men working parties. Remainder of battn under company arrangements	9.7.67
ST AMAND	Nov 26		Battn relieved the 13th ROYAL FUSILIERS in the trenches at HANNESCAMPS. The relief was safely effected as regards the 11th ROYAL WARWICKSHIRE REGT but as the 13th ROYAL FUSILIERS were retiring along the BANNESCAMPS — BIENVILLERS road the enemy opened fire on the road with field guns, however only one casualty was sustained by the 13th ROYAL FUSILIERS.	

Army Form C. 2118.

WAR DIARY
or
INTELLIGENCE SUMMARY.

(Erase heading not required.)

Sheet 25   11th Service Battalion Royal Warwickshire Regt

Place	Date	Hour	Summary of Events and Information	Remarks and references to Appendices
	1915			
HANNESCAMPS	Nov 27		A Winter normal, weather very cold. 2Lt AE BOUCHER accompanied by Lee Cpl DE ST CROIX and Pte EDGINGTON made a successful reconnaissance of the enemy wire north of the MONCHY ROAD. The patrol was fired on from a German sap which they in turn successfully bombed with two mills grenades. The patrol then returned safely to our own lines.	¶ 3-9
HANNESCAMPS	Nov 28		Situation normal, weather very cold, German snipers active.	¶ 7-13
HANNESCAMPS	Nov 29		Weather wet but warmer. A. D coys were relieved in the trenches by B and C coys.	¶ 7-B
HANNESCAMPS	Nov 30		Weather very wet. much rain during the night causing considerable damage to trenches. At 8.15 AM enemy commenced shelling our trenches with Minenwerfen. It is estimated that between thirty and forty of these projectiles were fired at our trench. Three bays in the trenches of the left sector were completely obliterated. Only one casualty was however sustained.	¶ I-3

J. Johns B. aty Capt., Adjutant
11th Royal Warwickshire Regt

112th Inf.Bde.
37th Div.

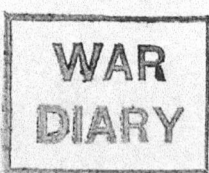

11th BATTN. THE ROYAL WARWICKSHIRE REGIMENT.

DECEMBER

1915

Confidential

War Diary

of

11th (Serv.) Bn., Royal Warwickshire Regt.

From 1st December 1915 To 31st December 1915

Volume I No. V

Army Form C. 2118.

WAR DIARY
or
INTELLIGENCE SUMMARY.

(Erase heading not required.) 11th Service Battalion Royal Warwickshire Regt

Sheet 2b

Instructions regarding War Diaries and Intelligence Summaries are contained in F. S. Regs., Part II. and the Staff Manual respectively. Title pages will be prepared in manuscript.

Place	Date	Hour	Summary of Events and Information	Remarks and references to Appendices
	1915			
HANNESCAMPS	Dec 1		Weather wet during day. Situation normal. Owing to the wet weather trenches continue to fall in. The necessity for an efficient system of revetting becomes daily more apparent. The system of digging small holes in the centre of trenches and placing wooden covers over them has not proved efficacious during the heavy rains which we have recently been experiencing. Lt Col. S. COLLISON proceeded on leave and is due back on December 11th During his absence Captain T.H.LLOYD will be in command of the Battalion.	J.J-B.
HANNESCAMPS	Dec 2		Weather very wet. All available men working on trenches which continue to fall in despite all efforts. Situation normal. A very minimal number of flares sent up from German trenches opposed to us	J J-B.
HANNESCAMPS	Dec 3		Weather very wet. Situation normal.	J J-B.
HANNESCAMPS	Dec 4		Weather wet. Our Artillery bombarded the enemy's trenches opposite to the trenches occupied by the battalion immediately on our right. The bombardment appeared to be very successful and sentries	J J-B.

Army Form C. 2118.

WAR DIARY
or
INTELLIGENCE SUMMARY.

(Erase heading not required.) 11th Service Battalion Royal Warwickshire Regt

Month 27

Place	Date	Hour	Summary of Events and Information	Remarks and references to Appendices
HANNESCAMPS	Dec 4		report seeing timber huts corrugated iron lying blown into the air after the explosion of our shells. The enemy retaliated by shelling BIENVILLERS. Major General Count CLEICHEN visited the trenches in the afternoon.	9.79
HANNESCAMPS	Dec 5		Wet weather continues. The parties carrying rations to the trenches experience the greatest difficulty in making their way along the communication trenches. Many cases occurred where men had to be dug out of the mud and clay into which they had sunk. Brigadier General ROBINSON visited Batta Headquarters during the afternoon. Inter company relief took place	9.79
HANNESCAMPS	Dec 6		Weather fine. Strong wind blowing which it is hoped will dry up the trenches. Situation normal. Occasional sniping	9.79
HANNESCAMPS	Dec 7		Situation normal. During afternoon snow reported to be very great	9.79
HANNESCAMPS	Dec 8		Situation very quiet. Occasional sniping by enemy from direction of MONCHY. Battalion was relieved by 13th ROYAL FUSILIERS and on relief marched to rest billets in ST AMAND.	9.79

Army Form C. 2118.

WAR DIARY
or
INTELLIGENCE SUMMARY.

(Erase heading not required.) 11th Service Battalion Royal Warwickshire Regt

Sheet 28

Place	Date	Hour	Summary of Events and Information	Remarks and references to Appendices
	1915			
ST AMAND	Dec 9		Companies at disposal of company commanders for purpose of cleaning up kit etc and resting the men	J.S.B.
ST AMAND	Dec 10		Battalion had the use of Divisional Baths at PAS.	J.S.B.
ST AMAND	Dec 11		Battn found working parties as follows. 100 men HANNESCAMPS. 100 men BIENVILLERS, 50 men coils line SOUASTRE	J.S.B.
ST AMAND	Dec 12		Church Parade service at 10A.M. Lieut Col COLLISON returned from leave.	J.S.B.
ST AMAND	Dec 13		Battn found working parties as follows 100 men HANNESCAMPS, 100 men BIENVILLERS, 50 men coils line SOUASTRE, 50 men Brigade grenade school.	J.S.B.
ST AMAND	Dec 14		Battn made a route march ST AMAND – HENU – PAS – GAUDIEMPRE – ST AMAND. The 37th Divisional Band accompanied the Battn.	J.S.B.
ST AMAND	Dec 15		Battn found working parties as follows 100 men HANNESCAMPS, 100 men BIENVILLERS, 50 men coils line SOUASTRE, 50 men Brigade grenade school	J.S.B.
ST AMAND	Dec 16		Battn found one working party of 50 men on Brigade grenade school, the remainder of the Battalion rested in billets	J.S.B.

Army Form C. 2118.

WAR DIARY
or
INTELLIGENCE SUMMARY.
(Erase heading not required.)

11th Service Battalion Royal Warwickshire Regt.

Sheet 29

Place	Date	Hour	Summary of Events and Information	Remarks and references to Appendices
	1915			
ST AMAND	Dec 17th		Battn found working parties as follows 100 men HANNESCAMPS 100 men BIENVILLERS, 50 men carrying line SOUASTRE, 50 men Brigade ground school	
ST AMAND	Dec 18		Battn found one working party of 50 on Brigade Grenade school	
ST AMAND	Dec 19		Remainder of men rested in billets	1.5.-17 1915
ST AMAND	Dec 20		Battalion moved in billets. 2 Lt TARLTON reported for duty from H.A.C. The Battalion relieved the 13th ROYAL FUSILIERS in the trenches at HANNESCAMPS. The trenches (69 & 77) were found to be in a very bad state and in many places impassable owing to the mud and water. The relief had to be carried out over the open ground as the communication trenches were impassable	
HANNESCAMPS	Dec 21		Situation normal; weather wet	9.5.-17 9.5.-15
HANNESCAMPS	Dec 22		Situation normal with the exception of continuous bursts of fire from enemy machine guns	9.7-15
HANNESCAMPS	Dec 23		Situation quiet. Our artillery bombarded enemy's trenches heavily. Artillery not being very	1.5.-13.
HANNESCAMPS	Dec 24		Situation normal weather wet. A few of enemy's howitzer shells fell on trenches 74 & 75	

WAR DIARY or INTELLIGENCE SUMMARY.

Army Form C. 2118.

11th Service Battalion Royal Warwickshire Regt

Sheet 30

Place	Date	Hour	Summary of Events and Information	Remarks and references to Appendices
	1915			
HANNESCAMPS	Dec 25		Situation normal. British aeroplanes seen looking the roof over German lines	J.S.B.
HANNESCAMPS	Dec 26		Situation normal. German 5.9 howitzer shell burst in trench 76 B wounding 4 men. Later enemy rifles effective SW.	J.S.B.
HANNESCAMPS	Dec 27		Situation very quiet	J.S.B.
HANNESCAMPS	Dec 28		British Artillery duel. Aerial activity and many shells fired at aeroplanes. The only apparent damage being a casualty in our left sector caused by dropping pieces of our own shells	J.S.B.
			Situation quiet. British artillery action on both sides during afternoon	J.S.B.
HANNESCAMPS	Dec 29		Situation normal during morning. Between 1.30PM and 3PM enemy fired about 40 trench mortar projectiles (about 15lbs each) into the trenches in our left sector	J.S.B.
HANNESCAMPS	Dec 30		Enemy field artillery active during morning. Enemy's trench mortars again fired into trenches in our left sector. Very heavy transport heard moving north of LA BRAYELLE.	J.S.B.
HANNESCAMPS	Dec 31			

(signature)
COMDG. 11th SERVICE BN. R. WARWICKSHIRE REGT.

112th Brigade,
37th Division.

11th BATTALION

ROYAL WARWICKSHIRE REGIMENT

JANUARY 1916

11th Dansville
rd. 6
Jan '16

37

Confidential

War Diary

of

11th (Ser) Bn Royal Warwickshire Regiment

from 1st January 1916 to 31st January 1916

(Volume 2, No. 1.)

Army Form C. 2118.

WAR DIARY
or
INTELLIGENCE SUMMARY.
(Erase heading not required.)

11th Service Battalion Royal Warwickshire Regt

Sheet 31

Place	Date	Hour	Summary of Events and Information	Remarks and references to Appendices
	1916			
HANNESCAMPS	Jan 1		Situation very quiet, Bttn was relieved by 13th ROYAL FUSILIERS and on relief marched to billets in ST AMAND. at about 5 PM an exceptionally strong S.W. wind sprung up	
ST AMAND	Jan 2		Battalion rested in billets. Conference of enterny commanders at 12 noon and Brigade conference of battalion commanders at 2 PM.	J.3.9 J.7-9
ST AMAND	Jan 3		One working party of 100 men at HANNESCAMPS, Bttn otherwise has the use of 37th Divisional Bath at PAS.	J.7.9
ST AMAND	Jan 4		Working party of 100 men for 13th ROYAL FUSILIERS at HANNESCAMPS	J.7-9
ST AMAND	Jan 5		Working party of 100 men for 13th ROYAL FUSILIERS at HANNESCAMPS	J.7-9
ST AMAND	Jan 6		Working party of 100 men ten north of Brigade Grenade School, also 100 men for 13th ROYAL FUSILIERS at HANNESCAMPS and 150 men for work on the Quarry at HENU	J.7.9
ST AMAND	Jan 7th		Working party of 100 men for 13th ROYAL FUSILIERS at HANNESCAMPS. 2nd FRENCH reported for duty	J.7-9
ST AMAND	Jan 8th		Working party of 100 men for 13th ROYAL FUSILIERS at HANNESCAMPS. Battn had the use of 37th Divisional Baths at PAS during the morning	J.7-9
ST AMAND	Jan 9th		Working party of 100 men for 13th ROYAL FUSILIERS at HANNESCAMPS. Church of England parade service held at 10 AM at ST AMAND. During this was a test alarm by 112th Bde. Battn were ordered to turn out to arms at 6 PM and paraded in 4.3 minutes.	J.73

Army Form C. 2118.

WAR DIARY
or
INTELLIGENCE SUMMARY.

(Erase heading not required.) 11th Service B Battalion Royal Warwickshire Regt

Place	Date	Hour	Summary of Events and Information	Remarks and references to Appendices
	1916			
ST AMAND	Jan 10		The following working parties were found by the battalion, 100 men for 13th ROYAL FUSILIERS at HANNESCAMPS. 150 men for work at HENU. 100 men for work on the trenches & the Bangalore grenade school. Riflemen were take debris for an hour while carrying on their work. It was was found that they in no way hindered the use of the telephone instruments.	J.J.D
ST AMAND	Jan 11		Working party of 100 men for 13th ROYAL FUSILIERS at HANNESCAMPS	J.J.D
ST AMAND	Jan 12		Working party of 150 men for 13th ROYAL FUSILIERS at HANNESCAMPS.	J.J.D
ST AMAND	Jan 13		Battn marched to HANNESCAMPS and relieved the 13th ROYAL FUSILIERS in trenches 69 to 76. The 10th LOYAL NORTH LANCASHIRE REGT being on our right and the 9th LEICESTERSHIRE. REGT on our left	J.J.D
HANNESCAMPS	Jan 14		Situation very quiet. Wind from the north westerly. Bristol aeroplanes active during morning	J.J.D
HANNESCAMPS	Jan 15		Situation generally quiet during morning. 4 enemy field gun shell fell close to trench 72 at 11 AM no damage. W eather fine and clear.	J.J.D
HANNESCAMPS	Jan 16		A few rifle grenades and trench mortar shells fell in our left sector during morning	J.J.D

Army Form C. 2118.

WAR DIARY
or
INTELLIGENCE SUMMARY.
(Erase heading not required.)

Instructions regarding War Diaries and Intelligence Summaries are contained in F. S. Regs., Part II. and the Staff Manual respectively. Title pages will be prepared in manuscript.

About 3 3   11R Service Battalion Royal Warwickshire Regt

Place	Date	Hour	Summary of Events and Information	Remarks and references to Appendices
	1916.			
HANNESCAMPS	Jan 16		Situation very quiet. B. reported visited trenches during afternoon. 2/Lt Webb joined for duty from 13th Bn	J.T.R
HANNESCAMPS	Jan 17		Situation normal. 4 HE shells fell in our left sector. 4 field gun	J.T.R
HANNESCAMPS	Jan 18		Shells fell near Company commanders dugout in night sector. Weather fine. Machine guns of 17th Division commenced on MONTHY but were no attempt noticed. Situation quiet. A few field gun shells fell near own support line and front.	J.T.R
HANNESCAMPS	Jan 19		B and C coys relieved A and D companies in the trenches.	J.T.R
HANNESCAMPS	Jan 20		Enemy artillery active during morning no damage to our trenches a hostile monoplane flew over our lines and dropped three bombs on BIENVILLERS. Line reported to be unusually quiet during afternoon	J.T.R
HANNESCAMPS	Jan 21		Situation normal. Weather fine. A few shells burst over our support line but effected no damage	J.T.R
HANNESCAMPS	Jan 22		Line very quiet. Wind S.W.	J.T.R
HANNESCAMPS	Jan 23		Hostile machine guns active otherwise the line was very quiet. Our artillery bombarded enemy front line opposite our trenches from 12.10 P.M to 2 P.M. Enemy retaliated on our front trenches but failed.	J.T.R
HANNESCAMPS	Jan 24		Line quiet. During afternoon the stillness was quite remarkable	J.T.R

Army Form C. 2118.

WAR DIARY
or
INTELLIGENCE SUMMARY.

(Erase heading not required.) 11th Service Battalion Royal Warwickshire Regt

Place	Date	Hour	Summary of Events and Information	Remarks and references to Appendices
	1916			
HANNESCAMPS	Jan 25		Line quiet. Battn was relieved and after relief marched back to billets at ST AMAND	9 F R
ST AMAND	Jan 26		Battn rested in billets and companies were at the disposal of company commanders	1 F B
ST AMAND	Jan 27		Battn found working parties as follows: 100 men for 13th ROYAL FUSILIERS at HANNESCAMPS. 150 men for work on quarry at HENU. 50 men for work on HENU-GAUDIEMPRE Rd. 30 men for work on Brigade grenade school and 30 men for work under O.C. Labour battn. At 6.50 PM a telephone message was received giving warning of a gas attack. All ranks were warned and companies stood to arms in their billets. A later message was to the effect that the gas attack was reported by the 48th Division and also by own own artillery at BIENVILLERS. Subsequently this was reported as being a false alarm and men were ordered to return to their billets. The alarm in the 48th Division was occasioned by some gas shells.	
~~ST AMAND~~	~~Jan 27~~			
ST AMAND	Jan 28		Battn found a working party of 100 men for the 13th ROYAL FUSILIERS	

Army Form C. 2118.

WAR DIARY
or
INTELLIGENCE SUMMARY.

(Erase heading not required.) 11th Service Battalion Royal Warwickshire Regt

Instructions regarding War Diaries and Intelligence Summaries are contained in F.S. Regs., Part II. and the Staff Manual respectively. Title pages will be prepared in manuscript.

Place	Date	Hour	Summary of Events and Information	Remarks and references to Appendices
	1916		About 35	
ST AMAND	Jan 30		Battn found a fa working party of 100 men for work under the 13th ROYAL FUSILIERS at HANNESCAMPS.	J.F.R.
ST AMAND	Jan 31		Battn furnished working parties as follows. 100 men for 13th ROYAL FUSILIERS at HANNESCAMPS. 150 men on the quarry at HENU. 50 men on the quarry on the HENU – GAUDIEMPRE road. 30 men on Brigade grenade school. 30 men on roads under 3rd Lothians D Walker	

Marwick
LT. COLONEL,
COMDG. 11th. SERVICE BN. R. WARWICKSHIRE REGT.

112th Brigade.
37th Division.

1/11th ROYAL WARWICKSHIRE REGIMENT

FEBRUARY 1 9 1 6::

11ᵗᵉ Wawrzecko Vol: 7

MN (4)

Confidential

War Diary
of
11th (S) Bn., Royal Warwickshire Regt.

From 1st February 1916   To 29th February 1916

(Volume II   No 2.)

Army Form C. 2118.

WAR DIARY
or
INTELLIGENCE SUMMARY.

(Erase heading not required.) 11th Service Battalion Royal Warwickshire Regt

Sheet 36

Place	Date 1916	Hour	Summary of Events and Information	Remarks and references to Appendices
ST AMAND	Feb 1		Battn found a working party of 100 men for 13th ROYAL FUSILIERS at HANNESCAMPS	9.7-R
ST AMAND	Feb 2		Weather cold. D company found a working party of 100 men for 13th ROYAL FUSILIERS at HANNESCAMPS	9.7-R
ST AMAND	Feb 3		Battn found a working party of 100 men for 13th ROYAL FUSILIERS at HANNESCAMPS	9.7-R
ST AMAND	Feb 4		Battn found working parties as follows: 100 men for 13th ROYAL FUSILIERS at HANNESCAMPS. 150 men for the quarry HENU. 50 men on the FLINT Quarry on the HENU – GAUDIEMPRÉ road. 30 men for work under 3rd labour Battalion. 30 men for work on the grenade school.	9.7-3
ST AMAND	Feb 5		Battn found a working party of 100 men to the 13th ROYAL FUSILIERS at HANNESCAMPS and a party of 50 men for work at the RE yard BIENVILLERS.	9.7-3
ST AMAND	Feb 6		The Battn marched to HANNESCAMPS and relieved the 13th ROYAL FUSILIERS in the trenches 69 to 76L. Trenches were found to be in excellent condition	9.7-3
HANNESCAMPS ST AMAND	Feb 7		Situation quiet	1.3-3
HANNESCAMPS	Feb 8		Activities normal. 2 men were wounded by a H.E. German Yeomitzer shell burst in bay 3 Trod 75. Major C.P. ROOKE returned to the battalion from 13th ROYAL WARWICKSHIRE. He was wounded on Sept 16th 1915 when serving with the 11th ROYAL WARWICKSHIRE.	9.7-3

Army Form C. 2118.

WAR DIARY
or
INTELLIGENCE SUMMARY.

(Erase heading not required.)

11th Service Battalion Royal Warwickshire Regt

Sheet 37

Place	Date	Hour	Summary of Events and Information	Remarks and references to Appendices
	1916			
HANNESCAMPS	Feb 9		Weather fine. Situation normal. Our artillery carried out an organised bombardment of the enemy's trenches in the neighbourhood of LA BRAYELLE FM. The Germans replied by shelling FONQUEVILLERS.	
HANNESCAMPS	Feb 10		Aviation normal.	
HANNESCAMPS	Feb 11		Situation quiet.	
HANNESCAMPS	Feb 12		Artillery active on both sides. 3 shells fell behind trench 73. No damage.	
HANNESCAMPS	Feb 13		The battalion was relieved in the trenches by the 1/6 GLOUCESTERSHIRE REGT. and the companies in HANNESCAMPS were relieved tenth by companies to HUMBERCAMPS mounted tenth by the 6th WORCESTERSHIRE REGT. After being relieved the battn marched to HUMBERCAMPS where it took over the billets of the 13th RIFLE BRIGADE.	
HUMBERCAMPS	Feb 14		Companies rested in billets. The commanding Officer, Adjutant and the four company commanders visited the billets held by the 8th LEICESTERSHIRE REGT at BERLES AU BOIS. The battalion is to take over these trenches on the night of Feb 16/17.	
HUMBERCAMPS	Feb 15		Companies rested. All platoon commanders visited the trenches at BERLES AU BOIS.	

WAR DIARY
INTELLIGENCE SUMMARY

Army Form C. 2118.

Sheet 38. 11th Service Battn Royal (W) Warwickshire Regt

Place	Date	Hour	Summary of Events and Information	Remarks and references to Appendices
HUMBERCAMPS	Feb 16 1916		Battn marched to BERLES AU BOIS and took over the trenches 109 to 116 from the 8th LEICESTERSHIRE REGT. The relief was not completed until 9.45 PM owing to the communication trenches being in such a bad condition. The Battn has the 8th E. LANCS REGT on its right and the 13th RIFLE BRIGADE on its left.	¶ 7-D
BERLES AU BOIS	Feb 17		Weather fine. Situation very quiet. The Battn is distributed as follows: two companies in fire trenches 109 to 116. One company in Fort 147 and one company billeted in BERLES.	¶ 7-D
BERLES AU BOIS	Feb 18		Weather very wet and windy. Some hostile Field Gun shells fell on open ground west of Fort 147. A Zeppelin appeared to come from ADINFER WOOD.	¶ 7-D
BERLES AU BOIS	Feb 19		A patrol under 2nd Lt FRENCH reconnoitred the ground in front of our right company and found the enemy quiet and working in his trenches. At about 11 PM one or more Zeppelins were seen moving towards POMMIER and fire was opened on them. B coy relieved A coy and C relieved D coy. A coy occupying the fort and D coy billets in BERLES.	¶ 7-D ¶ 7-D ¶ 7-D
BERLES AU BOIS	Feb 20		A very fine day. Great aeroplane activity on both sides.	¶ 7-D

Army Form C. 2118.

WAR DIARY
or
INTELLIGENCE SUMMARY.
(Erase heading not required.)

11th Service Battalion Royal Warwickshire Regt   Sheet 29

Place	Date	Hour	Summary of Events and Information	Remarks and references to Appendices
	1916			
BEALES AU BOIS	Feb 21		Weather fine - cold situation normal	7F-R
BERLES AU BOIS	Feb 22		Weather very cold. Snowstorm commenced at 11AM. Lt Col COLLISON took over command of 112th Infantry Brigade owing to Brigadier General ROBINSON proceeding on leave to ENGLAND. Major C P ROOKE assumed command of the Battalion. Battalion relieved in trenches by 8th LEICESTERSHIRE REGT and marched to billets in HUMBERCAMPS.	7.3-03
HUMBERCAMPS	Feb 23		Snowstorm continued. Battn at church at embarking officers in the afternoon. Major ROOKE held an Officers conference.	7F-17
HUMBERCAMPS	Feb 24		Snow lying deep on ground and a hard frost prevailing	7F-4
HUMBERCAMPS	Feb 25		More snow and weather very cold	1F-0
HUMBERCAMPS	Feb 26		Thaw set in	75-R
HUMBERCAMPS	Feb 27		Nothing to report	
HUMBERCAMPS	Feb 28		Nothing to report	
HUMBERCAMPS	Feb 29		Battn marched to HANNESCAMPS and took over trenches 66 & 77 from 4th GLOUCESTER regt. 10th L.N.LANCS regt being on our right and 7th LEICESTER on our left	

J Falay - 2nd Lt Capt Adjt
for.
LT. COLONEL,
COMDG. 11th. SERVICE BN. R. WARWICKSHIRE REGT.

112th Brigade.
37th Division.

1/11th ROYAL WARWICKSHIRE REGIMENT

MARCH 1 9 1 6

XXXVII / 11 Warwick Vol 8

Confidential.

War Diary

of

11th (S) Bn., Royal Warwickshire Regiment.

from 1st March 1916.   to 31st March 1916.

(Volume II. No 3).

Army Form C. 2118.

WAR DIARY
or
INTELLIGENCE SUMMARY.

(Erase heading not required.) 11th Service Battalion Royal Warwickshire Regt

Sheet 40

Place	Date	Hour	Summary of Events and Information	Remarks and references to Appendices
	1916			
HANNESCAMPS	March 1		A situation quiet, weather cold ? wind from south east at P.A.S	App ? - ?
HANNESCAMPS	March 2		Weather cold no wind. A British ? plane flew very low over our lines enemy opened very heavy rifle and machine gun fire on it but without any apparent result. A few rifle grenades fired into our left trenches and several field gun shells during the course of the day	App ? - ?
HANNESCAMPS	March 3		Weather dull wind light SW situation very quiet	App ? - ?
HANNESCAMPS	March 4		Weather very cold wind N much snow falling. Line quiet	App ? - ?
HANNESCAMPS	March 5		Weather cold snow falling wind north situation quiet	App ? - ?
HANNESCAMPS	March 6		Weather cold snow still falling. Situation normal. Battalion was relieved in the trenches by 6th BEDFORDSHIRE REGT and after relief marched to POMMIER where it went into billets vacated by the 6th BEDFORDSHIRE REGT. Lt Col COLLISON returned to the Battalion from commanding 112th Brigade owing to the return from leave of Gen ROBINSON	
POMMIER	March 7		Battn rested in billets.	App ? - ?
POMMIER	March 8		Battn rested	App ? - ?
POMMIER	March 9		Battn had the use of the 37th Divisional baths at PAS	App ? - ?

Army Form C. 2118.

WAR DIARY
or
INTELLIGENCE SUMMARY.
(Erase heading not required.) 11th Service Battalion Royal Warwickshire Regt

Place	Date 1916	Hour	Summary of Events and Information	Remarks and references to Appendices
POMMIER	Mar 10		Battn had the use of the 37th Divisional Baths at PAS	J. G. 13
POMMIER	Mar 11		Battn rested. Companies under company arrangements	J. G. 12
POMMIER	Mar 12		Battalion relieved the 6th BEDFORDSHIRE REGT in the trenches at HANNESCAMPS	J. G. 3
HANNESCAMPS	Mar 13		Wind south westerly fine situation quiet	J. G. B
HANNESCAMPS	Mar 14		Wind south west. A few howitzer shells burst killing trench 76 Also field gun shells fell in rear of trench 67 about midday. About 2.30 PM seven 4.2 howitzer shells fell near COLLINGBOURNE AVENUE enemy appeared to be registering	J. G. 3
HANNESCAMPS	Mar 15		Wind NNE. Two heavy Canister bombs fell in rear of trench 75 otherwise the line was very quiet	J. G. 3
HANNESCAMPS	Mar 16		Between 1 & 3 PM a number of 42 howitzer shells and also a number of rifle grenades fell behind 76 A. 3 men & one NCO wounded by a rifle grenade	J. G. 3
HANNESCAMPS	Mar 17		Situation unusually quiet General ALLENBY 3rd Army Commander inspected trenches	J. G. 3
HANNESCAMPS	Mar 18		Situation normal. The Battn was relieved in the trenches by the 1st Battn The Somerset Light Infantry and on being relieved marched to ST AMAND where it went into billets	J. G. R

Army Form C. 2118.

WAR DIARY
or
INTELLIGENCE SUMMARY.

(Erase heading not required.) 11th Service Battn Royal Warwickshire Regt

Sheet 42

Place	Date	Hour	Summary of Events and Information	Remarks and references to Appendices
	1916			
ST AMAND	Mar 19		Battn rested in billets	¶ 7-B
ST AMAND	Mar 20		Battn rested in billets	¶ 3-B
ST AMAND	Mar 21		Battn rested in billets. Lt Col C.S. COLLISON proceeded on leave, during his absence the Battn will be commanded by Major C.P. ROGKE	¶ 4-?
9T AMAND	Mar 22		Battn worked on the corps line	¶ 4-B
ST AMAND	Mar 23		Battn had the use of the 37th Divisional Baths at PAS	¶ 4-B
ST AMAND	Mar 24		Battn had the use of the rifle range at GAUDIEMPRE	¶ 7-B
ST AMAND	Mar 25		Battn working on corps line and flank quarries	¶ 1 FB
ST AMAND	Mar 26		Battn less A Coy and 70 men of C Coy marched to MONDICOURT and took over the billets of the 8th E LANCASHIRE REGT. A Coy plus and 70 men of C marched to LA HERLIERE when they took over the billets of the detachment of the E LANCASHIRE REGT. This detachment is for work on a new railway line being constructed between LA HERLIERE and BIENVILLERS	¶ 7-B ¶ 7-B
MONDICOURT ST AMAND	Mar 27		Battn found a working party of 200 men at No 5 RE Park MONDICOURT and 20 men at Faillen MONDICOURT	¶ 7-3
MONDICOURT	Mar 28		Battn found working party as on March 27th	¶ 7-?

WAR DIARY
or
INTELLIGENCE SUMMARY.

11th Service Batt. Royal Warwickshire Regt.

Army Form C. 2118.

Place	Date	Hour	Summary of Events and Information	Remarks and references to Appendices
MONDICOURT	March 29		Baltn found some working parties as on March 27th	1/3/03
MONDICOURT	March 30		Baltn found some working parties as on March 27th	1/3/03
MONDICOURT	March 31		Baltn found some working parties as on March 27th	1/3/03
			J. Fahey-Bayt Captain, Adjutant for OC 11th Royal Warwickshire Regt	

Sheet 43

112th Brigade.
37th Division.

1/11th ROYAL WARWICKSHIRE REGIMENT

APRIL 1916

11 Warwick
Vol 9

XXXVI

Confidential

War Diary

of

11th (S) Bn, Royal Warwickshire Regt.

From 1st April 1916. to 30th April 1916.

(Volume II, No 4).

Army Form C. 2118.

WAR DIARY
or
INTELLIGENCE SUMMARY.
(Erase heading not required.) 11th Service Battn Royal Warwickshire Regt

Sheet 44

Place	Date	Hour	Summary of Events and Information	Remarks and references to Appendices
	1916			
MONDICOURT	April 1		Battn found a working party of 200 men for work at no 5 RE Park MONDICOURT and 20 men for Ordnance Officer railhead MONDICOURT	f.7.R
MONDICOURT	April 2		Battn found working parties as on April 1st	f.7.-R.
MONDICOURT	April 3		Working parties as on April 1. 2—2Lt V.W. ALABASTER reported for duty.	f.7.R.
MONDICOURT	April 4		Working parties as before and an extra party of 5 men on quarry at GRINCOURT	f.7.R
MONDICOURT	April 5		Working parties as on April 4	f.7.R.
MONDICOURT	April 6		Working parties as on April 5th	f.7.R. —
MONDICOURT	April 7		Working parties as before	f.7.R.
MONDICOURT	April 8		Working parties as usual. Lt Col C.S. COLLISON returned from leave to the United Kingdom	f.7.R.
MONDICOURT	April 9		Working parties until 12 noon when they were relieved by parties from the 9th Batn LEICESTERSHIRE REGT. Lt Col Collison proceeded to AUXI LE CHATEAU to attend a conference at the 3rd Army School of Instruction Battn marched to LE SOUICH where it took over billets vacated by the 9th LEICESTERSHIRE REGT. A coy and 70 men of C coy rejoined the Battn	f.7-R. f.7.R f.7.R.
LE SOUICH	April 10		Battn at disposal of company commanders	

WAR DIARY
or
INTELLIGENCE SUMMARY

(Erase heading not required.) 11th Service Battn. Royal Warwickshire Regt.

Sheets 145

Army Form C. 2118.

Place	Date	Hour	Summary of Events and Information	Remarks and references to Appendices
	1916			
LE SOUICH	April 11		Battn attended a plane projector demonstration at the 112th Brigade Bombing school	1-7-3
LE SOUICH	April 12		Battn under company commanders for training	8-7-3
LE SOUICH	April 13		Battn under company arrangements as regards training, Major ROOKE the Adjutant and all company commanders visited the Corps line in the neighbourhood of BEAUMETZ	9-7-3
				1-7-3
LE SOUICH	April 14		Battn was inspected by Brigadier General P.M. ROBINSON 112th Bde Commander who expressed himself as being very satisfied at the state of the Battn	1-5-9
LE SOUICH	April 15		Battn training under company arrangements and also special training in Bayonet fighting under 2nd Lt KEMSEY-BOURNE. and in Bombing under 2nd Lt CRITCHLEY	9-7-3
LE SOUICH	April 16		Battn training as on April 15th	9-7-3
LE SOUICH	April 17		Battn found working party of 400 men for hurdle making in ROBERMONT wood	9-7-3
LE SOUICH	April 18		Working party as on April 17th	
LE SOUICH	April 19		Battn found working party of 500 men for hurdle making in ROBERMONT WOOD	9-7-3
LE SOUICH	April 20		Working party as on April 19th	9-7-3

Army Form C. 2118.

WAR DIARY
or
INTELLIGENCE SUMMARY.
(Erase heading not required.)

Sheet 46 11th Service Batn Royal Warwickshire Regt

Instructions regarding War Diaries and Intelligence Summaries are contained in F. S. Regs., Part II. and the Staff Manual respectively. Title pages will be prepared in manuscript.

Place	Date	Hour	Summary of Events and Information	Remarks and references to Appendices
	1916			
LE SOUICH	April 21		Battn found working parties of 500 men for hurdle making in ROBERMONT Wood	G.S.O
LE SOUICH	April 22		Working party as on April 21st	G.S.O
LE SOUICH	April 23		EASTER SUNDAY: The Battn rec'd Capt. & Adj. J.FALVEY-BETTS proceeded to D.H.Q as acting G.S.O.3: 2nd Lt LITTLE, Adj. Batt's Training under Company arrangements and also special training in Bayonet fighting under 2nd Lt. KEMSLEY-BOURNE and in Bombing under 2nd Lt. CRITCHLEY. "D" Company had the	G.S. M.C.
LE SOUICH	April 24		use of the Rifle Range to carry out a Course of Musketry laid down by 112th BDE.	M.C.
LE SOUICH	April 25		Battn Training as on April 23rd. Lewis Gun classes had the use of the Range.	M.C.
LE SOUICH	April 26		Battn Training as on April 24th. "B" Coy. had the use of the Range. 2nd Lt. G.F.WALEY reported for duty.	M.C.
LE SOUICH	April 27		Battn Training as on April 25th. "A" Coy. had the use of the Range. Inoculation was resumed by the M.O.	M.C.
LE SOUICH	April 28		Battn Training as on April 26th, but marching took the place of Bombing. "B" Coy. had the use of the Range. Inoculation was continued.	M.C.
LE SOUICH	April 29		Battn Training as on April 27th. "C" Coy. had the use of the Range. Inoculation was continued	M.C.
LE SOUICH	April 30		Battn rested.	

W.H.W.Little
Lt
o.c. Capt.
Adj. 11th SERVICE BN. R. WARWICKSHIRE REGT.

112th Brigade.
37th Division.

1/11th ROYAL WARWICKSHIRE REGIMENT

M A Y 1 9 1 6:

Confidential

War Diary

of

11th (S) Bn., Royal Warwickshire Regt.

From 1st May 1916 to 31st May 1916

(Volume II No 5).

Army Form C. 2118.

WAR DIARY
or
INTELLIGENCE SUMMARY.
(Erase heading not required.) 11th Service Battalion Royal Warwickshire Regiment

Sheet 57 47

Instructions regarding War Diaries and Intelligence Summaries are contained in F.S. Regs., Part II. and the Staff Manual respectively. Title pages will be prepared in manuscript.

Place	Date	Hour	Summary of Events and Information	Remarks and references to Appendices
LE SOUICH	May 1st		Batt.⁰ moved out of LE SOUICH, the head of Batt.ⁿ passing the starting point at 9.a.m. A 2 hour halt was made at COUTURELLE at 12.30 p.m. HUMBERCAMPS was reached at 5 p.m. and the Batt.ⁿ passed the night there.	Nil.
HUMBERCAMPS	May 2.		Batt.ⁿ marched to HANNESCAMPS to relieve the 1st RIFLE BRIGADE in the trenches. Head of Batt.ⁿ passed starting point at 7.30 pm. the Relief was completed by 10 p.m. A hostile patrol threw 12 bombs towards Sap from T.65 on ESSARTS RD. All fell short. No damage. Hostile Artillery active at some time & place,' also at 11 p.m. on T.76A. Batt.⁰ occupied trenches 64/77 with 3 Companies, having the 8th EAST LANCASHIRE REGT on our Right, and the 13th RIFLE BRIGADE on our left. Some bombs thrown at Sap in T.65 at about 10 pm otherwise situation very quiet. Wind from South. Weather hot and fine.	Nil.
HANNESCAMPS	May 3.		Some hostile shells on COLLINGBOURNE AV. during forenoon. Retaliation by our Howard Hill Guns on ESSARTS. Weather fine, wind South. situation normal.	Nil.
HANNESCAMPS	May 4.	2.30 am	An intense bombardment by enemy along the front immediately N/E of us, from T.71. to about T.92. Last night we observed our line handing over on our left Company front from T.74 to T.77 to the 6th BEDFORDSHIRE REGT. and ourselves occupying a 2 Company front (A & B) from T.60 to T.71. The bombardment continued until 3.25 AM	

T2134. W⁺. W708–776. 500000. 4/15. Sir J. C. & B.

Army Form C. 2118.

WAR DIARY
or
INTELLIGENCE SUMMARY.
(Erase heading not required.)

Sheet 48. 11th Service Battalion Royal Warwickshire Regiment

Place	Date	Hour	Summary of Events and Information	Remarks and references to Appendices
HANNESCAMPS	May 4		During the bombardment a patrol was sent out from our right Company to prevent a surprise on this front. For the remainder of the 24 hrs. situation was normal. Very hot weather. Wind S.W.	6 atts.
HANNESCAMPS	May 5		Hostile shells, 77 m/m and 4.2 fell on our front line and communication trenches at intervals during the day. A patrol went out from the left Company & another from the right Company at 9.45 p.m. Nothing was seen of the enemy. Both parties returned about 10 p.m. A strong S.W. wind sprung up about midnight & there was some rain. The night was very quiet. Weather fine. Wind S.E. Situation very quiet.	M.G. M.G.
HANNESCAMPS	May 6		"A" Company was relieved in the trenches by "C" Company, and "B" by "D". A draft of 37 N.C.O.s and men arrived from the 12th Bn. Weather continued fine. The situation was quiet. Wind S.W.	M.G.
HANNESCAMPS	May 7		Rain. Situation quiet. Wind S.	M.G.
HANNESCAMPS	May 8			
HANNESCAMPS	May 9		A hostile patrol about 30 strong was seen at about 8 p.m. proceeding from the hostile trenches to the O.S.E.D.H.E. Artillery and Lewis Gun fire were opened by us. Nothing further was seen of the enemy. The situation was very quiet during the early morning & forenoon. Between 12.45 v.1 p.m. about 40 T.M. bombs fell about T.62 and COLLINGBOURNE Av. at a range of about 800 x. Our field guns retaliated effectively. Weather mild and wet. Wind N. by S.	M.G.
HANNESCAMPS	May 10		Sgt. de St Croix and Pte Brandish were in observation in front of our line for nearly 18 hrs on the 9th inst.	M.G.

Army Form C. 2118.

WAR DIARY
or
INTELLIGENCE SUMMARY.
(Erase heading not required.)

11th Service Battalion Royal Warwickshire Regt

Sheet No 9.

Place	Date	Hour	Summary of Events and Information	Remarks and references to Appendices
HANNESCAMPS	May 10 (contd.)		Owing to unfavourable weather observation was difficult, but some useful information was obtained. More than usual activity on part of hostile Artillery. 36 4.2 shells falling about right Company front. No damage. Majority of shells failed to burst. 4 O.T.M. bombs again on T62 and COLLINGBOURNE Av. A Patrol consisting of Capt E.L. ROUTH, 2nd Lt STALKER, 2nd Lt JENKINS and 52 other ranks encountered an equally strong hostile patrol in the RAVINE. A brisk action ensued in which our patrol inflicted about 10 casualties among the enemy killed, and 10 wounded. We had 9 wounded (1 only seriously) and 1 missing (killed). A dead German was brought in. Our Artillery assisted on given signals. A full report of the affair was sent in to H.Q. Otherwise situation quiet, wind fresh & from West.	Nil.
HANNESCAMPS	May 11		Hostile 4.2 shells fell about our front line trenches at intervals during the forenoon and between 7 and 9 p.m. At 2 a.m. an intense bombardment could be heard about 12 miles South of us. At 7 a.m. HANNESCAMPS received about 6 4.2" shells. No damage was caused. Machine guns have been more active of late. Our Artillery retaliated effectively to the hostile shelling. Weather fine. Wind nil. On the 10th inst. Lt Col N.A.I. FLETCHER, 2/6 Bn. LIVERPOOL REGT., became attached to the Bn. for a period of 3 days. A working party of 50 men of the BEDFORD REGT. reports daily for work (commencing 9th inst). They are constructing Grenade Store under the direction of Lt CROSS, B.O.	Nil.
HANNESCAMPS	May 12		Rain. Situation quiet. Wind W. A patrol consisting of 2nd Lt H. SHEWRING and 3 other ranks, left	

Army Form C. 2118.

WAR DIARY
or
INTELLIGENCE SUMMARY.
(Erase heading not required.)

1/1th Service Battalion Royal Warwickshire Regiment.

Sheet 50.

Place	Date	Hour	Summary of Events and Information	Remarks and references to Appendices
HANNESCAMPS	May 12 (cont'd)		Left the Sap in Trench 58 at 6 p.m. in order to examine the wire in our right Company front and also to reconnoitre the ground to a distance of about 100 in front of our wire. Very useful information was obtained, a full report of which was sent in. The patrol returned to Trench 62 at 9.45 p.m.	WTC.
HANNESCAMPS	May 13		The wire in front of our Left Company was examined by a patrol under 2nd Lt. ALABASTER, last night, 12 inst. Rain and cold. Wind N. Situation quiet. Very dark night. Lt.-Col. De VOEUX, C.R.E. reconnoitred the ground in front of our right Company from ESSARTS ROAD to the POPLAR on the HANNESCAMPS — LA BRAYELLE Rd. He was accompanied by Capt. E.I. ROUTH, Sgt. de Ste CROIX and 4 men.	WTC.
HANNESCAMPS	May 14		Situation quiet. Wind N. Rain in evening. Bn. relieved by the 8th Leicester Regiment. Went into Billets at LA CAUCHIE.	WTC.
LA CAUCHIE	May 15		Bn. rested in Billets. Lt.-Col. C.S. COLLISON took over Command of the 112th B.D.E., Brigadier-General P.M. ROBINSON proceeding to ENGLAND on leave. Major C.P. ROOKE took over Command of the Battalion; Capt. E.H. BROCKSOPP, acting 2nd in Command, 2nd Lt. C.H. FRENCH acting O.C. "A" Coy.	WTC.
LA CAUCHIE	May 16		Battalion supplied a working party of 200 for the Corps Line, and another of 250 for work on the new Railway from LA HERLIERE to BIENVILLERS. Training in Signalling was carried on under 2nd Lt. R.M. HARRISON; in Lewis Guns under Lt. J.K. JONES; in Bombing under 2nd Lt. J. CRITCHLEY; in Sketcher-Bearer duties under Sgt. HICKENBOTTOM.	WTC.

Army Form C. 2118.

WAR DIARY
or
INTELLIGENCE SUMMARY.

(Erase heading not required.)

11th Service Battalion Royal Warwickshire Regiment

Sheet 51.

Instructions regarding War Diaries and Intelligence Summaries are contained in F.S. Regs., Part II. and the Staff Manual respectively. Title pages will be prepared in manuscript.

Place	Date	Hour	Summary of Events and Information	Remarks and references to Appendices
LA CAUCHIE	May 17		Battalion supplied working parties as on 16th inst. Courses continued as on 16th inst.	N.K.
LA CAUCHIE	May 18		Battalion supplied working parties, and Courses continued as on 17th inst.	N.K.
LA CAUCHIE	May 19		Battalion supplied working parties, and Courses continued as on 18th inst. An additional working party of 20 men under an N.C.O. had to be found for work under the O.C. North STAFFORD Regt.	N.K.
LA CAUCHIE	May 20		Battalion supplied working parties as on 19th and an additional one of 75 for work under 37th Bde Signal Coy. Courses in Signalling, Bombing and duties of Station Bearer were stopped in order to find the men required. At 9.20 pm Orders were received from Brigade to "Stand to". The Battalion was dismissed at 11 pm.	N.K.
LA CAUCHIE	May 21		Battalion supplied working parties as on 20th inst.	N.K.
LA CAUCHIE	May 22		Battalion supplied working parties as on 21st inst.	N.K.
LA CAUCHIE	May 23		A recently trained detachment of Lewis Gunners had the use of a Range. Battalion supplied working parties as on 22nd inst.	N.K.
LA CAUCHIE	May 24		Capt. J. FALVEY-BEYTS promoted Major from 18th April 1916, & relinquished appointment of Adjutant from that date. Battalion supplied working parties as on 23rd inst.	N.K.
LA CAUCHIE	May 25		Battalion supplied working parties as on 24th inst.	N.K.
LA CAUCHIE	May 26 am		Battalion supplied working party of 125 for Railway. Bde. Gen. P.M ROBINSON returned from leave and Lt. Col. C.S. COLLISON resumed command of the Battalion.	N.K.
HANNESCAMPS	May 26 pm		Battalion relieved the 8th Bn. LEICESTERSHIRE REGT. in the trenches, having the 4th DIVISION on our right,	N.K.

Army Form C. 2118.

WAR DIARY
or
INTELLIGENCE SUMMARY.
(Erase heading not required.)

11th Service Battalion Royal Warwickshire Regiment

Sheet 52.

Place	Date	Hour	Summary of Events and Information	Remarks and references to Appendices
HANNESCAMPS	May 26 (cont'd)		and the 8th Bn. EAST LANCASHIRE REGT. on our left. Situation normal. Weather hot and fine.	MH.
HANNESCAMPS	May 27		A large working party of about 450 was supplied by the Brigade for work on new front line trenches about 200x in advance of existing line on the Right Company front. The Battalion supplied 150 men for work of a similar nature on the Left Company front. This party was heavily shelled and 5 casualties were caused. (Work was carried on from 9 p.m. to 1 a.m.) Otherwise, situation normal, weather hot and fine. Considerable hostile artillery activity immediately South during the night.	MH.
HANNESCAMPS	May 28		Hostile Artillery activity was not above normal during the day. By night our new works received 105 mm shells every half hour from 11 p.m. to 2.30 a.m. Situation on our front generally normal. Heavy gun fire for prolonged periods several times during night immediately South of us. HANNESCAMPS received heavy shells about 4 p.m. In the early hours of the morning a small party became detached from a large party covering the front during the progress of new work. One man was discovered killed, and two are missing. Hostile Artillery was less active than usual. In the morning 5.9 How. Shells fell in some profusion about COLLINGBOURNE AV. Our 6" and 9.2 Hows. retaliated with effect on hostile Communication trenches. Otherwise situation quiet. Weather very wet : wind West.	MH.
HANNESCAMPS	May 30		Situation normal : weather fine; wind West. Some hostile Artillery activity on new trenches in front of trench 66; no men were at work there; Artillery ceased at about 11 p.m. A patrol consisting of	MH.

Army Form C. 2118.

WAR DIARY
or
INTELLIGENCE SUMMARY.

(Erase heading not required.) 11 "A" Service Battalion Royal Warwickshire Regiment

Instructions regarding War Diaries and Intelligence Summaries are contained in F. S. Regs., Part II. and the Staff Manual respectively. Title pages will be prepared in manuscript. Sheet 53.

Place	Date	Hour	Summary of Events and Information	Remarks and references to Appendices
HAMNESCAMPS	May 30 (contd)		L/Sgt. de St CROIX and two others searched the RAVINE for the 2 missing men. No signs of them were seen, and no hostile patrols encountered. The enemy appeared to be carrying on much work and later our Artillery fired on the locality. Work was continued on the new trenches in front of our right Company by 150 of our own men and 200 of the 10th LOYAL NORTH LANCS REGT. No hostile fire was opened.	NSR.
HAMNESCAMPS	May 31		Situation very quiet during day. Weather warm & fine; wind, mild W.N. From 11.40 pm until 12.30 am about 30 77 mm shells burst over the new trenches in front of Trench 66. No damage, no casualties. During the past six nights large working parties ranging from 140 to 250 men have been supplied by the 6th LEICESTER REGT and the 10th LOYAL NORTH LANCS REGT for work on a new front line about 200 yards in advance of the present line, under Brigade arrangements. The ourselves have supplied 150 men nightly for the same work.	NSR.

Wilfrid Little Lt. Col for
LT. COLONEL,
COMDG. 11th. SERVICE BN. R. WARWICKSHIRE REGT.

112th Brigade.
37th Division.

The battalion was attached to 34th
Division from 5th July 1916 to
21st August 1916

1/11th ROYAL WARWICKSHIRE REGIMENT

J U N E 1 9 1 6

34/ JUNE
11 Warwick
VOL II

11.N (7)

Confidential

War Diary

of

11th (S) Battalion, Royal Warwickshire Regiment

from 1st June 1916. to 30th June 1916.

(Volume II No 6.)

Army Form C. 2118.

WAR DIARY
or
INTELLIGENCE SUMMARY.

(Erase heading not required.) 11th Service Battalion Royal Warwickshire Regiment.

Instructions regarding War Diaries and Intelligence Summaries are contained in F.S. Regs., Part II. and the Staff Manual respectively. Title pages will be prepared in manuscript. Sheet 54.

Place	Date	Hour	Summary of Events and Information	Remarks and references to Appendices
HANNESCAMPS	June 1.		Hostile machine Guns were active at morning dawning stood to "Their positions have been located and reported to the artillery. 5,105 am shells fell about COLLINGBOURNE AVENUE and 4,77 mm. on an O.P. in trench 63, at about 8 a.m. No damage nor casualties. Between 8 a.m. & 11 p.m. about 40, 77 mm. and 15, 105 am. shells fell about the new work in front of trenches 65 and 66. 3 R.E. casualties. Generally, situation very quiet. Weather fine, wind, gentle S.W.	NRC.
HANNESCAMPS	June 2.		Hostile 77 mm. shells, H.E. and Shrapnel fell about the new works throughout the morning. COLLINGBOURNE AVENUE and the Sap in trench 66 were shelled with 5.9 How. from 5 p.m. to 7.30 p.m. Six casualties occurred, among them being Major B. R. MAGRATH, 2nd F. LANCS REGT. and Capt. HALLETT, 125 D. R.F.A., both killed. New works were intermittently shelled during the night. Two 5.9 shells fell near CHURCH END in HANNESCAMPS. A groom & 2 horses were killed. Weather fine. Wind, gentle S.W.	NRC.
HANNESCAMPS	June 3		New trenches between trench 59 and NORTH FORTIN registered by hostile 77 mm. gun during forenoon. COLLINGBOURNE AVENUE and vicinity again received about 20, 5.9 shells and about 50, 77 mm. shells. The trench was blown down in several places but no very material damage was done. Hostile machine Guns were again active. Weather fine. Wind, gentle S.W. Until 12 m/n the situation was extraordinarily quiet.	NRC.
HANNESCAMPS	June 4		Heavy bombardments were opened both N. and S. of us in the early hours of the morning. Raids were made on the hostile trenches by the Unit of the Brigade North of ours, and by a Unit of that on our right.	

Army Form C. 2118.

WAR DIARY
or
INTELLIGENCE SUMMARY.
(Erase heading not required.) 11th Service Battalion Royal Warwickshire Regiment

Instructions regarding War Diaries and Intelligence Summaries are contained in F.S. Regs., Part II. and the Staff Manual respectively. Title pages will be prepared in manuscript. Sheet 55.

Place	Date	Hour	Summary of Events and Information	Remarks and references to Appendices
HANNESCAMPS	June 4 (contd)		Hostile batteries replied, but our front was not touched. The situation otherwise was exceptionally quiet. Weather fine; wind gentle S.W. Lt Col C.S. COLLISON proceeded on leave to IRELAND; Maj ROOKE Cmdg Bn.	MAL
HANNESCAMPS	June 5		Situation very quiet. Weather dull and showery. Wind fresh S.W.	MAL
HANNESCAMPS	June 6		Situation normal. Wind fresh S.W. Heavy showers in morning. Some later Battalion was relieved in the trenches by 8th Bn. LEICESTERSHIRE REGT, the Battalion proceeded to billets in LA CAUCHIE except for "B" Coy which went into billets in POMMIER for the purpose of supplying a working party of 150 for the Rifle Butts of the Brigade front in the Trenches. The London Gazette of the 10th June contained among the "Birthday Honours" an award of the D.S.O to Lt Col C.S. COLLISON, Cmdg 11th ROYAL WARWICKSHIRE REGT, the MILITARY CROSS to 2nd Lt A.E. BOUCHER and the D.C.M. to R/Sgt DE STE CROIX, of the same Battalion.	MAL
LA CAUCHIE	June 7		The Battalion rested in billets.	MAL
LA CAUCHIE	June 8		Battalion supplied various working parties, 450 men being employed altogether, including the 150 at POMMIER. A course of instruction for 4 Officers was started under 2nd Lt ALABASTER. Signallers training was continued.	MAL
LA CAUCHIE	June 9		Battalion supplied working parties as on 8th inst. The London Gazette dated 3rd June 1916 contained the name of No.11056, Cpl. H.C. BAGLEY, 11 R. WAR. R. - MILITARY MEDAL.	MAL
LA CAUCHIE	June 10		Battalion supplied working parties as on 8th inst. A draft of 42 men joined the Battalion. 3 officers and 3 N.C.Os proceeded for a 7 day course to the BDE. GRENADE School.	MAL

Army Form C. 2118.

WAR DIARY
or
INTELLIGENCE SUMMARY.

(Erase heading not required.) 11th Battalion (Service) Royal Warwickshire Regiment

Sheet 56.

Place	Date	Hour	Summary of Events and Information	Remarks and references to Appendices
LA CAUCHIE	June 11		Working parties supplied by Battalion as on 10th inst.	
LA CAUCHIE	June 12		Working parties again supplied by Battalion. Capt. E.H. BROCKOPP & 2nd Lt. L. HORTON proceeded on leave.	
LA CAUCHIE	June 13		Working parties again supplied by Battalion.	
LA CAUCHIE	June 14		Working parties again supplied by Battalion.	
LA CAUCHIE	June 15		As on 14th inst. Lt. Col. C.S. COLLISON D.S.O. returned from leave.	
LA CAUCHIE	June 16		As on 15th inst.	
LA CAUCHIE	June 17		As on 16th inst.	
LA CAUCHIE	June 18		The Battalion relieved the 8th Bn. LEICESTER REGT. in the trenches, "A" & "B" Coys taking up their former positions on right and left respectively. "C" Company relieved a Company of the 1/5 LINCOLN REGT, taking up thereby a new set of trenches on the right of "A" Coy. "D" Company supplied ration carrying parties for the three Companies in the front line.	
HANNESCAMPS	June 19		Situation normal last night. Some activity on part of hostile Machine Guns. Wind S.W. Weather fine but cold. Some artillery activity on both sides throughout the day principally dealing with GOMMECOURT.	
HANNESCAMPS	June 20		Situation normal. Hostile machine guns active at various on new works throughout the night. Hostile shells at intervals throughout day at points along our Battalion front. No damage. Weather fine Wind W.	

Army Form C. 2118.

WAR DIARY
or
INTELLIGENCE SUMMARY.

(Erase heading not required.) 11th Service Battalion Royal Warwickshire Regiment

Instructions regarding War Diaries and Intelligence Summaries are contained in F. S. Regs., Part II. and the Staff Manual respectively. Title pages will be prepared in manuscript. Sheet 57.

Place	Date	Hour	Summary of Events and Information	Remarks and references to Appendices
HANNESCAMPS	June 21		Situation normal. Hostile Artillery active at intervals on various points. Very quiet night. Weather fine & warmer. Wind N.N.W.	WSC.
HANNESCAMPS	22.		More than usual activity on the part of our Artillery. Shells of various calibre were fired intermittently all day on GOMMECOURT WOOD & hostile lines throughout. Hostile Artillery retaliation inconsiderable. 150mm. battery registering during forenoon on old & new trenches held by our right Company. Very few shells fell on our centre & left Company. At night enemy very quiet. Hostile parties seen by party covering new work in progress & dispersed by rapid fire. No traces found on reconnaissance. Weather very warm. Wind S.W. British aeroplanes very active throughout daylight.	WSC.
HANNESCAMPS	23		Considerable artillery activity on both sides, principally on our immediate right. Our right Company received "attention" but only 2 casualties were caused. Our field batteries were active throughout the morning & after-noon cutting wire in front of hostile front line facing FONQUEVILLERS. At about 3 p.m. a very heavy downpour of rain & hail came on, & a gale of wind. Trenches dugouts quickly flooded. Rain continued practically throughout the night. Throughout the night our field guns and machine guns worried the enemy with intermittent shooting.	WSC.
HANNESCAMPS	24		Continued activity of our Artillery on our immediate right. Field batteries also cutting wire opposite our lines. Bombardment of GOMMECOURT WOOD & hostile works in front of it increasingly. At	WSC.

WAR DIARY
or
INTELLIGENCE SUMMARY.

(Erase heading not required.)   11th Service Battalion Royal Warwickshire Regiment.

Army Form C. 2118.

Place	Date	Hour	Summary of Events and Information	Remarks and references to Appendices
HANNESCAMPS	June 24	(contd)	Times this bombardment was intense but generally only moderate. Field Batteries continued to cut wire successfully. At about 11 p.m. there was a very intense bombardment further South. On our own particular front the line was quiet except for an occasional shell, & at night machine gun fire, but our right Company came in for the hostile Artillery fire on FONQUEVILLERS –	MCK
HANNESCAMPS	25		VILLERS. British aeroplanes were active throughout daylight. Weather fine throughout daylight. Wind N. Bombarded by our Artillery continued throughout the night & became particularly heavy at dawn. During forenoon we continued to actively shell works from Pigeon Wood to GOMMECOURT. Some very heavy shells were used, resulting explosions being terrific. Enemy retaliated actively on FONQUEVILLERS, principally with 150 & 77 mm shells, but the retaliation was insignificant compared to our fire. This continued incessantly from before, at times being very intense. S.	M.W.
HANNESCAMPS	26		Bombardment continued. Very heavy Artillery fire could also be heard further South. It is impossible to say how far down the line the bombardment is being made. During the forenoon a raid was made, only an extract from letter GOMMECOURT and FONQUEVILLERS of smoke. It worked admirably. The town be turned at the same time was terrific. 3 hostile balloons were today brought down in flames. Some Rain.	WKL

Army Form C. 2118.

WAR DIARY
or
INTELLIGENCE SUMMARY

(Erase heading not required.)

Title Pages Sheet 59. 11th Service Battalion Royal Warwickshire Regt.

Place	Date	Hour	Summary of Events and Information	Remarks and references to Appendices
HANNESCAMPS	June 27		Between 5 and 6 a.m. the bombardment on both sides was very heavy. Our right Company received the heaviest yet experienced. Shelling was again heavy between 8 a.m. & 9 a.m. and between 9 and 10 a.m. Much damage was caused to hostile works by our heavy guns. At 3.30 p.m. Gas was discharged from the lines of the 2 battalions on our left. It drifted over MONCHY and QUESNOY FARM. Little rifle & machine gun fire came from the enemy. At 6.30 p.m. our Artillery opened an intense bombardment on hostile lines from the Z to COMMECOURT WOOD. 97s and 105s retaliated with intense fire on FONQUEVILLERS, which our right Company again received attention. Our Artillery has kept up an incessant intermittent fire throughout day and night. Hostile retaliation generally is very feeble. Bombardment of intensity was also in progress from our side south of HEBUTERNE at midnight. Weather - heavy showers. Wind N.S.W.	W.S.D. H.H.
HANNESCAMPS	28		Bombardment of hostile lines continued during the early hours with some intensity; later on diminishing to intermittent but persistent shelling from our side. Retaliation at times considerable but generally feeble. Our right Company again came in for the overflow of the hostile shelling on FONQUEVILLERS. The Centre & left Companies remaining quiet. Effect of our bombardment on hostile lines is very clear. The hostile trenches are scarcely distinguishable: the trees in the woods are becoming considerably thinned out; the enemy is very quiet - very little machine gun and no rifle fire. It is possible to walk out in the open in front of our lines where previously one would have been certainly sniped probably shelled. Weather dull & showery. Wind changeable, generally S.W. H.H.

Army Form C. 2118.

WAR DIARY
or
INTELLIGENCE SUMMARY

(Erase heading not required.)

11th Service Battalion Royal Warwickshire Regiment

Sheet 60.

Instructions regarding War Diaries and Intelligence Summaries are contained in F. S. Regs., Part II. and the Staff Manual respectively. Title Pages will be prepared in manuscript.

Place	Date	Hour	Summary of Events and Information	Remarks and references to Appendices
HANNESCAMPS	June 29.	1.45 to 2.30 a.m.	Numerous red and other flares were sent up by the enemy, & his artillery opened on HEBUTERNE. No M.G. or rifle fire was opened from the Z and LITTLE Z. Gas was seen going slowly across the hostile lines in the direction of DOUCHY from our trenches in HANNESCAMPS salient. Heavy rifle fire was heard &	
		4 a.m.	intense Artillery fire on both sides. The wire cutting by our Field Guns opposite GOMMECOURT continued & heavier also fired at intervals throughout the day. No hostile retaliation in morning. At 4.40 p.m.	
		5 p.m. to 11 p.m.	the bombardment by our Artillery became intense and activity continued on both sides until after 8 p.m. About 10 p.m. our guns opened heavy fire, and machine & Lewis guns were very active. A heavy bombardment could be heard South of HEBUTERNE. We sent out a patrol to examine a new hostile trench across the RAVINE. It was found to be incomplete & unoccupied. No sound of the enemy could be heard. 2nd Lt. JENKINS & 2nd Lt. CRITCHLEY led the patrol.	WK.
HANNESCAMPS	30.		Our Artillery continued bombarding GOMMECOURT at intervals; wire-cutting continued. Enemy showed little activity; retaliated at times with 5.9s, 4.2s and 77mm. Our fire was unusually heavy after dark; hostile batteries dropped several salvos into FONQUEVILLERS between 10 p.m. and 11 p.m. Bombarded also heavily opposite MONCHY from 10 p.m. to m/n. Weather fine. Wind W.	WK. ditto.

37th Division.
34th Division from 5.7.16.
112th Infantry Brigade

Transferred with 112th Brigade from
37th to 34th Division 5th July 1916.

1/11th BATTALION

ROYAL WARWICKSHIRE REGIMENT

JULY 1916

WAR DIARY or INTELLIGENCE SUMMARY

Army Form C. 2118

(Erase heading not required.) 1/1th Service Battalion Royal Warwickshire Regiment

Sheet 61.

Place	Date	Hour	Summary of Events and Information	Remarks and references to Appendices
HANNESCAMPS	July 1	6.30 am	Intense Bombardment on GOMMECOURT Salient. At 7.25 am Smoke was discharged all along our line, & Division on our immediate right attacked at 7.30 am, all went well except on right of 46th Division opposite Southern end of FONQUEVILLERS. There was a check. Observation was rendered exceedingly difficult owing to the dense smoke. Our right Company reports having seen some of our men about the hostile trenches which had been attacked. Later it was reported that the 46th Division attacking troops had occupied the hostile third line except for the check already mentioned. At 3.30 pm our artillery again bombarded that sector but apparently our troops could not advance further. In the meantime the 56th Division was reported to have secured its objectives. At midnight information came to hand that the 46th Division had been ordered to withdraw to its original front line. We were very fortunate during the bombardments having only 6 casualties (one killed). Weather fine and hot. Wind W.	NH.
HANNESCAMPS	2.		No further attacks were made. Intermittent shelling by our Artillery continued. Capt. E.H.BROCKSOPP took out a patrol and examined our front but no sign of hostile patrols was found. A hostile cap marked by a cavalry group was handed by L/Sgt. de la CROIX D.C.M.	NH
HANNESCAMPS	3		The night of 2nd/3rd passed quietly. 2/Lt. BARWELL took out a patrol 15 strong but no sign of the enemy patrols was found. During the day there was intermittent shelling on both sides. The Battalion was relieved in the trenches by the 1/5 LINCOLN REGT. and proceeded for the night to WLch in BIENVILLERS.	NH.
BIENVILLERS HALLOY	4.	10 am 3 pm	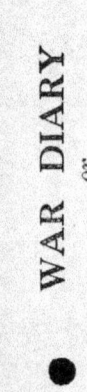 Battalion marched from BIENVILLERS and proceeded via SEAMAND, HENU, PAS to HALLOY. Battalion reached HALLOY and went into billets. Very heavy rain came on during the march and all got drenched through. Very bad billets - leaking huts. Weather cleared for night. N.W.

WAR DIARY or INTELLIGENCE SUMMARY

(Erase heading not required.) 11th Service Battalion Royal Warwickshire Regiment

Army Form C. 2118

Sheet 62.

Place	Date	Hour	Summary of Events and Information	Remarks and references to Appendices
HALLOY	July 5.		Battalion rested in billets. Orders were received in afternoon to be ready to move off at short notice.	NIL.
		12 p.m.	Orders received to be ready to move by motor buses at 6 a.m.	NIL.
VALLOY	6	6 a.m.	Battalion ready to move. Motor buses did not begin to arrive until 8.30 a.m.	NIL.
MEILMONT	6	4 p.m.	Arrival of Battalion completed. Tents pitched.	NIL.
		12 m/n	Orders to proceed to ALBERT starting at 5.20 a.m.	
ALBERT	7	7 a.m.	Battalion marched through ALBERT & proceeded to reserve trenches at TARA REDOUBT.	NIL.
		7.30 a.m.	Bombardment started. Battalion standing-to ready to move forward.	
ALBERT (Battle of the SOMME)	8	1 a.m.	Orders received for 2 Companies to proceed to trenches known as HELIGOLAND.	
		12 noon	Orders received for Battalion to proceed to front line trenches to relieve the 58th B.D.E. (Remarks the 112 Bde. has become part of 34th DIVISION).	NIL.
		8.30 p.m.	Battalion marched up to front line trenches from TARA REDOUBT & occupied trenches along CONTALMAISON - LA BOISELLE road (taken from the enemy at noon today) with its Right about 300x W of the former still occupied by the enemy.	W.T.Hunt Capt acting adjt
	9.	2.30 p.m	A patrol of B.Coy reconnoitred the ground leading to CONTALMAISON WOOD & found 3 abandoned 77 m.m. guns also made 3 prisoners in the Battery dugout. Half a Platoon was left to hold the Battery position. Many useful maps were also	

Army Form C. 2118

WAR DIARY
or
INTELLIGENCE SUMMARY
(Erase heading not required.)

Instructions regarding War Diaries and Intelligence Summaries are contained in F.S. Regs., Part II. and the Staff Manual respectively. Title Pages will be prepared in manuscript.

Place	Date	Hour	Summary of Events and Information	Remarks and references to Appendices
Battle of the SOMME.	9/7/16		found, our marking the defences of OVILLERS on our left still held by the enemy. During the afternoon our position was heavily shelled. The detachment guarding the Sunna being partially surrounded was withdrawn. Heavy shell fire (chiefly 150 m.m.) on our position continued throughout the night. Our casualties during the day were 4 officers (2nd Lt Horton, 2nd Lt Jenkins, 2nd Lt Beswick + 2nd Lt Alabaster) wounded 2nd Lt Keller	O.T.A.
"	10th	10 + about 86 wounded. mainly from shell fire		
		1.30p.m.	Bde ordered to push strong patrols to certain points immediately N of CONTALMAISON with a view to the re-adjustment of our line. The 111 Bde on our left conforming. The operation was cancelled, as it was daylight before orders which had to be carefully examined were ready for issue by O.C. Corps. Our position was heavily shelled the whole day.	
		4.30.	The 69th Bde assembled in our trenches + attacked CONTALMAISON from the W. The attack was prevented by an intense bombardment. The village was successfully carried	
		5 p.m.	C Coy proceeded to establish strong patrol posts on a line running S.W. of CONTALMAISON WOOD in conjunction with the 13th R. Bde (111 Bde) on our left. The 13th R. Bde was late making it impossible	

WAR DIARY or INTELLIGENCE SUMMARY

Army Form C. 2118

Place	Date	Hour	Summary of Events and Information	Remarks and references to Appendices
Battle of the SOMME	July 10	5PM	for "C" Coy to make good its object owing to heavy Machine Gun & rifle fire from its front & left flank. Two Officers & 50 O.R's were sent from "A" Coy to assist in the consolidation. "C" Coy lost in Officers 2nd Lt Hemsey-Browne Killed, 2nd Lt Fleuring & 2nd Lt Webb wounded. Capt. Reath O.B's Coy was also wounded, while assisting in the evacuation as he knew the ground. The 13th R.F. Bde could not make their ground good & lost heavily in the attempt. During the latter retirement to its original position, our "D" Coy on the left of our line repulsed enemy's forces, that followed the 13th R.F. Bde in their retirement making one unwounded prisoner. The losses of the Batt throughout the day from heavy shell fire & the above action was considerable. "D" Coy especially were very heavily shelled but remained steady throughout. 2nd Lt YORKIN'S was killed also 2nd Lt. CRITCHLEY (Batt Bombing Officer). L.S.Mjr CANTON. The losses for the day were 3 Officers killed 3 officers wounded 6 O.R's killed & 34 wounded & 6 missing.	
"	10			N.A.
"	11	6AM	Relieved by the 101 N. Lanc Regt. & returned to TARA-USNA	

WAR DIARY
INTELLIGENCE SUMMARY

(Erase heading not required.)

Army Form C. 2118

Instructions regarding War Diaries and Intelligence Summaries are contained in F. S. Regs., Part II. and the Staff Manual respectively. Title Pages will be prepared in manuscript.

Place	Date 1916	Hour	Summary of Events and Information	Remarks and references to Appendices
BATTLE of the SOMME	July 11	6 AM	Ridge. During the night a very heavy Artillery action about our front & in the region of THIEPVAL. No prist.	WDH.
"	12		Heavy Artillery action throughout the day. A 150 MM. shell hit C. Coy Field Kitchen, killing 3 of its cooks & a prisoner. Batt. moved from bivouacs to trenches near for the night	
"	13	10 PM	Moved up to trenches & relieved the 8th E. Lancs Regt in first support. Intense Artillery action throughout the day, we were not worried very much.	WDH. WDH.
"	14			
"	15	3 AM	OPERATION ORDERS arrived, that the 112 Bde would attack POZIERES at 9. 20 AM. Friday Conference of Commanding Officers at 6.30 AM. The dispositions were that the 8th E. Lancs Regt were to clear that part of the Village S. of the ALBERT–POZIERES road the 6th Bedfd Regt the area N of that road. The 11. R. War. R. to take up tools & assist the two Battalions to consolidate the ground gained. The 15 K. W. Lancs Regt was to carry bombs & stores &c. The order of attack was each Battalion with 2 Coys in the front line + 2 in support each Battalion to follows the other in the following order. 8th E. Lancs, 6th Bedfs, 11 R War.R.	

Place	Date	Hour	Summary of Events and Information	Remarks and references to Appendices
BATTLE of the SOMME.	July 15		under cover of an intense bombardment. The distance to the objective in view of the enemy was about 1100x. POZIERES was reported thinly held with no wire to contend with. The Bde. advanced seemingly in order, but was held up quite near to its objective by enemy M/G's which were in great force, also it was found that the wire on the front to be attacked was not cut. The Bde found itself immobilised in front of the village with its unwilling more or less intermixed. Capt Brocksopp & 2nd Lt French of "A" Coy, 2nd Lt Walker of "C" Coy & 2nd Lt Bower of "B" Coy. were wounded very early in the action, "A" Coy was then without officers & 2nd Lt C.S. Major Freeman was with Capt Brocksopp in an anger-at-Atta position. Sergt Tyson took Command. Batt H.Qrs were caught when moving from the trenches by an Artillery barrage M/G fire were obliged to take shelter in a shell hole where it established communication by telephone with Bde H.Qrs. Batt H.Qrs. were subsequently moved to a trench off the CONTALMAISON - POZIERES road, whence touch with the Companies was maintained by runners with Bde H.Qrs by telephone (the latter was cut by shell fire during the day about 6 times repaired each time	

Army Form C. 2118

WAR DIARY
or
INTELLIGENCE SUMMARY
(Erase heading not required.)

Place	Date 1916	Hour	Summary of Events and Information	Remarks and references to Appendices
Battle of the SOMME POZIERES	July 1/15		with very little delay) Meanwhile the Coy on the left (B.C. Coys) had made the attempt to formed the post over available & remained in action, but were unable to advance. "A" Coy had ensconced itself in shell holes.	
		5 PM	The artillery again bombarded the Village & the infantry 2nd assault was timed for 6 P.M. The signal for the 2nd assault being a red rocket. The bombardment tho intense failed to put out the hostile M/Gs & the assault was met with such a fierce fire that it collapsed, though our infantry did not give way but held their ground with great tenacity. An attempt by the enemy to advance against the flank of A. Coy was caught by the Lewis Gun of that Coy & was easily crushed. Here Sergt HITCH. MAN behaved with great coolness straying even when killed at his gun. Capt McCleod of D Coy was wounded in the latter assault under cover of night the Battn was relieved by the 10th L.N. Lanc Regt & returned to the support trenches & occupied the previous night. OTRs out of 8 any Officers who went into the action 5 were shot & 270 OTRs out of 580, a percentage of 48. The Casualties since the Battn arrived in this Sector have been 15 Officers & 450 OTRs	

WAR DIARY or INTELLIGENCE SUMMARY

Army Form C. 2118

Place	Date 1916	Hour	Summary of Events and Information	Remarks and references to Appendices
Battle of the SOMME.	July 16	3.15 P.M.	The Batt. was relieved by the 11th Batt Northumberland Fusiliers & proceeded to billets in ALBERT.	WTH
ALBERT	17		Resting. Batts. releases undertaking afforded by 34th Res Batts	WTH
"	18	12.30AM	Batt ordered to proceed to trench system called HELIGOLAND as a support to 68th Bde who were to attack POZIERES at dawn. Attack cancelled, the Batt ordered to return to its billets where it arrived at 8.30AM. Resting.	WTH
BRESLE	19	3.30PM	Batt proceeded to billets in BRESLE about 5 miles W.S.W. of ALBERT.	WTH
LA HOUSSOYE	20	10.AM	Batt proceeded to LA HOUSSOYE on the main ALBERT-AMIENS road. Full 1st line Motor Transport. Accommodation by billets bad, especially for Officers. Billet accommodation improved by leaving the "Pillage" Corp.	WTH
"	21		Very wet. Inspections & returns to refitted in accordance with Instructions when other Regts of the Bde leaving the front. Tactical — Deficiencies found to be few — Reorganising Companies. Very few instruction left. (Officers or NCOs) to train new Lewis Gun Sections & Bombing purposes. Losses in Senior NCO's particularly serious.	WTH
"	22		Batt commenced training. Programme of Instruction. Running Drill, Steady Drill, 1½ km Route march daily (full marching order on alternate days). Special classes	

WAR DIARY or INTELLIGENCE SUMMARY

Army Form C. 2118

Place	Date 1916 July	Hour	Summary of Events and Information	Remarks and references to Appendices
LA HOUSSOYE	22		Instruction for Lewis Gun, Bombing, Signalling also Sketches Drawing.	W7/4
"	23	10 AM	Divine Service. Officers attended. Mounted Officer attended funeral of Major General E.C. INGOUVILLE WILLIAMS CB D.S.O. (Killed in action MAMETZ WOOD July 22-7-16)	A7/4
"	24		Batt training under Company arrangements. 34th "Div" School instituted for training - found to be good on the training Ground.	W7/4
"		6 PM	(Guide close) Draft of 388 O.R's arrived posted to Coys as follows:- A. Coy 106 "B" Coy 108 "C" Coy 109 "D" Coy 65	W7/4
"	25	10 AM	Draft inspected by the Commanding Officer & afterwards by the Brigadier General. The draft comprised 25 N.C.Os, 253 Privates (including 5 signallers) 63 had seen previous active service during the war. The majority had only received 13-14 weeks training. Very few had ever handled a Mills bomb - none had received instruction in the Lewis Gun. Batt training under Coy arrangements.	W7/4
"		3.45 PM until 12 Noon	The 112 Bde inspected by Lt General Sir W.P. PULTENEY K.C.B. D.S.O. Commanding III Corps. The R.W. was congratulated on its work since its arrival in the present Sector with the Corps. The General commented on the fact the Bde was at on July 1st on POZIERES on the 9th the most difficult ever set to any troops. (All new to active service conditions)	W7/4
"		6 PM	Draft of 9 Officers arrived (2 Lieutenants)	W7/4

Army Form C. 2118

WAR DIARY
or
INTELLIGENCE SUMMARY
(Erase heading not required.)

Instructions regarding War Diaries and Intelligence Summaries are contained in F. S. Regs., Part II. and the Staff Manual respectively. Title Pages will be prepared in manuscript.

Place	Date	Hour	Summary of Events and Information	Remarks and references to Appendices
LA HOUSSOYE	July 1916 26		Batt training under Coy arrangement. Skirmishing attacking troops there with to an Artillery barrage even at the expense of a few casualties from same. This was practised today in so be proceeded with daily.	WT/A
"	27		Batt training under Coy arrangements & it also attended a Anti-Gas lecture by the Army Gas Expert at 4 PM.	WT/A WT/A
"	28		Batt training under Coy arrangements.	WT/A
"	29		Batt training under Coy arrangements.	
"	30	AM 6:30	Batt attended Church Parade. At 4.45 PM. The Batt proceeded to Billets at BRESLE. 112 Bde all billeted here.	WT/A
"	31	PM 6:15	Batt proceeded with the Brigade to bivouac in BECOURT WOOD as Brigade in Divisional Reserve in BECOURT WOOD, relieving 101st Bde. 101st Bde relieving Front Bde (57th Bde) 19th Div. on Line running E & S.W. of BAZENTIN-le-Petit. 111 Bde relieving Supporting Bde (56 Bde) 19 Div in MAMETZ WOOD Area.	67/A
"		M/N	Batt landed in FRANCE on this date three last Year.	67/A

W.T. Hart
CAPTAIN
ADJ. 11th SERVICE BN. R. WARWICKSHIRE REGT.

112th Brigade.
34th Division till 22nd.
37th Division from 22nd Aug.

1/11th BATTALION

THE ROYAL WARWICKSHIRE REGIMENT

AUGUST 1 9 1 6

Attached:-
 Operation Orders.
 Report on Operations 12/13th August 1916.

WAR DIARY or INTELLIGENCE SUMMARY

Army Form C 2118.

Place	Date 1916	Hour	Summary of Events and Information	Remarks and references to Appendices
BECOURT WOOD	Aug. 1	10-11am	Hostile H.E. Shells from a heavy gun dropped & exploded in quick succession among the companies in close bivouacs, involving many casualties before the Batt. could take cover in the adjoining trenches allotted to the Companies. 8 Officers viz:- Batt. Chaplain (C.of E.) Capt. J. GARFIELD - ROBERTS, 2nd Lt. P.A. THORSON & 2nd Lt. F.W. ALLAM were wounded. O.R's Killed 10, wounded 39, missing 2. Total 52. Previous to this date no serious shelling of the wood had taken place. The Batt. was at once moved about 300x outside the EASTERN edge of wood, where a line of good deep trenches exist. Batt. training in Lewis Gun & Bombing etc continued. Batt. provided a working party to the C.R.E. to dig trenches immediately EAST of FRICOURT.	W.T.H. W.T.H. W.T.H.
" "	2			
" "	3	Noon	Operation Orders received from 112 Bde. that the Div (34th) was to extend its right & to take over the line now held by the left of the 51st Div. up to the WESTERN end of HIGH WOOD. (Exclusive). The new sub-sector to be occupied by the 111th Bde. who relieve the 152nd Bde. today. The 111th Bde. in first support to be replaced by the 8th E. Lanc. & 6th Bed Rifle & 13th Rifle Bde. & 13 R. Fusiliers of the	

WAR DIARY
or
INTELLIGENCE SUMMARY
(Erase heading not required.)

Army Form C.2118.

Place	Date 1916	Hour	Summary of Events and Information	Remarks and references to Appendices
BECOURT WOOD	Aug 3rd		of the 112th Bde. The remainder of the Bde to stay in its present position. The 34th Divisional front now runs approx from a point 250 x N of BAZENTIN--le-Petit to the S. Western edge of HIGH WOOD.	65TH
"	" 4		Batt training continued.	65TH
"	" 5		Operation Orders received from 112th Bde H.Q." that the Bde was to prepare to relieve the 107th Bde tomorrow. Conference of Commanding Officers at 2.30 PM. C.O.s reconnoitred their prospective trench lines to be taken over.	65TH
"	6		112 Bde relieved the 101st Bde. 8th E. Lanc & 6 Bedf Regt in the front line. 11 R. War. R. in Support. 10th N. Lanc Regt in reserve. The Batt. occupied trenches. "A" Coy. with Batt H.Q. on the S.E. edge of BAZENTIN-le-Petit. WOOD. "B" Coy in trench line made N. edge of. D. Coy inside W. edge of MAMETZ WOOD. Relief complete 7 PM.	65TH
BAZENTIN-Le-Petit	7		Intermittent shelling on both sides throughout the day. MAMETZ WOOD was heavily shelled by 8" & 5.9" How.s & 77 mm Guns	65TH
"	8		Very heavy Artillery duel throughout the night. T/R MAMETZ WOOD heavily shelled as on the previous day. D. Coy suffered from this losing 1 Officer (2nd Lieut E.J. PUSCH) Killed. 1 O.R. Killed & nine wounded. The shelling con-	

WAR DIARY or INTELLIGENCE SUMMARY

(Erase heading not required.)

Place	Date 1916	Hour	Summary of Events and Information	Remarks and references to Appendices
BAZENTIN-Le-Petit	Aug. 8		Quiet throughout the day. D. Coy. was moved to the RIGHT flank of Batt H.Q. trench. Hostile aeroplanes (one) came over our lines during the evening & were engaged by British machines for about an hour.	WD4
"	9		Hostile artillery activity increased. HAMETZ WOOD & vicinity heavily shelled with 8" & 5.9 How & 77mm guns throughout the day. A large number of gas shells being used. B. Coy. was moved to Batt H.Q. trench system. 1 Officer 2nd Lieut COOPER & 4 O.R.'s wounded this day.	WD4
"	10		Hostile artillery less active during today. Batt. relieved the 6th Bedford Regt. on the FRONT LINE. About 500 x of trench running E & W 200 x N of BAZENTIN-le-Petit, & facing Germans in 300 x of intermediate line being tenaciously held. This intermediate trench was part of a line taken by a previous Division, in length about 500 x. The 107th Bde tried but failed to take it with heavy losses. The 6 Bedford Regt next tried & failed with about 75 casualties. The 10th K.R. Lancs. were successful in taking about 200 x of the right of it on morning of 10th inst (it cut out them about 120 casualties) leaving 3 hrs hard fighting mostly with soft bombs. During the evening the hostile artillery fire was very intense. D. Coy in close support on N.W. edge of BAZENTIN-Le-Petit, sustained casualties, 1 Officer killed	WD4

INTELLIGENCE SUMMARY

(Erase heading not required.)

Place	Date 1916	Hour	Summary of Events and Information	Remarks and references to Appendices
BAZENTIN-Le-Petit	Aug 10.		(2nd Lieut WARD 1 wounded (Shell shock) 2nd Lieut VAUGHTON. Hostile Artillery very active throughout the day. 8" & 5.9 Hows + 77 M.M. Guns searching our support trenches mostly. Our casualties were O.R. Killed 13, Wounded 43, Missing 7. Total 63. A large number of men were buried by H.E. shells this account for the missing, 4 bodies were afterwards dug out + pieces of other men unrecognisable.	W.T.A.
"	11. 12	1 PM	This was a very trying day for the Troops. Intense hostile artillery fire on our trenches throughout the day early morning, but below normal during the remainder of the day. Operation Orders received from Bde H.Q. that the Batt would attack at 10.30 P.M. the remaining 300× of Intermediate line running EAST of the direct BAZENTIN-Le-Petit — MARTINPUICH road. Artillery Cooperation. Intense 3 hrs bombardment with heavies up to 7 P.M. then 3 mins intense shelling by 18 pdrs before ZERO (10.30 p.m.) + lastly to Lift + continue for an hour. Order of attack A. Coy on the RIGHT C. Coy on the LEFT each on a half Company frontage, Platoons in line, the remaining half companies in same formation to follow at 100× distance. B + D	

25

WAR DIARY
or
INTELLIGENCE SUMMARY

(Erase heading not required.)

Place	Date	Hour	Summary of Events and Information	Remarks and references to Appendices
DAZENTIN-le-PETIT	May 1916	12½	Companies to reoccupy trenches of those left by C"A" & to support the attack if called upon. B.Coy to supply one section to follow each half company assaulting, with consolidating material. The bombardment of the hostile trench by our heavies no doubt attracted our intended attack. Directly darkness set in our front & trenches also Batt H.Q. were subjected to an intense shelling by 77 m/m. Shrapnel fire, which increased in intensity directly the assault issued over our parapet, also considerable M/G fire was turned on our men. The attack was held up within 20 x of the hostile trench, also the flank. Cooperation of bombing parties by the 10th Royal Scots on the left & the 10th R.N.Lancs on the right. The assaulting troops were obliged to return to their original trenches. Our casualties were Officers Killed 1. (2nd Lieut Orcton) Wounded 2. (Lieut LITTLE) & (Lieut CHAMBERS) Missing 2.(2nd Lieut Roberts & 2nd Lieut VIGOR) (the former believed killed) O.R. Killed 11 Wounded 109 Missing 37. The Signal Officer (2nd Lieut HARRISON) was also wounded while laying lines during the previous afternoon.	W.S.H.

INTELLIGENCE SUMMARY

(Erase heading not required.)

Place	Date 1916	Hour	Summary of Events and Information	Remarks and references to Appendices
BAZENTIN-le-Petit.	Aug 13		At daybreak many of our men were still finding their way back to our trenches. The Germans showed themselves & shouted friendly remarks to our men & appeared anxious for a peaceful spell. Our stretcher bearers went out & fetched in wounded men. For some hours the situation was very quiet & both sides set on firing at anything seen moving. The distance between the line being 80–200 yds.	WTH.
"	14		Generally quiet throughout the day. Intermittent artillery activity on both sides. At 7 PM Batt relieved by the 10 Lincoln Regt & proceeded to the Reserve Trenches in MAMETZ WOOD.	WTH.
MAMETZ WOOD.	15		Quiet day. 5.30 PM. relieved by 8th Royal Berkshire Regt. & proceeded to bivouac in BECOURT WOOD. 34th Division relieved by the 1st Division	WTH
BECOURT WOOD	16	5 AM	Batt moved off & and proceeded to billets at LA-HOUSSOYE	WTH.
LA HOUSSOYE	17		Batt preparing to move tomorrow to new Divisional Area.	WTH
"	18	5 PM	Batt less transport entrained at FRECHENCOURT & detrained at LONGPRÉ. Transport proceeded by road	WTH

INTELLIGENCE SUMMARY

(Erase heading not required.)

Place	Date	Hour	Summary of Events and Information	Remarks and references to Appendices
LONGPRE	Aug 19/6 18	N/N	Detrained marched into billets at LONGPRE.	10TH 6TH
"	19		Resting	
"	20	1:30PM	Batt entrained & proceeded to BAILLEUL where it detrained at 10PM & marched to billets in NEUF BERQUIN	10TH
NEUF BER-QUIN	21		Commanding Officer took over temporary command of the Bde during the absence of the Brigadier General proceeding on leave. Operation Orders received from the Bde, that the Bde will rejoin the 39th Division tomorrow at DIVION.	10TH
"	22	3 PM	Batt marched to LA GORGUE & entrained at CALONNE-RICOUART at 5:30PM marched to billets in BRUAY.	10TH
BRUAY	23		Operation Orders received from the Bde, that the Bde will march tomorrow to MAZINGARBE where it would come under the orders of the G.O.C. 16th Division. On the 25th inst, it will take over the 14th BIS Section of the FRONT LINE & on completion of the relief, will come under the orders of the G.O.C. 40th Division. 4th Corps.	
"	24	2 PM	Batt marched at head of Bde to MAZINGARBE, where it went into billets	10TH 10TH
MAZIN-GARBE	25	2:30PM	Operation Orders received from Bde, that the Bde will relieve the 49th Bde today in the 14th BIS Section. The 8th East Lanc Regt to relieve the RIGHT Batt. 7th R. Inniskilling Fus. The 6 Bed Regt the LEFT Batt, 7th R. Irish Fus. The 11 R. War. R. the SUPPORT Batt, 8th R. Irish Fus. & the 10th L. N. Lancs in RESERVE at MAZINGARBE.	

Instructions regarding War Diaries and Intelligence Summaries are contained in F.S. Regs., Part II and the Staff Manual respectively. Title Pages will be prepared in manuscript.

INTELLIGENCE SUMMARY

(Erase heading not required.)

Place	Date 1916	Hour	Summary of Events and Information	Remarks and references to Appendices
14th B'IS LOOS	Aug 25	7.PM	Relief of the 8th R. Irish Fusiliers completed in SUPPORT Trenches, immediately NORTH of LOOS & running parrael with the LOOS-HULLUCH Road in two lines. The FRONT LINE system runs approx NORTH & SOUTH & EAST of the road.	WTH
"	26		Quiet day. Batt. supplying working parties.	WTH
"	27		About 30 shells from a 120 m.m. Howitzer dropped near our trenches, otherwise Quiet. Batt supplying working parties.	WTH
"	28		OPERATION ORDERS received from Bde that the Batt would relieve the 8th E. Lancs Regt in the FRONT LINE tomorrow. Quiet day. Batt supplying working parties.	WTH
"	29	7.30PM	Batt relieved the 8th E. Lancs Regt. LINE Quiet but weather very wet, trenches 60cm. Except for slight T.M. Battery & Rifle Grenade activity, the day was Quiet.	WTH
"	30		Operation Orders received from Bde Hqrs that the Bde will be relieved by the 15th Infantry Bde tomorrow. Some hostile artillery activity, towards evening to North of our T.M. Battery. The locality of this was shelled with a considerable number of 77 M.M, 120 M.M & 10 Heavy How H.E. shells. Our patrols have not encountered any hostile patrols during the tour the hostile lines have been swept with	WTH
"	31		Quiet day - a few rifle F.E. guns shots, T.M. & rifle grenade exchanges	

W.T. Hart
CAPTAIN.
ADJ. 11th SERVICE BN. R. WARWICKSHIRE REGT.

WAR DIARY or INTELLIGENCE SUMMARY

Place	Date	Hour	Summary of Events and Information	Remarks and references to Appendices
BATTLE of the SOMME	July 1st to August 18th 1916 inclusive		The total casualties sustained by the Battalion during these operations were as follows:—	

OFFICERS.   OTHER RANKS

Killed   6   87
Wounded   19   524
Missing   2   61
Sick (mostly nervous complaints) 5   55
              ——   ——
              32   727

Total 759

Honours and Awards:— Immediate.

The Distinguished Conduct Medal awarded to No 8311 Pte. B. WARD. This Stretcher Bearer behaved with extraordinary courage throughout the action of POZIÈRES, 15 July 1916, in bringing wounded men to cover from places where a stretcher could not have been taken owing to the intensity of the hostile fire. The lives of many men were saved owing to Private WARD'S conspicuous gallantry. On August 6th 1916 Private WARD was killed in action unfortunately.

W.A.

"A" Form. Form C. 2121.
MESSAGES AND SIGNALS.

Prefix * Code m.	Words	Charge	This message is on a/c of:	Recd. at m.
Office of Origin and Service Instructions.	Sent		Service.	Date
Secret	At m.			From
	To			
	By		(Signature of "Franking Officer.")	By

TO { 11/R Warwick Regt

| Sender's Number. | Day of Month. | In reply to Number. | |
| * BM 329 | 11 | | AAA |

It is probable that you will be required to-night to make a bombing attack supported by at least one company along the German Intermediate Line Westwards. aaa This attack would start from the LEFT flank of the 10/R N Lancs Regt and would have for its object the capture of that portion of the Intermediate Line still in possession of Germans aaa It is possible that the 46 H Bde will attack simultaneously from the other end of the trench aaa No orders have as yet been received +

From
Place
Time

The above may be forwarded as now corrected. (Z)

Censor. Signature of Addressor or person authorised to telegraph in his name.
* This line should be erased if not required.

"A" Form.
MESSAGES AND SIGNALS.

Prefix	Code	m.	Words	Charge	This message is on a/c of:	Recd. at	m.
Office of Origin and Service Instructions.					Service.	Date	
			Sent			From	
			At	m.			
			To			By	
			By		(Signature of "Franking Officer.")		

TO

| Sender's Number. | Day of Month. | In reply to Number. | A A A |

No details are known aaa But notice of this probable attack is given you so that you may be able to consider the matter & make some arrangements aaa Further instructions will be issued aaa Acknowledge

From 112 Bde
Place
Time 11.40 a.m.

E Stanton Major
Signature of Addressor or person authorised to telegraph in his name.

| "A" Form. | Army Form C. 2121. |
| MESSAGES AND SIGNALS. | |

TO: D. G

Sender's Number: A.10.29. Day of Month: 11th In reply to Number: BM 829 AAA

Noted but personally I favour a frontal attack as most of my bombers (trained ones) are non-existent, and I think a trench mortar firing in enfilade from about the Centre of the Left Coys of the 10th L.N.L. Regt wd be of material assistance.

Morrison Lt/C

BM 355

11th Rog. Warwick. Regt.

After consultation with the B.G.C. 46th
Inf. Bde. 15th Division the following
arrangements have been made for co-
operation in tonight's operations and you
will find them referred to in op. orders
order N2 45 of today —

(a) Stokes mortars and Machine
Guns, guns will fire up on the Trench
junction Northwards from S.2.c.8.45
from Zero hour onwards —

(b) Immediately your objective is
reached a [illegible] will be dug by 1/7 R.W.
15th Bde. across the road to [illegible]
the new front line Westwards with the S.E.
which you must dig toward S.2.c.8.05

(c) Two bombing parties will be
ready at the base of the above mentioned
sap at zero ready to cooperate with
you in [illegible] you reach your objective —

(d) An officer will be in liaison with
your Batt. H.Q. Commander —

(e) The 15th I.Bde. will give protection
Support on a [illegible] your objective
and the position of this Bde. is
not known to me — etc

Success of the operations is as important from the point of view of the 15th Bde as from that of the [?] Bde.

12
8
11

9.55 a.m.

F. Mukherji
Bde Major
11th [?] Bde

NOT TO BE TAKEN BEYOND PRESENT FRONT TRENCHES

Dispositions for Attack

DISPOSITIONS

1. 'A' and 'C' Comp^{ies} in line, each on a 2-Platoon frontage, with 2 Platoons following in the same formation at 25 yards distance.

2. 'B' Comp^y will hold the front trenches of 'C' Comp^y, but will be prepared to advance at a moment's notice & complete the attack.

3. 'D' Comp^y will take over the line now held by 'A' Comp^y by 9.30 pm.

ARTILLERY ACTION.

1. At 10.30 pm (ZERO) light artillery will shrapnel No Man's Land (on a line 50 yds S. of the objective) for 30 secs:

2. At 10.33 pm it will lift from the objective-trench & form a curtain 150 yards N. of it. (This barrage will continue for about 1 hour.

3. The ADVANCE.
  (1) By 10.30pm (ZERO) 'A' and 'C' Comp^ies will be outside their trenches. 'A' Comp^ys leading platoon being advanced to a line with those of 'C' Comp^y.
  (2) At 10.35 pm the enemy trench will be attacked & carried.
  (3) The 4 Sections of 'B' Comp^y (in addition to the orderlies connecting with O.C. 'B' Comp^y) will follow the SUPPORTING platoons of 'A' and 'C'. The Bombs will be placed in the Captured trench, and the wire loose about 30 yds. N of it.

4. BOMBS
  (1) Each man of 'A' 'B' and 'C' Comp^s will carry 2 bombs
  (2) Bombers on the flanks of the leading Platoons will carry 5 bombs each, but on the LEFT

3. (cont:) FLANK of the TWO LEFT PLATOONS of of 'C' Coy's. there will be complete Bombing groups, each carrying 100 bombs. It is the duty of these latter to block the trench that runs N and S from the W. flank of the objective, at a distance of about 60 yards from this flank.

5. AMMUNITION
   (a) Every NCO & man will carry 170 rounds, except bombers who will carry 50 only.
   (b) A reserve of S.A. Ammunition will be stored in the present (B' Coy's R) trenches

6. ACTION of LEWIS GUNS
   The Lewis Guns of A & C Coy's will accompany the supporting platoons of these Companies, then cross the captured trench, and establish themselves in shell holes about 40 yards N. of it. They will not be withdrawn without written orders from their Coys. Comdrs:

7. TOOLS, SANDBAGS, &c:
 ① Each man of the 4 Supporting Platoons will carry either a PICK or a SHOVEL in the proportion of 1 PICK to 2 Shovels.
 ② Each man should carry 2 empty Sandbags.

8. WATER
 Water-bottles will be filled.

9. Very-Lights, &c: &c:
 ① 2 White Very-lights and 1 pistol will be carried by each platoon
 ② Green Very-lights & flares will also be taken, the latter will be shown at SIX am in the bottom of the captured trench when the aeroplane sounds its Klaxon horn at about SIX am.

10 COMMUNICATION
 An advanced Battⁿ Battle Centre will be established in the Communication trench

10 (cont)
running S from about the centre of 'C' Company's line of advance. The 2nd in Command will be established here & will be in touch with Battn. H.Q. by telephone & orderly.

11. CO-OPERATION of FLANK UNITS

① The 10th Loyal N. Lancashire Regt. is cooperating on our RIGHT by engaging hostile M.Guns that may contest our advance from positions N. of the objective, and by engaging the enemy's LEFT up to the road running N & S. at that point

② The 10th Scottish Rifles will cover our left & oppose a hostile counter attack from the West

12. ASSISTANCE to BOMBING ATTACK

After the capture of the trench the leading Platoons will assist the LEWIS gun teams

12 (Cont.).
in covering the trench from the N, and a party should be detailed to cooperate if possible from the EAST in 'C' Company's bombing action mentioned in 4(3) above.

12.8.16.

Headquarters 112th Inf Bde.

I have to report as follows on the action of this Battalion in the operations of the night 12th/13th — in so far as I am able to collate them, now.

(1) The 2 Assaulting Companies left their trenches, according to arrangements, about 1 minute before ZERO.

(2) When our Artillery barrage was put up they moved forward. It then appears that (on the "lift" taking place) they came under an exceedingly fierce hostile curtain fire, and a certain amount of Machine Gun fire, and through

this the assaulting troops were unable to penetrate. Some of them, in spite of it, reached the enemy's trench, and many are to be seen lying from 15 to 20 yards from it. — I may mention that I saw no man lying otherwise than with his face to the enemy.

3. There was at least one instance of a Platoon approaching too closely behind our Artillery barage, & suffering appreciable losses. I understand that this happened during the barage put up for 30 Secs: in No Man's Land.

4. The Company in Support was also caught, before Zero time, under very heavy fire from Shrapnel & Field-Guns as it was moving to its position up the communication trench. It was however, in touch with the 2 assaulting Companies, and as the latter had left the trenches for the attack & had not returned, its Commander considered that they had been successful, & so reported to me; and

5. it was not till a considerable time afterwards that wounded, & others, of the attacking Companies began

82

to return to our lines, and it was known that the attack had not succeeded.

6. The hostile Artillery fire remained so hot over our Communications in rear, and especially about Battn Hd Qrs, that successive attempts by orderlies to obtain information as to the situation were fruitless. This fire commenced at about 9pm & continued till the early hours of the morning.

7. I am at present unable to give an accurate forecast of the casualties, and there are many details that I must

enquire into before I can give an
really
^accurate description of this affair.

                    C W Trombold (?)
13.8.16   Crig M. R. Warwick Rg

I attach a short summary of the
principle orders I gave previous to
the attack.

ACTION N. of BAZENTIN LE PETIT (Night 12th/13th)

Headquarters 112th Inf Bde.

1. I have examined the action of this Battn in the the attack last night & find that its want of success can only be attributed to the fact that the Left assaulting Company lost direction in the advance. All the Officers of this Company were either killed or wounded, so that my finding is only based upon the evidence of other ranks; but the facts appear to be these:—

    (a) The RIGHT Company was ordered to direct (vide Battn Orders).

    (b) The LEFT Compy Commander, who had received these orders, had pointed out to me that if his left was in touch with the BAZENTIN LE PETIT – MARTINPUICH road, the right direction would be maintained, & I agreed with him.

(c.) It appears, however, that this Company neither maintained touch with the road, nor with the RIGHT (directing) Compy, as it crossed the road in a N.W. direction & eventually became involved in the trench-system of the 46th Inf/Bde

(d.) The O.C. Company would then appear to have walked Eastwards in an attempt to locate the LEFT flank of the directing Company. He was seriously wounded when so engaged.

(e.) The Company now without Officers — of the others, 1 had been killed & 1 was missing — & much reduced in strength, eventually returned to our Line, and I have no evidence to show that any portion of it entered the German trench (as has been reported)

(f.) From other evidence I am satisfied that but for this regrettable error the objective of the LEFT attack would have been attained, as the hostile opposition was apparently not so pronounced at this point.

(q) The behaviour of the men, not excepting those of the new draft, was very good. Altho' the hostile barrage was very intense, it was pierced at several points by small parties & individuals of the RIGHT Company.

13.8.16.   CMorrisonLt/A

B.M.884

Headquarters,
112th Inf. Bde.

Copy

I have to report as follows on the action of this Battalion in the operations of the night 12th/13th - in so far as I am able to collate them now.

(1) The 2 Assaulting Companies left their trenches, according to arrangements, about 1 minute before ZERO.

(2) When our artillery barrage was put up they moved forward. It then appears that (on the "lift" taking place) they came under an exceedingly fierce hostile curtain fire, and a certain amount of machine gun fire, and through this the assaulting troops were unable to penetrate. Some of them, in spite of it, reached the enemy's trench, and many are to be seen lying from 15 to 20 yards from it. I may mention that I saw no man lying otherwise than with his face to the enemy.

(3) There was at least one instance of a platoon approaching too closely our artillery barrage, and suffering appreciable losses. I understand that this happened during the barrage put up for 30 secs. in No Man's Land.

(4) The Company in support was also caught, before Zero time, under very heavy fire from shrapnel and field guns as it was moving to its position up the communication trench. It was, however, in touch with the 2 Assaulting Companies, and as the latter had left the trenches for the attack and had not returned, its Commander considered that they had been successful and so reported to me, and

(5) It was not till a considerable time afterwards that wounded, and others, of the attacking Companies began to return to our lines and it was known that the attack had not succeeded.

(6) The hostile artillery fire remained so hot over our communications in rear, and especially over Bn. Hd. Qrs., that successive attempts by orderlies to obtain information as to the situation were fruitless. This fire commenced at about 9 pm and continued till the early hours of the morning.

(7) I am at present unable to give an accurate forecast of the casualties and there are many details that I must enquire into before I can give a really accurate description of this affair.

13/8/16.

(sd) C.S.Collison, Lt.-Col.
Comdg. 11 R.Warwick Regt.

H.Q. 39th Division
Forwarded for information.
P.M.Robinson B.Genl.
Comdg 112th Infy Bde

13.8.16.

112th Brigade.
37th Division.

1/11th ROYAL WARWICKSHIRE REGIMENT

SEPTEMBER 1 9 1 6

Vol 14

11. Warwick

112/31

Confidential

War Diary

of

11th (S) Bn, Royal Warwickshire Regiment

from 1st September 1916 to 30th September 1916

(Volume II. No 9)

Army Form C. 2118.

WAR DIARY
or
INTELLIGENCE SUMMARY

(Erase heading not required.)

Instructions regarding War Diaries and Intelligence Summaries are contained in F.S. Regs., Part II. and the Staff Manual respectively. Title Pages will be prepared in manuscript.

Place	Date	Hour	Summary of Events and Information	Remarks and references to Appendices
14 BDE LOOS	July 1/16		Batt relieved by the 2nd Bn Suffolk Regt proceeded to billets in MAZINGARBE. The day has been quiet. A few slight O.F. Shells, T.M. rifle Grenades exchanged	WTH
MAZINGARBE	2	7.P.M. 7.30	Batt marched to LA COMTE where it went into billets	WTH
LA COMTE	3		Batt resting	WTH
LA COMTE	4		Batt cleaning up generally. Orders received from 112 Bde that the Batt would be inspected tomorrow at 10 A.M. by the G.O.C. 37th Division	WTH
	5	10 A.M.	Batt inspected by Major General Count GLEICHEN, K.C.V.O., C.B., C.M.G., D.S.O. The Batt was congratulated on its good work in the 'Battle of the SOMME'.	WTH
	6		The reorganisation and training of specialists commenced with i.e. Lewis Gunners, Bombers, Snipers, Signallers. Very little other training possible owing to the demand on the Battalion for various working parties.	WTH
	7		Battalion Training	WTH
	8		do do	
	9		do do Officers attended a lecture at Brigade H.Qrs by Lieut General Sir H.H. WILSON, K.C.B. D.S.O. Commanding 4th Corps. on the EUROPEAN SITUATION	WTH
	10		Batt resting. Attended 112 Bde Sports in the afternoon	WTH
	11		Battalion Training	WTH

WAR DIARY
or
INTELLIGENCE SUMMARY

Army Form C. 2118.

Place	Date	Hour	Summary of Events and Information	Remarks and references to Appendices
LA COMTE	1916 Sept 12		Battalion Training.	W.T.H.
"	13		Battalion Training. Senior officers attended a Conference Bde H.Q. to discuss lessons gained in the SOMME.	W.T.H.
"	14		Battalion Training.	W.T.H.
"	15		Battalion Training.	W.T.H.
"	16		Battalion Training.	W.T.H.
"	17		Battalion Resting. Operation Orders received from the Bde. That the 3rd Division would relieve the 63rd Division in the SOUCHEZ, ANGRES and CALONNE Sections of the LEFT Section, IV Corps Front on September 20th. The 112 Bde to relieve the 188 Bde in the ANGRES (Centre) Sector on September 19th. (The 63rd Bde will be on the RIGHT, the 111 Bde on the LEFT.)	W.T.H.
"			The 112 Bde to move into forward area tomorrow the 18th September.	W.T.H.
"	18	4 P.M. 8.15	Batt marched via HOHOHN-BARLIN to COUPIGNY where it went into billets.	W.T.H.
COUPIGNY	19	8 PM	Batt moved up into SUPPORT relieving the Howe Battalion R.N. Division with Two companies and Bn Head Quarters in BULLY GRENAY. One Company in CORONS d'AIX & the fourth company in MECHANICS Trench in close support.	W.T.H.
BULLY-GRE-NAY	20		Batt supplying working parties. Sector quiet throughout the day.	W.T.H.
"	21		Do	W.T.H.

WAR DIARY
INTELLIGENCE SUMMARY
(Erase heading not required.)

Army Form C. 2118.

Place	Date 1916	Hour	Summary of Events and Information	Remarks and references to Appendices
BULLY-GRE-NAY.	Sept. 22		Battalion employing working parties. Sector quiet throughout the day	607.H.
"	23		Do Do Do	607.H.
"	24		Do Do Do	607.H.
ANGRES II. Sector	25	8 A.M	Batt relieved the 8th East Lancs Regt in the FRONT LINE ANGRES II. 2 Companies in the FRONT LINE & 2 Companies in Support. During the day 4. 120 m.m. How Shells fell on our line, the entrance to one dugout being damaged. Our T.M. Batteries fired numerous mortars & rifle grenades into the hostile trenches. Little retaliation was made. Our Patrol report no hostile activity whatever. Weather very fine.	607.H.
"	26		Artillery activity almost Nil. Intermittent hostile minenwerfers (small) fell on our line doing very slight damage. Our 2" Trench Mortars & Stokes guns were active & and considerable damage to hostile works during the day. Officers Patrol made a reconnaissance of the hostile front though took useful information. Weather very fine.	607.H.
"	27		Extract from Battalion Orders of today. Lieut-Colonel C.S. COLLISON D.S.O. proceeded to ENGLAND on sick leave on the 25th inst Major C.P. ROOKE assumed command of the Battalion from the 25th inst.	607.H.

Army Form C. 2118.

WAR DIARY
or
INTELLIGENCE SUMMARY
(Erase heading not required.)

Instructions regarding War Diaries and Intelligence Summaries are contained in F. S. Regs., Part II. and the Staff Manual respectively. Title Pages will be prepared in manuscript.

Place	Date 1916	Hour	Summary of Events and Information	Remarks and references to Appendices
ANGRES II	SEPTY 27		Artillery on both sides inactive. A few hostile minenwerfer (small medium) & rifle grenades fell in our trenches doing little damage. Our 2" T.M. & Stokes Batteries showed considerable activity with apparent result. Our M/G's played on the hostile communication during the night. Our patrols report very little hostile activity. Weather fine.	WTH.
"	28		Our 2" T.M. & Stokes Batteries fired several hundred rounds with good result on the hostile works. Our Rifle grenade M/G's were also active. Hostile minenwerfer showed increased activity with little result & a few rounds of 120mm. shells fell near C.T. (BULLY ALLEY). Our aeroplanes were particularly active. Hostile aeroplanes fly very occasionally over our line & then at a great altitude.	WTH.
"	29 29		Our patrol report enemy holding their front line but very little movement. Weather fine. Trench mortars on both sides less active during the day. About 2.30 P.M. a lively interchange of rifle grenades took place. Artillery activity below normal. One hostile small minenwerfer got into our front trench, killing 1 man & wounding 3 others on the 28th bn.-Northn. fus.	WTH.
"	30 30		Our patrol report all quiet in the hostile line. Unusually quiet throughout the day. Our Lewis Gun obtained a hostile working party before daybreak. In the evening our aeroplane fired their Lewis Guns.	WTH.

Army Form C. 2118.

WAR DIARY
or
INTELLIGENCE SUMMARY
(Erase heading not required.)

Instructions regarding War Diaries and Intelligence Summaries are contained in F. S. Regs., Part II. and the Staff Manual respectively. Title Pages will be prepared in manuscript.

Place	Date	Hour	Summary of Events and Information	Remarks and references to Appendices
ANGRES	Sept 1916 30		N of the Fosse Liors. Our patrol made a reconnaissance of BULLY CRATE, useful information was found. Got a little minenwerfer came into the front trench, killing 5 N.C.O. men. Weather fine	WIH

E. P. Rooke
Major
Comdg 11th Royal Warwickshire Regt

112th Brigade.
37th Division.

1/11th ROYAL WARWICKSHIRE REGIMENT

OCTOBER 1 9 1 6 ::::

Confidential

War Diary

of

11th (S) Bn, Royal Warwickshire Regiment.

from 1st October 1916.   to 31st October 1916.

(Volume II.   Nº 10.)

WAR DIARY
or
INTELLIGENCE SUMMARY

(Erase heading not required.)

Place	Date 1916	Hour	Summary of Events and Information	Remarks and references to Appendices
ANGRES II	Oct 1	9 AM	Battalion relieved by the 8th East Lancs Regt. Battalion marched into "Reserve" billets with Battn. H.Qrs. & 2 Companies at FOSSE.10. and 2 companies in BULLY-GRENAY. Programme of Training while in Reserve proposed to commence tomorrow. "Battalion Training - Musketry, Bombing, Sniping, Signalling, Drill etc".	WT.A WT.A WT.A WT.A
FOSSE. 10	2		Do	
"	3		Do	
"	4		Do	
"	5		Do	
"	6			
ANGRES II	7	8 AM	Battalion relieved the 8th East Lancs Regt in the front line, "D" Coy on the right, "B" Coy on the left, with "C" and "A" in right and left supports. Enemy trench mortars active, causing some damage to trenches at the head of BULLY ALLEY. Orders received that on the next day the Division would extend its front northwards, the 112th BDE to hand over to 63rd BDE the southern portion of its line as far as M.32. a.20.65 and to take over the southern portion of the front held by the 111th BDE as far as M.20. b.2.5. The new inter-battalion boundary would be from M.25. b.95.95 along BULLY LANE and BULLY ALLEY to MECHANICS, the battalion front north of this being the new ANGRES II sector.	A.D.? A.O.?

WAR DIARY
or
INTELLIGENCE SUMMARY
(Erase heading not required.)

Place	Date	Hour	Summary of Events and Information	Remarks and references to Appendices
ANGRES II	9		Line quiet during the morning.	
		2 pm	The battalion took up its new positions. "D" Coy handed over its line to the 10th Loyal North Lancashire Regt and relieved the 10th Royal Fusiliers from Trench 203 - 210 inclusive, thus becoming the left Company of the battalion. "B" Coy extended its front westwards to Trench 203, taking over its extra frontage from the 10th Fusiliers. "C" Coy moved into ANGIERS NORTH with its left on CHAPLET ALLEY and its right on BOVRIL ALLEY. "A" Coy remained in MOROCCO NORTH. Battalion HQ remained in MECHANICS.	
"	10		Our field guns were active during the afternoon, both on the enemy trenches and our own. 7 shells dropping short in RICHARD ALLEY. Our Stokes guns did good work during the night, without retaliation. All the artillery activity and most of the Trench-mortar activity was on our side during the day. During the night our machine-guns traversed the hostile trenches, and our LEWIS guns dispersed a digging-party, which failed to do any more digging.	
"	11	12.15 pm	Enemy's trench-mortars very active during the day. Between 12.45 pm and 1.30 pm 60 TM shells fell in the neighbourhood of BULLY CRATER. At 1.15 pm the Southern	

WAR DIARY
or
INTELLIGENCE SUMMARY

(Erase heading not required.)

Instructions regarding War Diaries and Intelligence Summaries are contained in F.S. Regs., Part II. and the Staff Manual respectively. Title Pages will be prepared in manuscript.

Place	Date	Hour	Summary of Events and Information	Remarks and references to Appendices
ANGRES W	11	1:15 PM	Sap of 11th CRATER was blown in, two men being killed and two wounded. Enemy salvoes from our trench guns put an end to this activity. Our Stokes guns fired at intervals during the night, and a wiring party was dispersed here turns by our Lewis guns.	app.
"	12		Enemy again very aggressive with trench-mortars and rifle grenades on our right Company, the front line near BULLY CRATER being blown in in five places. Our artillery retaliation was not successful on this occasion. A draft of 10 men (all signallers) arrived from the 3rd and 4th Bns.	app.
"	13	8 AM	Battalion relieved by the 8th East Lancashire Regt and went into support at BULLY GRENAY, one Company in CORONS D'AIX and one in close support in MECHANICS as before.	app.
"	14		Orders received that the 112th Bde would be relieved on the next day by the 5th Canadian Bde, the battalion being relieved by the 25th Canadian Bn. A draft of 42 other ranks from the 1/8 Worcestershire Regt and the 1/4 and 1/5 Gloucester Regts arrived in the afternoon.	app.
"	15	11 AM	Battalion relieved by the 25th Canadian Bn and marched into billets at FRESNICOURT. Draft of 79 other ranks arrived from the R.S.L.I.	app.

WAR DIARY
or
INTELLIGENCE SUMMARY

(Erase heading not required.)

Place	Date	Hour	Summary of Events and Information	Remarks and references to Appendices
	Oct			
FRESNICOURT	16	10 AM	Battalion marched into billets at BAJUS.	appx
BAJUS	17		Resting. Company training. 65 other ranks from the 2nd and 14th Bns. joined the battalion.	appx
"	18		Battalion marched into billets at NEUVILLE AU CORNET and MAISNIL ST PR. Battalion HQ at NEUVILLE AU CORNET.	appx
NEUVILLE AU CORNET	19		Resting. Company training. Draft of 6 O.R. joined the battalion.	appx
"	20		Battalion marched into billets at BOURET-SUR-CANCHE.	appx
BOURET	21		Battalion marched into billets at LONGUEVILLETTE.	appx
LONGUEVILLETTE	22		Battalion marched into billets at SARTON. Orders received to proceed on the next day to BERTRANCOURT.	appx
SARTON	23		Battalion marched to BERTRANCOURT. On arrival it was found that there were no billets available, whereupon battalion marched into billets at MAILLY-MAILLET.	appx
MAILLY-MAILLET	24		Battalion training in bombing, bayonet fighting, extended order and artillery formation. Wire reconnoitred.	appx

WAR DIARY
or
INTELLIGENCE SUMMARY

(Erase heading not required.)

Instructions regarding War Diaries and Intelligence Summaries are contained in F. S. Regs., Part II. and the Staff Manual respectively. Title Pages will be prepared in manuscript.

Place	Date	Hour	Summary of Events and Information	Remarks and references to Appendices
MAILLY-MAILLET	25		Battalion marched into billets at ACHEUX.	
ACHEUX	26		Battalion training. Extended order, artillery formation, bombing etc.	
"	27		Battalion training.	
"	28		Battalion training.	
"	29		Battalion training.	
"	30		Battalion warned to be ready to march at 9.30 a.m. On receiving further orders battalion marched at 2 p.m. into billets at AMPLIER.	
AMPLIER	31		Battalion marched into billets at DOULLENS.	

J. Strathmann........... CAPTAIN.
ADJ. 11th SERVICE BN. R. WARWICKSHIRE REGT.

112th Brigade.
37th Division.

1/11th BATTALION ROYAL WARWICKSHIRE REGIMENT

NOVEMBER 1916

Confidential

11/37 8 Oct 16

War Diary
of
11th (S) Bn, Royal Warwickshire Regiment.

from 1st November 1916 to 30th November 1916

(Volume V, N° 11).

WAR DIARY
or
INTELLIGENCE SUMMARY

(Erase heading not required.)

Instructions regarding War Diaries and Intelligence Summaries are contained in F. S. Regs., Part II. and the Staff Manual respectively. Title Pages will be prepared in manuscript.

Place	Date 1916	Hour	Summary of Events and Information	Remarks and references to Appendices
DOULLENS	1.XI.16		Battalion Training.	107.H.
"	2.XI.16		Battalion Training.	107.H.
"	3.XI.16		Battalion Training. 112 Bde. Exercise. 107.H. Battalion warned to be in readiness to move tomorrow.	107.H.
"	4.XI.16		Heavy rain, movement order cancelled. Battalion Church Parade 107.H. Battalion Training continued	107.H.
"	5.XI.16		Battalion Training. Capt. J.S. Thain M.C. appointed Adjutant vice Capt. 107.H Hunt promoted	107.H.
"	6.XI.16		Battalion Training. Lt Colonel. C.E. Arthur D.S.O. Struck off Strength. Authority:- C.R. 36815 of 1.6.9.16	107.H.
"	7.XI.16		Battalion Exercise	107.H.
"	8.XI.16		Battalion Training.	107.H.
"	9.XI.16		Battalion Training. Training inspected by G.O.C. 37th Division	107.H.
"	10.XI.16		Battalion Training. Operation Order received from Bde. that the 112 Bde will move to the VAUCHELLES – LOUVENCOURT Area tomorrow	107.H.
"	11.XI.16			107.H.
"	12.XI.16		Battalion marched into billets at LOUVENCOURT.	107.H.
LOUVEN-COURT	13.XI.16	3PM	Battalion moved off with an hours notice to BERTEENCOURT & after two hours in but-ment, it proceeded to MAILLY-MAILLET in billets for two hours.	107.H.
MAILLY-MAILLET	14.XI.16	3AM	The Battalion moved forward in "battle order" to WHITE CITY where it arrived at 6AM. "Stood to" in a Communication Trench until 1PM. awaiting further orders. at 1PM.	

WAR DIARY or INTELLIGENCE SUMMARY

(Erase heading not required.)

Instructions regarding War Diaries and Intelligence Summaries are contained in F.S. Regs., Part II. and the Staff Manual respectively. Title Pages will be prepared in manuscript.

Place	Date	Hour	Summary of Events and Information	Remarks and references to Appendices
WHITE CITY	14/XI/16	1 PM	Battalion under orders of the 99th Brigade to which it was attached, moved forward to attack FRANKFORT TRENCH passing over MUNICH TRENCH which was previously reported to be in the British hands now held by the 2nd K.R.R.C. The attack was held up by hostile M/G rifle fire from MUNICH TRENCH. The Batt retired to MINDEN TRENCH, which it established its Hd Quarters. During the operation R.S. Major Sheer was killed, also 2nd Lt. C.W. LUSH.	107 H
"MINDEN TR"	15/XI/16	7 AM 8.30	Orders received from the 99th Bat. that MUNICH TR. would be attacked at 9 AM. The attack to be carried out by the 9th East Lanc + 10th L.N. Lanc Regts, supported by the 11th R. War. R. MUNICH TRENCH was found to be very strongly held, the attack was held up under cover of dark the Batt reorganised in LEAVE TR. and WAGON ROAD with Batt. Hd Quarters in BEAUCOURT TR. Capt J.S. THAIN M.C. slightly wounded.	107 H
BEAUCOURT TR.	16/XI/16		The Batt held on in WAGON ROAD. During the afternoon a heavy hostile barrage was experienced.	107 H
"	17/XI/16	1 AM	The Batt being relieved by R.W. BOLTON. wounded. moved into billets in MAILLE-MAILLET. At 2.10 PM it Batt marched into billets at ENGLEBELMER.	
ENGLEBELMER	18/XI/16	7 AM 6.30 AM	Operation Orders received from 112th Brigade that the Brigade would move to HAMEL today. The Batt. marched out of billets to HAMEL via MESNIL. After a short rest it moved forward to STATION ROAD. During the operation C. Coy suffered about 40 casualties from shell fire	107 H

INTELLIGENCE SUMMARY

(Erase heading not required.)

Instructions regarding War Diaries and Intelligence Summaries are contained in F.S. Regs., Part II. and the Staff Manual respectively. Title Pages will be prepared in manuscript.

Place	Date	Hour	Summary of Events and Information	Remarks and references to Appendices
STATION Rd	18.XI.16		2nd Lieut. A.E. BOUCHER M.C. was killed. Two sections of the 112th M.G.C. were attached to the Batt.	WT/A
"	19.XI.16		The Batt. remained in Reserve in STATION Rd.	WT/A
"	20.XI.16	5 PM	The Batt. moved to re-occupied Trenches adjoining REDOUBT ALLEY, relieving the 13th K.R.R.C.. During the relief, the hostile artillery fire was intense. 2nd Lt. T.O.L. DRAKE was wounded, also 2nd Lt. H.R. SPRANGER.	WT/A
REDOUBT ALLEY	21.XI.16		Intense intermittent hostile shell fire on our trenches the whole day. Trenches in a very wet condition, men suffered from exposure. Draft of 200 O.Rs arrived	WT/A
"	22.XI.16		Conditions as on previous day. At 7.30 PM. the Batt. was relieved by the 8th East Lancs Regt. The Batt retired to STATION Rd. in Reserve.	WT/A
"	23.XI.16		The Batt. remained in Reserve in STATION Rd.	WT/A
STATION Rd	24.XI.16	7 PM	The Batt relieved the 8th East Lancs Regt in Trenches adjoining REDOUBT ALLEY.	WT/A
REDOUBT ALLEY	25.XI.16		Quiet day, but very wet, everybody wet through, covered in mud, very tired.	WT/A
"	26.XI.16	2 AM	Batt relieved by the 21st MANCHESTER Regt & marched into billets at MAILLY MAILLET.	WT/A
MAILLY-MAILLET	27.XI.16	11 AM	Batt. Marched into billets at LOUVENCOURT. The total Casualties for period 14-11-16 to 27-11-16 are as follows :- Officers 3 Killed 4 wounded. Other Ranks. 32 Killed, 153 wounded 31 Missing 11 Shell Shock 93 Sick to F.A. Total. 9 Officers 320 Other Ranks.	WT/A

INTELLIGENCE SUMMARY

or

(*Erase heading not required.*)

Instructions regarding War Diaries and Intelligence Summaries are contained in F.S. Regs., Part II. and the Staff Manual respectively. Title Pages will be prepared in manuscript.

Place	Date	Hour	Summary of Events and Information	Remarks and references to Appendices
MOLLENCOURT	28.XI.16		Batt cleaning up refitting. Draft of 200 OR's posted to companies. Lt Jenkins reported for duty.	WT.4
"	29.XI.16		Reorganization of Battalion, checking Mobilization stores etc	WT.4
"	30.XI.16	9am	Battalion marched off proceeded to billets in LAVIGOGNE	107.4

E. P. ROOKE
Lt Col
Comy 11 R. Warwickshire Regt

112th Brigade
37th Division.

1/11th ROYAL WARWICKSHIRE REGIMENT

DECEMBER 1916 :::

Vol 17

War Diary

of

11th (Service) Battalion, Royal Warwickshire Regiment.

from 1st December 1916 to 31st December 1916

(Volume II. No IX)

WAR DIARY or INTELLIGENCE SUMMARY

Army Form C. 2118.

Place	Date	Hour	Summary of Events and Information	Remarks and references to Appendices
LAVICOGNE	1/7/16		Battalion Commenced Training	SH)
"	2/7/16		Battalion Training	SH)
"	3/7/16	9.30 am	Battalion Church Parade	SH)
"	4/7/16		Battalion Training	Do.
"	5/7/16		" and Bathing. 2/Lt BLUNDEN appointed (temporary) Intelligence officer.	EH) PH)
"	6/7/16		" "	PH)
"	7/7/16	11 am	Battalion was inspected by Brigadier General A. St Q. RICARDO D.S.O	PH)
"	8/7/16		Battalion Training. Surgeon received under 2/Lt BLUNDEN.	PH)
"	9/7/16		" " Re-organisation	PH)
"	10/7/16	9.30am	Battalion Church Parade. 2/Lt H.C.B. BOWEN (wounded) rejoined the Battalion and 2/Lt H.B.BIRD joined for duty.	PH)
"	11/7/16		Battalion Training. Battalion to be inspected by Corps Commander tomorrow.	PH)
"	12/7/16		Corps Commanders Inspection Cancelled. Orders received for Batt. to concentrate at BEAUVAL further. Strgth 7/29 NCO & OR's around	PH)
BEAUVAL	13/7/16	9.30am	Battalion marched to BEAUVAL and went into Billets	PH)
"	14/7/16	12 noon	" " " FORTEL " " " "	PH)
FORTEL	15/7/16	12 noon	" " " BLANGERVAL " " " "	EH)

WAR DIARY
or
INTELLIGENCE SUMMARY

(Erase heading not required.)

Place	Date	Hour	Summary of Events and Information	Remarks and references to Appendices
BLANGERVAL	16/17/14	8.15am	Battalion marched to BOYOVAL and went into billets.	
BOYOVAL	17/11/14	9.30am	" " " WESTREHEM " " "	
WESTREHEM	18/11/14	8 am	" " " ROBECQ "	
"	19/11/14		Battalion resting and cleaning up. Box respirators of two Coys tested by M.O.	
"	20/11/14		Battalion marched to BETHUNE and went into billets.	
BETHUNE	21/11/14		Battalion resting and cleaning up. Box respirators tested of two Coys at 6"48th Section	
"	22/		Orders received that Bat. will take over the FERME DU BOIS N. front line and Battalion to take over billets of Batt. RIGHT RESERVE Battalion at LE TOURET tomorrow	
"	22/11/14	9.30am	Battalion marched to LE TOURET and went into Billets. 2/Lt WITHERS EMERSON and HUMPHERSON joined for duty. Battalion Training. Battalion officers have now formed Two Coy. battery	
LE TOURET	23/11/14		" "	
"	24/11/14		" " Two Coy battery	
"	25/11/14		Battalion Church Parade. Cancelled owing to bad weather.	
"	26/11/14		Battalion Training. Coy. formations in open warfare. Found 3 Armed working parties	
"	27/11/14		" " Seven Military Medals awarded to NCO's & men of the Batt.	
"	28/11/14	10 noon	Battalion relieved the 2 K.S.Lanc. Regt in the FERME DU BOIS RIGHT Sub-	
FERME DU BOIS Section (RIGHT Sub- Section)			Section of the front line. Quiet day, Except for 20 rounds of H.E. Shrapnel. Relief of infantry & Lewis Guns over, after Relief was completed	

INTELLIGENCE SUMMARY

(Erase heading not required.)

Place	Date	Hour	Summary of Events and Information	Remarks and references to Appendices
FERME DU BOIS (Right Section)	29/9/16		Quiet day. Our Artillery fired into the enemy's support line intermittently throughout the day. Very slight retaliation. After dark boys improving the wire. Artillery activity about nil. Heavy rain during the day. the left of the trenches is in a bad condition generally. Enemy snipers busy where parapet had fallen in. R.E. and other working parties repairing front line.	
	30/9/16			
	3/1/16		Section very quiet.	

E. P. Rooke Lt. Colonel
COMDG. 11th SERVICE BN. R. WARWICKSHIRE REGT.

Vol 18

18N. (3)

Confidential
War Diary
of

11th (Service) Battalion, Royal Warwickshire Regiment.

from 1st January 1917 to 31st January 1917

(Volume VI, No. I.)

Army Form C. 2118.

WAR DIARY
or
INTELLIGENCE SUMMARY
(Erase heading not required.)

Instructions regarding War Diaries and Intelligence Summaries are contained in F. S. Regs., Part II. and the Staff Manual respectively. Title Pages will be prepared in manuscript.

Place	Date	Hour	Summary of Events and Information	Remarks and references to Appendices
FERME DU BOIS Right Sub Section	1/1/17		Our Artillery active throughout the day. Enemy did not retaliate.	DAD
	2/1/17		Our Artillery registering on enemy front line. Enemy artillery active about H.Q. Cellar. Fell behind the Flat British line. Lt Col Rooke awarded the D.S.O.	DAD
	3/1/17		Relieved by 21st & 2nd Lancs Regt. Battalion proceeded to Rest Billets at LE TOURET. Battalion cleaning up and resting.	DAD
LE TOURET	4/1/17		Battalion finding working parties. Ball debut commenced a composite Coy. of 133 O.R's under 2/Lt Reed was sent from the Battn.	DAD
	5/1/17			DAD
	6/1/17		Battalion finding working parties. H.Col Rorke sto'n leave to England. Major Hart took command of Battn.	DAD
	7/1/17		Church Parade. Battalion finding working parts. 2/Lt Sample joined for duty. CSM Chalinor, l/Sgt de St Croix returned from England. CSM Chadwick appointed R.S.M.	DAD
	8/1/17		Battalion finding working parties.	DAD
	9/1/17	10 am	Battalion relieved 1st R. Welsh. Regt in the FERME-DU-BOIS Right Sub-Section. Capt Routh M.C. rejoined from England	DAD
FERME DU BOIS Right Sub Section	10/1/17	7 am	A combined Artillery and Trench mortar shoot was carried out. A great deal of damage appears to have been done to enemy trenches. Enemy retaliated with 77 minenwerfer.	DAD
	11/1/17		Very quiet. Our Howitzers shelled points in rear of enemy's lines.	DAD

Army Form C. 2118.

WAR DIARY
or
INTELLIGENCE SUMMARY

(Erase heading not required.)

Instructions regarding War Diaries and Intelligence Summaries are contained in F. S. Regs., Part II. and the Staff Manual respectively. Title Pages will be prepared in manuscript.

Place	Date	Hour	Summary of Events and Information	Remarks and references to Appendices
FERME DU BOIS (Right Sub Section	12/1/17		Our Artillery fired intermittently during the day.	Appx
	13/1/17	12 noon	A bombardment was carried out by Artillery and Trench Mortars. Enemy retaliated with about 90 minenwerfer sent to H.E. shells on our left Coy. Very little damage done. No casualties.	Appx
"	14/1/17		Artillery inactive. Quiet day.	Appx
"	15/1/17	12 noon	Battalion was relieved by 2nd K.E. Horse Regt. and proceeded to LE TOURET. Cleaning up and inspections	Appx
LE TOURET	16/1/17		Battalion Training. Col Poole S.I.O. returned from leave.	Appx
"	17/1/17		"	Appx
"	18/1/17		" 2nd Lieut Rothwell, Baugh and Fife and Drews Brand was formed.	Appx
"	19/1/17		" Capt J.R. Jones rejoined from England.	Appx
"	20/1/17		" Experts by returned from Base School	Appx
"	21/1/17		Battalion relieved the 8th K.E. Horse Regt. in the FERME DU BOIS Right Sub Section	Appx
FERME DU BOIS Right Sub- Section	22/1/17		A composite Coy of 133 O.R.s under 2/Lt Brand proceeded to Base School for training. Enemy Artillery fortunately active. Several jno shells fired behind the old British line. A number of howitzer H.E. fell with left Coy. Our "heavies" retaliated with effect.	Appx
	23/1/17		Our Artillery was normally active during the day. Artillery inactive in the afternoon. 15 minenwerfer fell on the extreme left of the left Coy doing no damage	Appx

Army Form C. 2118.

WAR DIARY
or
INTELLIGENCE SUMMARY
(Erase heading not required.)

Instructions regarding War Diaries and Intelligence Summaries are contained in F. S. Regs., Part II. and the Staff Manual respectively. Title Pages will be prepared in manuscript.

Place	Date	Hour	Summary of Events and Information	Remarks and references to Appendices
FERME DU BOIS Right Sub-Section	24/1/17		Quiet.	Appx 1
	25/1/17		6" Howitzer registering on enemy front line. Artillery activity normal. Battalion relieved by 1st 8th Warwick Regt. Battalion proceeded to Pont Billot at	Appx 2
	26/1/17		LE TOURET. Cleaning up and inspection.	Appx 3
LE TOURET	27/1/17		Battalion marched to Reserve Pile area and went into billets in the LE LOBES — LE VERT LANNOT area. (B'Amn.) 4 officers + 200 men left on working party at HAVERSKERQUE. Battalion resting and cleaning up.	Appx 4
B'Amn	28/1/17			Appx 5
"	29/1/17		Battalion training.	Appx 6
"	30/1/17		Battalion at "inspection" of 2/Lt Brett & 20 O.R. proceeded to MERVILLE to represent Battalion at presentation of Meritorious Ribbon by Army Commander. Capt Revere and C.S.M Farrington received the Military Cross ribbon at this parade.	Appx 7
"	31/1/17		Battalion training. Orders received that Division will be withdrawn from the line into G.H.Q. Reserve shortly.	Appx 8

31-1-17

C. P. Rokes
Lieut Col
Comdg. 11 R. Warwickshire Regt

No 19

Confidential

War Diary
of

11th (Service) Battalion, Royal Warwickshire Regiment.

from 1st February 1917 to 28th February 1917.

(Volume III, No 2)

<u>SECRET</u>

Subject :- War Diary, Feb. 1917.   W/66/R.

Headquarters,
      112th Inf Brigade.

Herewith War Diary of this bn for February 1917.

<u>Kindly</u> acknowledge receipt.

Llewellin Dane Lt/c
                LT. COLONEL,
COMDG. 11th. SERVICE BN. R. WARWICKSHIRE REGT.

28/2/17

Army Form C. 2118.

WAR DIARY
or
INTELLIGENCE SUMMARY
(Erase heading not required.)

Instructions regarding War Diaries and Intelligence Summaries are contained in F. S. Regs., Part II. and the Staff Manual respectively. Title Pages will be prepared in manuscript.

Place	Date	Hour	Summary of Events and Information	Remarks and references to Appendices
BAREA	May 1/17		Battalion training. Orders received that the Division was hereby ready to move at an hour's notice from the morning of the 3rd.	
	2/2/17			
	3/2/17			
	4/2/17	9 a.m.	Battalion inspected by MAJOR GENERAL BRUCE WILLIAMS C.B, D.S.O. & followed by short route march.	
	5/2/17		Battalion training. Orders received that the Batt. was to be ready to move by Lateral train or by road at 24 hours notice.	
	6/2/17		Elylord at 24 hours notice.	
	7/2/17		Battalion re-organising on the French system of organisation.	
	8/2/17		Battalion route march.	
	9/2/17		Operations Orders received that 112th Brigade would relieve 93rd Brigade in the LOOS SECTION on the 11th inst.	
PETIT SAINS	10/2/17		Batt. marched to PETIT SAINS via its billets there.	
	11/2/17	1 p.m.	Battalion marched to MAROC & relieved 2nd LEINSTER REGT. in support there.	
MAROC	12/2/17		Battalion in support at MAROC.	
	13/2/17		2 Lt. SIMMS & 119 O.R's joined for duty.	
	14/2/17		CAPT. BARWELL M.C, proceeded to 3rd ARMY H.Q. & received etc.	
	15/2/17		Croix du Bourgeois from GEN: NIVELLE.	
	16/2/17		Battalion relieved the 8th EAST LANCS. REGT. in the LOOS (RIGHT SUB-SECTION).	W.J.B.
	17/2/17	2 p.m.	Very little artillery activity on either side. Night quiet.	

Army Form C. 2118.

WAR DIARY
or
INTELLIGENCE SUMMARY

(Erase heading not required.)

Instructions regarding War Diaries and Intelligence Summaries are contained in F. S. Regs., Part II. and the Staff Manual respectively. Title Pages will be prepared in manuscript.

Place	Date	Hour	Summary of Events and Information	Remarks and references to Appendices
LOOS (Rt Sub-Sec[tio]n)	18/2/17		Enemy artillery inactive. Our heavy T.M's fired from 1.30 p.m to 5 p.m, several hits being made on the top of N. CRASSIER. The enemy retaliated by searching for the gun. Enemy fairly active with aerial darts. Our snipers claimed three hits. Patrols went out from CRASSIER SAP & BARRICADE SAP found no mans land in heavy condition. No hostile patrols encountered.	
	19/2/17		Enemy artillery very inactive during the 24 hours. Enemy T.M's fired intermittently hits were silenced by our heavy T.M. & Stokes mortars. Our snipers claimed five hits. Patrols went out from SAPS G & H & BARRICADE SAP. The party recorded no mans land between SAPS G & H. The enemy approached enemy wire at M5.c.90.55. found it occupied. A dummy raid was carried out against the enemy lines. Our artillery bombarded successfully with very little retaliation by the enemy.	
	20/2/17 3 a.m		The enemy right again active with aerial darts during the 24 hours. Our snipers claimed three hits. Patrol left CRASSIER SAP & reconnoitred no mans land between that point & SAP G. Artillery inactive on both sides. The enemy aerial darts were silenced by rifle grenades. Enemy M.G's active during the night. Our Lewis guns disposed a working party opposite SAP G. Our snipers claimed three hits.	
	21/2/17		The enemy sprung a mine, presumably a camouflet, in front of Rt. PLATOON, Rt. COT. Patrol reconnoitred this at night. found a deep crack along the centre. Enemy T.M's active during the night but were silenced by our artillery. Our snipers claimed one hit.	
	22/2/17 2.55pm		Hostile patrol approached RUSSIAN SAP then fired at by the sentry & dispersed.	M.S.B.

2449 Wt. W14957/M90 750,000 1/16 J.B.C. & A. Forms/C.2118/12.

Army Form C. 2118.

WAR DIARY
or
INTELLIGENCE SUMMARY
(Erase heading not required.)

Instructions regarding War Diaries and Intelligence Summaries are contained in F. S. Regs., Part II. and the Staff Manual respectively. Title Pages will be prepared in manuscript.

Place	Date	Hour	Summary of Events and Information	Remarks and references to Appendices
LOOS (A SUB SECTION)	23/2/17	12 Noon	Battalion relieved by 8th EAST LANCS. REGT. & went into billets at LES BREBIS.	
LES BREBIS	24/2/17		Cleaning up & Inspections. 2 LT. J.G. WELLER rejoined the Battalion from England. Battalion Church Parade.	
	25/2/17			
	26/2/17	10 p.m.	Battalion relieved 8th EAST LANCS. REGT., in the LOOS (RIGHT SUB - SECTION) Relief complete 12 mn.	
LOOS (A SUB SECTION)	27/2/17		Artillery of both sides inactive during the day. A dummy raid took place at 10 pm by the Brigade on our left & our artillery took part effectively, while the enemy retaliated slightly on KING ST. & QUEEN ST., very little damage being done. The enemy also put up a barrage between the front & support lines on RIGHT COY: front, also down MIDDLE ALLEY. No damage was done & the shooting was very bad. Patrols went out from RUSSIAN SAP to a point between SAPS 6 & 4. The former reconnoitred the old front line between RUSSIAN SAP & BARRICADE SAP the latter, the ground to within 40 yards of the enemy's wire. No hostile patrols were encountered.	
	28/2/17		2 LT. M. HARPER + 23 O.R's joined the Battalion for duty. Orders received that the 96th Brigade will relieve 112th Brigade with the LOOS SECTION on the 2nd & 3rd MARCH. 2 LT. WELLER inadvertently wounded himself by stepping on his bayonet in returning from patrol & was evacuated to hospital.	W.B.

E. P. Rowe .... LT. COLONEL
COMDG. 11th. SERVICE BN. R. WARWICKSHIRE REGT.

Confidential.

War Diary

of

11th (S) Bn, Royal Warwickshire Regiment.

from 1st March 1914. to 31st March 1914.

(Volume III, No 3).

WAR DIARY
or
INTELLIGENCE SUMMARY.
(Erase heading not required.)

Army Form C. 2118.

Place	Date	Hour	Summary of Events and Information	Remarks and references to Appendices
LOOS (Lt. Sub-Section)	1/3/19		Enemy artillery more active than usual. Appeared to be registering with 77 m/m field guns on our LEFT Co'y front & JERMYN STREET. During the evening about 10 "the enemy's M.G." intermittent was active on both Company fronts. We retaliated with heavy artillery & Stokes mortars & effectively silenced the enemy. Our snipers claim one hit. Two patrols went out from RUSSIAN SAP & SAP G (?) the former to lie in wait for hostile patrols in the disused trench running across No Man's Land. None of the enemy were met.	
	2/3/19	8.45 a.m.	Two Germans of the 93rd REGT. were found wandering near RUSSIAN SAP. There blocken prisoner by our sentry. They were men of the 1912 Class - one of them were the ribands of the 2nd Class & Orders Frederick.	
		11 p.m.	The Battalion was relieved by the 2nd YORK & LANCASTER REGT, went into Billets at LES BREBIS.	
LES BREBIS	3/3/19		Battalion marched to BETHUNE - went into billets.	
BETHUNE	4/3/19		" " " ROBECQ	
ROBECQ	5/3/19		" " " ALLOUAGNE - went into Billets. LT. COL. E.P. ROOKE, D.S.O, evacuated to hospital, sick.	
ALLOUAGNE	6/3/19		" " " FEBVIN - PALFART went into billets.	
FEBVIN PALFART	7/3/19		Re-organisation of the Battalion under the new system. Hardening of the feet with FORMALIN solution. Cleaning up & Inspections.	
FEBVIN PALFART	8/3/19		LT. COL. F.S.N. SAVAGE-ARMSTRONG, D.S.O, took over command of the Battalion. Battalion marched to HESTRUS v ERS went into billets.	MSR

Army Form C. 2118.

WAR DIARY
or
INTELLIGENCE SUMMARY.
(Erase heading not required.)

Instructions regarding War Diaries and Intelligence Summaries are contained in F.S. Regs., Part II. and the Staff Manual respectively. Title pages will be prepared in manuscript.

Place	Date	Hour	Summary of Events and Information	Remarks and references to Appendices
HESDRUS	9/3/17		Battalion marched to CANETTEMONT went into Billets. Shortening of fee continued under the M.O.	
CANETTEMONT	10/3/17		Cleaning up & Inspections. 2 Lt. WELLER rejoined from hospital. Shortening of feet continued	
"	11/3/17	9.30 am	Battalion Church Parade.	
"	12/3/17		Battalion training commenced.	
"	13/3/17		Battalion training	
"	14/3/17	8.30 am	Battalion Route March to REBREUVIETTE, FREVENT, HOUVIN.	
"	15/3/17		Battalion training	
"	16/3/17		" " 2 Lt. LATYMAN, 2 Lts WILSON & BROWN joined the Battalion for duty from England	
"	17/3/17	8.0 am	Brigade Routemarch to EAREE-WAMIN, LIENCOURT, BERLENCOURT, MAGNICOURT & HOUVIN.	
"	18/3/17	9.30 am	Battalion Church Parade.	
"	19/3/17		Battalion Training.	
"	20/3/17		" "	
"	21/3/17		" " Battalion gained 2nd place in Brigade Transport Competition.	
"	22/3/17		" " Battalion won the Brigade Cross Country Race (B Company team).	
"	23/3/17		" " Battalion gained 3rd place in Brigade Bombing Competition (B Company team) 2 Lt. BIRD & 31 O.R. proceeded to HOUVIN to represent Battalion at the presentation of Medal Ribbons by the 5th Army Commander.	Int/3

Army Form C. 2118.

WAR DIARY
or
INTELLIGENCE SUMMARY.
(Erase heading not required.)

Instructions regarding War Diaries and Intelligence Summaries are contained in F. S. Regs., Part II. and the Staff Manual respectively. Title pages will be prepared in manuscript.

Place	Date	Hour	Summary of Events and Information	Remarks and references to Appendices
CANETTEMONT	24/3/14	8.30 am	Brigade Route March to ETREE-WAMIN, BEAUDRICOURT, IVERGNY, LE SOUICH, REBREUVIETTE.	
	25/3/14		2nd Lt. WEBB (wounded) & 34 O.R. joined the Battalion from England. Battalion Church Parade.	
	26/3/14		Battalion gained 2nd place in Brigade Relay Race for Bethune.	
	27/3/14		Battalion training. Battalion won the Brigade Lewis Gun Competition (B Company team).	
	28/3/14	9 am	Battalion Route March to HOUVIN, MAGNICOURT, GOUY-EN-TERNOIS, MONTS, MONCHEAUX & HOUVIN.	
	29/3/14		Battalion training.	
	30/3/14	12 noon	Brigade Operations at LIENCOURT.	
	"		Lt. BROOKE (wounded) rejoined the Battalion from England. MAJOR W.T. HART left the Battalion for Command Course at ALDERSHOT.	
	31/3/14		Battalion training.	

Hawkinson
LT. COLONEL
COMDG. 11th SERVICE BN. R. WARWICKSHIRE REGT.

Confidential.

112/37

Vol 21

War Diary
of
11th (Service) Bn, Royal Warwickshire Regiment.

from 1st April 1917. to 30th April 1917.

(Volume III, No IV).

Army Form C. 2118.

WAR DIARY
or
INTELLIGENCE SUMMARY.
(Erase heading not required.)

Instructions regarding War Diaries and Intelligence Summaries are contained in F. S. Regs., Part II. and the Staff Manual respectively. Title pages will be prepared in manuscript.

Place	Date	Hour	Summary of Events and Information	Remarks and references to Appendices
CANNETTEMONT	1-4-17		Battalion Church Parade	
"	2-4-17		Battalion operations at LIENCOURT. — March to point of assembly — Advance in Artillery Formation — deploy & attack. Contact patrol aeroplane co-operated.	
"	3-4-17		Battalion Training. 2nd Lieut. M. W. KNIGHT joined for duty. Posted from 3rd (Res) Bn. R. War. R.	
"	4-4-17		Battalion inspected by the Commanding Officer, training continued.	
NOYELLETTE	5-4-17		Battalion marched to NOYELLETTE & went into Billets	
"	6-4-17		Battalion Training continued	
MONTENESCOURT	7-4-17		Battalion marched to MONTENESCOURT & went into Billets. Major P. GROVE-WHITE (4th Middlesex Regt) joined for duty as 2nd in command. N° 1338 A/RegtSgt Major J. Beatty admitted to hospital, Sick.	
WARLUS	8-4-17		Battalion marched to WARLUS & went under canvas.	

WAR DIARY
or
INTELLIGENCE SUMMARY.
(Erase heading not required.)

Army Form C. 2118.

Place	Date	Hour	Summary of Events and Information	Remarks and references to Appendices
WARLUS	9/4/17	2.30	Battⁿ paraded & marched to PORT D'AMIENS, ARRAS, via DAINVILLE. Bde. transport & Reinforcements to L.29.a. north of DAINVILLE (Reg^{tl}. trsp S.L.C.)	
(Apr^l)	5.30	On arrival equipment was drawn at Bde. Dump & also meal served. Attaching weather which had been hitherto untoward. Orders received to proceed to Assembly Area.		
	10.30	Battⁿ took position in Sⁿ & 2nd Phoenix trenches with night flank		
	12 noon	resting on CAMBRAI R^d. German artillery fire at this time weak & very erratic. Ist line; A. Coy. right; B. Coy. (Huthamp) left 2nd " R. Coy. & Reserve Lewis Gunners in support. Battⁿ H.Q. at junction of 2nd Res. Line trench & INNERNESS TR. D. Coy at Rds. dump (carrying party). Disposition of Brigade as follows:— Right, C^o. Bedfords; 10th Royal N. Lancs in support Right, " 8th E. Lancs, 11th Royal Warwicks in support Left flank, 6^{3rd} Bde. Right flank, 3rd Division.	
	2.30	Battⁿ received orders to move to German front line trench south of CAMBRAI R^d. in rear of 6th Bedfords	

WAR DIARY or INTELLIGENCE SUMMARY

Army Form C. 2118.

Place	Date	Hour	Summary of Events and Information	Remarks and references to Appendices
	9th	8.30h	Brigade advancing. Batts in touch with 102 L. hott. howrs, on left & 6 R.Scots Fus. Head Qrs to old german front line, 200 Southly of CAMBRAI RD. Up to the time, no barrage had been observed but there was no seen on our right or of action. Cavalry was seen to be moving behind filling & some batteries of field artillery was moving forward. Batts had for a short while on the "Blue line" running north to south between TILLOY and the BOIS DES BOEUFS. Dispositions as follows :—
Right of A. Coy on CAMBRAI RD; C. Coy astride CAMBRAI RD with R.Coy echeloned in rear to the right. Batt. H.Q. in HARFLEUR TR. at H.31.c.5.5. At this time a Batt of the Queens passed through us to attack the "Brown line" - (position running north & south along high ground about 2000 yds West of MONCHY LE PREUX).	
	10th		Batts advanced as far as line of sunken road at N.3.b+d. Southly of FEUCHY CHAPEL on left resting on CAMBRAI RD. Here we dug in & remained until 11.30 A.M. on the 10th inst. The Batts was in touch with North hants on the left but no connection with	

WAR DIARY
or
INTELLIGENCE SUMMARY.

(Erase heading not required.)

Army Form C. 2118.

Instructions regarding War Diaries and Intelligence Summaries are contained in F.S. Regs., Part II. and the Staff Manual respectively. Title pages will be prepared in manuscript.

Place	Date	Hour	Summary of Events and Information	Remarks and references to Appendices
			(Ref. Map 51.c. N.W. & S.W.) Troops on our right were had two Lewis Guns now suddenly Ref. h Reserve to help cover the flank. Batt. H.Q. now moved to old German gun emplacements at N.1.b.8.5	
	10th Feb.	2.30	and at 2.30 A.M. on the 10th proceeded to N.3.c.65.85. Very little artillery activity on this side during the night.	
		5.40 A.M.	Orders received to withdraw to N.3.a south of MAISON ROUGE preparatory to the attack on the Brown Line.	
		12.0 noon	Attack on Brown Line started. Heavy enemy artillery retaliation. The W.E.R. Hampshires moved forward in artillery formation echeloned to the right rear of 10th L.N. Lancs.	
		1.0 P.M	At 1 P.M. Battn displayed in rear of the 6th Brigade west of Brown River. Advance continued till about 500 yds west of LES FOSSES FARM. The O.C. Coy. (2 Lieut. J.M. Stalker) finding that the Batts on the Left were held up had out two Lewis Guns and covered their advance by enfilading the German position west of MONCHY.	
		6.0 P.M.	By 6 P.M. Batts. had reinforced our front line & had advanced as far as	

WAR DIARY or INTELLIGENCE SUMMARY

(Ref: Maps S.I.C. N.W. & S.W.)

Place	Date	Hour	Summary of Events and Information	Remarks and references to Appendices
LES FOSSE'S FARM	10/4/17	6 P.M.	From CAMBRAI R⁰. South the line was now held as follows:— A.Coy. R.Ivanniere; C.Coy. R.Ivanniere; Some Cyclists; Redfords (62R₁); B.Coy. R.Ivanniere. Batt: H.Q. at N.11.a.2.7. A further advance was temporarily impossible on account of:— with 3ʳᵈ Bde: which owing to Cyclist Rath & enemy (62 Redfords having been forced to fall back. 2) The barrage at this time available. Batt: Therefore dug in, outer position forming a defensive flank to the right. During the afternoon of advance on the 1st and following Officers became casualties:— Capt. E.L. North M.C.; 2ⁿᵈ Lieut. E.E. Brett; 2Lᵗ P.T. Brown who were all the officers with A.Coy.— 2ⁿᵈ Lieut N.C. Dutchie, C.Coy; Lieut A.G.Jenour, D.Coy.— all wounded.	
	11.4.17	2 A.M.	Battⁿ ordered to become the leading right battalion in attack on high ground between MONCHY LE PREUX and GUEMAPPE.	

WAR DIARY
or
INTELLIGENCE SUMMARY.

(Erase heading not required.)

Army Form C. 2118.

Place	Date	Hour	Summary of Events and Information	Remarks and references to Appendices
	11.4.17		Batt'n: crossed to north of CAMBRAI R'd in artillery formation by short rushes in rear of LES FOSSES FARM. Batt'n: reforming along a shallow ridge at N.12.a (Left) Batt'n: advanced + occupied position about 50 yards East of MONT and parallel to MONCHY LE PREUX – LA BERGERE R'd covering a frontage of about 450 yds. The right resting on CAMBRAI R'd. Outposts were posted. Batt's H.Q. moved to LES FOSSES FARM. About 2.30 P.M. Enemy counter-attacked in strength after heavy artillery preparation but was everywhere repulsed with heavy losses. Outposts were put out + positions consolidated. Enemy Snipers & M.G. remained very active throughout the rest of the day. Enemy of'machine on the day (11.4.17) also guns were very heavy(?) were taken South of LES FOSSES FARM. The following officers were casualties:— 2/Lt. J.W. Alabaster, R.G.C., Lieut. S.A. Rayman A.Coy, 2/Lt. R.E. Pearson A.Coy, all wounded and 2/Lt. R.W.J. Threadgold while on his way up to reinforce B.Coy, was slightly wounded in the leg just outside ARRAS	

Army Form C. 2118.

WAR DIARY
or
INTELLIGENCE SUMMARY.
(Erase heading not required.)

Instructions regarding War Diaries and Intelligence Summaries are contained in F. S. Regs., Part II. and the Staff Manual respectively. Title pages will be prepared in manuscript.

Places	Date	Hour	Summary of Events and Information	Remarks and references to Appendices
	11.4.17	11 P.M.	The Batts were relieved by the 11th Royal Sussex Regt and marched back to TILLOY where they remained in cellars & dugouts till the morning of the 12.2.	
	12.4.17		Battalion formed up by Companies and marched back to ARRAS along the Artillery track north of CAMBRAI RD and occupied cellars in the GRANDE PLACE. Received orders that Battalion would proceed in busses to WANQUETIN to-night. Owing to congestion of traffic busses did not arrive till 3-0 a.m. on the 13th.	
	13.4.17		Battalion arrived at WANQUETIN at daybreak and went into billets.	
	14.4.17		Battalion marched to DENIER and went into billets.	
	15.4.17		Training and Reorganization by Companies. Battalion Church Parade. Following Officers rejoined the Battalion:— 2nd Lieutenant Chambers from 29th I.B.D. Rouen	

WAR DIARY
or
INTELLIGENCE SUMMARY.
(Erase heading not required.)

Army Form C. 2118.

Place	Date	Hour	Summary of Events and Information	Remarks and references to Appendices
(Maps 51 c. N.W. & S.W.)	15.4.17		Lieutenant R. Shaw from 1st Army course, Boulogne. 2nd Lieutenant H.H. L. Hallett from leave	
	16.4.17		Battalion Training	
	17.4.17		"	
	18.4.17		"	
	19.4.17		Battalion marched to NOYELETTE and went into huts	
	20.4.17		Battalion Training	
	21.4.17		Marched to point G.11.b.0.7 N.E. of St NICHOLAS. Battalion in tents and old British trenches. Transport at St CATHERINES	
	22.4.17		Battalion marched off at midnight to position of Assembly in LAUREL TRENCH (H.9.c.10.25 - H.9.c.5.1)	
	23.4.17 3.BaHH		Battalion in position of Assembly took in LAUREL TRENCH indrehint (42 Brigade in EFFIE TRENCH. Batt. H.Q at junction of EFFIE and LAUREL TRS.	
	4.30 (44th) + 1.35		Orders received to move to HURRUM-HUSSAR TRENCH. Batt=moved forward in artillery formation of platoons front line, B. Coy (right); C.Coy (left), Second Line, A.Coy (right), D.Coy (left). Very heavy enemy artillery barrage. Heavy shelling on Brokenleigth area third throughout the day	

WAR DIARY
or
INTELLIGENCE SUMMARY
(Erase heading not required.)

Army Form C. 2118.

Place	Date	Hour	Summary of Events and Information	Remarks and references to Appendices
	23.4.17	1/10 to 2.40	(Ref. Maps 57.b N.W. & N.E. Special sheet) Battalion in position as follows:— Bn. C. Coys in HALCYON and part of HAWTHORN from H.12.a.1.9 – H.6.c.5.5. R. Coy on right, C. Coy on left. A. Coy (right), D Coy (left) in HURRUM TR. overlaying the whole trench. Batt. H.Q. in new trench at about H.5.c.8.6. Bn. in touch with 6/R Staffords on the right. (Scottish were just south of GAYRELLE. Two M.G.s held intervening space behind walls + two platoons of D. Coy. including two Lewis Guns were sent up to 10 Royal Irish on our left at H.6.d.1.1 on their request	
		2.50	Orders received for attack on GREENLAND HILL	
		5.45	Batt. formed up for attack on Black Line (re CHILI TR.) in H.12.b.9.2 to H.12.b.8.0 as follows:— Front Line : R. Coy. Right, C. Coy. Left Support line : A. Coy. " , D. Coy. " In touch with 8/2 E. Lancs on right. Bn. Right (6/R.B.) appeared to be too slow in advance. Allies half an hours artillery preparation (25 mins Shrapnel, 5 mins H.E.)	
	6.9 hr			

WAR DIARY
or
INTELLIGENCE SUMMARY.
(Erase heading not required.)

Army Form C. 2118.

Place	Date	Hour	Summary of Events and Information	Remarks and references to Appendices
		6 P.M.	The Batt. moved forward in artillery formation in close order as to go east of GAVRELLE - ROEUX Rd. and dug in on a line running through I.7.a.7.3 to I.7.a.7.0 Batt. was unable to advance further owing to heavy M.G. fire from the CHEMICAL WORKS on our right and also owing to the fact that the Div. on the right was held up. Batt. consolidated the line. In the evening Lieut. Col. A.S.M. Savage Armstrong was killed by a shell when on his way back from meeting the Brigadier. Lieut. W.R. Rumsden being wounded at the same time. In addition the following casualties amongst the officers of the Batt. occurred during the advance in the morning Capt. F.W.G. Chambers "B" Coy, 2 Lt. E. Knight "B" Coy, 2 Lt. P. Willans + 2 Lt. E.A. Waley — A. Coy wounded. 2 Lt. M.D. Farrington of A. Coy was killed	
	2.4.17		Batt. intended with a battalion of the York + Lancs Rgt on the left + 8 E. Lancs on the right. Continue to hold above position until 3. Ath. night of 24.25 when relieved by 6th Bedfords. 2 Lt. A.C.B. Bowen wounded. Nothing else of importance occurred during this period.	

WAR DIARY
or
INTELLIGENCE SUMMARY.
(Erase heading not required.)

Army Form C. 2118.

Place	Date	Hour	Summary of Events and Information	Remarks and references to Appendices
	25/4/17		Ref. Maps. S.16 N.W. & N.E. (Special Sheet) When relieved Batt. took up position of support in CHILI TR. Bults, Vickers + two platoons of D. Coy including two Lewis Guns assigned from 10 R.F's.	
	26/4/17 to 27/4/17		Batt. held the trench until night of 27/2/28. During this period Communicating trench was dug from CHILI TR. to new front trench (CLASP TR.) Trenches were deepened, fire steps + L.G. emplacements made. Snipers were placed in suitable positions. On night of 27/2/28 a jumping off trench was dug 50 yds. west of GAVRELLE - ROEUX Rd on the Batt's frontage. Artillery on both sides continued very active. Enemy aeroplanes appeared several occasions and heavy artillery fire opened on our positions. Gnd. aerial activity particularly on side.	
	28/4/17	4:20 AM	Batt. in position to attack GREENLAND HILL :- front line, D. Coy right, B. Coy left in CLASP TR from I.7.0.7.3 — I.7.a.7.0 — In touch with 2nd Essex on right + 4th Middlesex on left. Support line, C. Coy left in Jumping I.7.a.3.3 — I.7.a.4.0 Batt. H.Q. at H.12.b.9.3	

WAR DIARY or INTELLIGENCE SUMMARY

Army Form C. 2118.

Place	Date	Hour	Summary of Events and Information	Remarks and references to Appendices
	28.4.17	4.45am	Batt's advance. After going about 100 yds the right front Coy (D Coy) hier R. Shew made a slight incline with the object of filling a gap which had occurred between us and the 6th Rde. on our left. B. Coy conformed to this movement. On both the officers with the leading Coy became casualties immediately after, & few men lost direction & became mixed up with the 112 Rde. The remainder advanced & owing to the fact that all the officers & senior N.C.O's with the exception of two Subalterns were either killed or wounded the battalion became very scattered. Scattered parties with Lewis guns occupied a general line 300 – 400 yds East of CURA TR. one party 6 or Rds on the left & remainder of this Rd. (1122) on the right. Battn. remained in this position until the Brigade was relieved by 102 Argyll + Sutherland Highlanders and before daybreak on the 29/2.	
	29.4.17		Marched back to transport lines at ST NICHOLAS	
	30.4.17		At 2 P.M. Batt embursed + proceeded to DENIER & went into huts. Batts rested	

J.H. Summerfield Lt. Major
Comdg. 11th. SERVICE BN. R. WARWICKSHIRE REGT.

WAR DIARY
or
INTELLIGENCE SUMMARY.
(Erase heading not required.)

Army Form C. 2118.

Place	Date	Hour	Summary of Events and Information	Remarks and references to Appendices
	30-4-17		Summary of Casualties sustained in the Battle of "ARRAS".	
			First Action, 9th to 13th April 1917.	
			Officers — Killed: NIL, Wounded: 9, Missing: NIL	
			Other Ranks — Killed & Died of Wounds: 25, Wounded: 142*, Missing: 8	* Includes 1 shell shock.
			Second Action, 23rd to 29th April 1917.	
			Officers — Killed: 2, Wounded: 8⊕, Missing: 1	⊕ Includes 1 shell shock, remained at duty.
			Other Ranks — Killed & Died of Wounds: 34, Wounded: 192⊙, Missing: 59	⊙ Includes 3 shell shock & 6 gassed.
			Total Casualties of all descriptions for the two actions:— 20 Officers + 463 Other Ranks.	

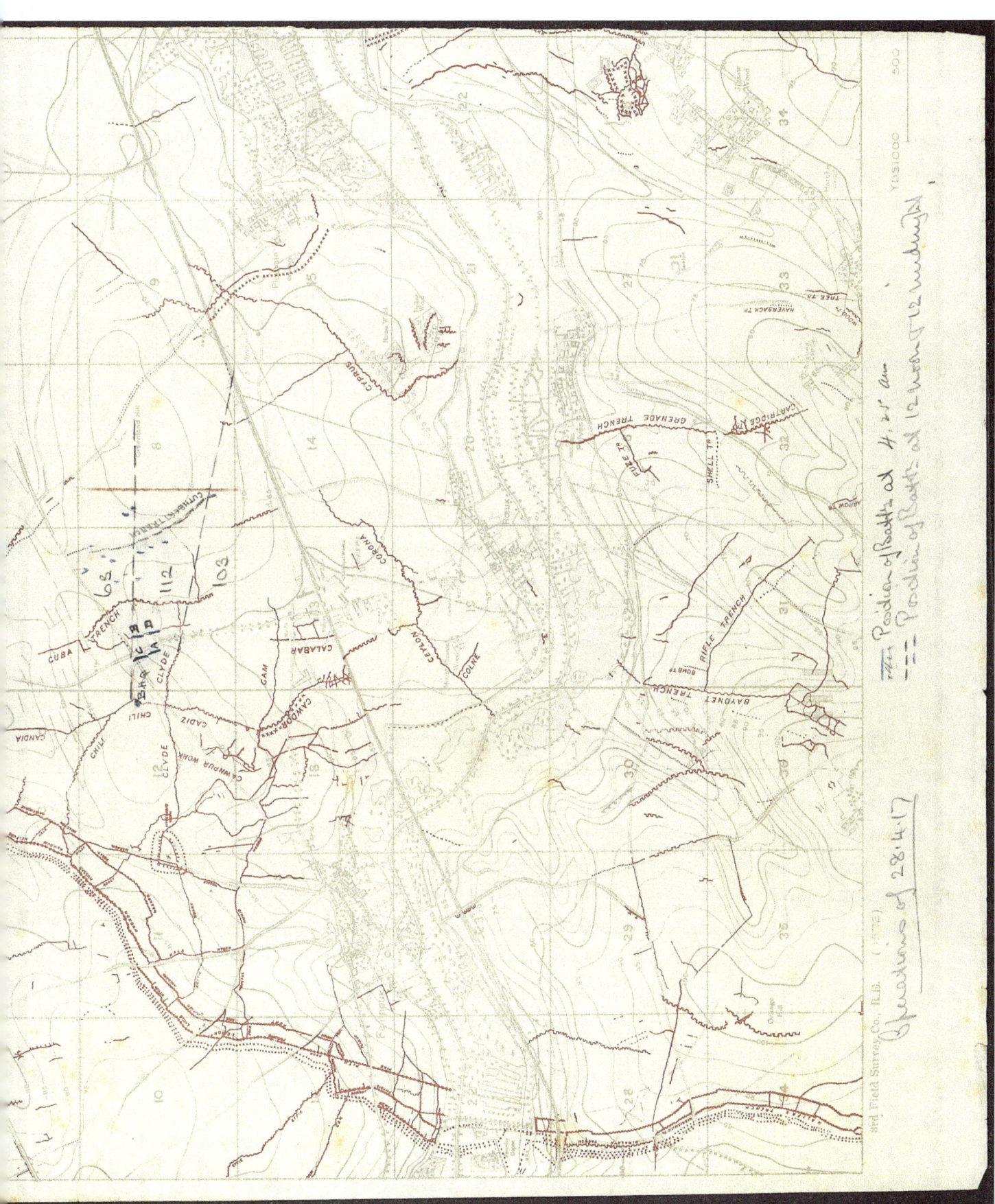

Confidential

112/37

Vol 22

War Diary

of

11th (S) Bn. Royal Warwickshire Regiment

From 1st May 1917 to 31st May 1917.

(Volume III. No V.)

WAR DIARY or INTELLIGENCE SUMMARY

Army Form C. 2118.

Place	Date	Hour	Summary of Events and Information	Remarks and references to Appendices
DENIER.	1/5/19	-	Battalion commenced training. Capt SHENNING rejoined from sick leave and took over the command of "C" Coy. 2/Lt F.H.WEBB took over the command of "B" Coy. The following Officers joined the Battalion for duty: 2/Lt P.L.SMITH & 2/Lt G.P.STUBBS - posted to "A" Company. 2/Lt R.B.WYNNE & 2/Lt A.H.MORCH - posted to "B" Company. 2/Lt R.FULLERLOVE - posted to "C" Company	
	2/5/19		Battalion training continued. Reorganisation of platoons & companies.	
	3/5/19		" " "	
	4/5/19		" " "	
	5/5/19		Battalion training at LIENCOURT. Attack formations.	
	6/5/19		Church parades for Church of England, Roman Catholic & Nonconformist men.	
	7/5/19		Battalion training and tactics.	
	8/5/19		Brigade wiring and field firing competitions. "D" Company which represented the Battalion gained the first place in the Brigade wiring. "C" Company gained the second place in the field firing competition and attack formation.	
	9/5/19		Brigade Transport competition, in which the Battalion gained second place. 2/Lt FOSSE rejoined from CANNETTEMONT, where he had been acting Town Major. He was appointed Battalion Bombing Officer. Night marching by compass for Officers.	

Army Form C. 2118.

WAR DIARY
or
INTELLIGENCE SUMMARY.

(Erase heading not required.)

Instructions regarding War Diaries and Intelligence Summaries are contained in F.S. Regs., Part II. and the Staff Manual respectively. Title pages will be prepared in manuscript.

Place	Date	Hour	Summary of Events and Information	Remarks and references to Appendices
DENIER	10/5/17		Brigade Route march HOUVIN - HOUVIGNEUL - MONCHEAUX - BUNEVILLE - GOUY-en-TERNOIS - MAGNICOURT. 'A' & 'B' Companies, commanded by MAJOR GROVE-WHITE, formed the Brigade Advance Guard and the Battalion was commanded by Capt SHERRING.	
	11/5/17		All drafts which had arrived since 1st inst were inspected by the C.O. 2/Lt J. MANSELL joined the Battalion from the 71 Corps Depot & was posted to "C" Coy.	
	12/5/17		Battalion training. Special courses commenced for Bombers and Lewis Gunners. Battalion Boxing Competition. Brigade Wiring Competition, in which wiring party from 'D' Company won second place.	
	13/5/17		Divisional Transport Competition in which Battalion Transport gained third place. A Brigade Church of England parade service was held at APISRINES.	
	14/5/17		Battalion took part in Brigade operations, including attack & formation of outpost line.	
	15/5/17		Battalion training. FIELD MARSHAL SIR DOUGLAS HAIG visited DENIER and saw the Battalion in training.	
	14/5/17 9 p.m.		Battalion carried out night operations, forming an outpost line covering LIGNEREUIL, on the assumption that enemy were reported at FREVENT and the Brigade was killed for the night at LIGNEREUIL.	
	18/5/17		Battalion moved to GOUVES today. The route of march was LIENCOURT - AVESNES - LES CONTE - HAUTEVILLE - MARQUENTIN. It was billeted for the night in huts at GOUVES.	

WAR DIARY
INTELLIGENCE SUMMARY

Army Form C. 2118.

Place	Date	Hour	Summary of Events and Information	Remarks and references to Appendices
GOUY-S.	19/5/17		Battalion moved to Tilloy. The route of march was AGNEZ – DAISANS – PORTE BAUDIMONT – FAUB. St SAUVEUR – TILLOY. The 112th Brigade relieved the 169th Brigade in trenches at Tilloy becoming the Brigade in reserve.	
TILLOY	20/5/17	4 a.m.	Battalion moved to HARCOURT – FEUCHY line, relieving the Queen Victoria Rifles.	
		8 p.m.	Battalion relieved 1/2 Middlesex Battalion in TOOL TRENCH, CAVALRY TRENCH, FARM TRENCH & RAKE TRENCH in front of GUEMAPPE, north of COJEUL RIVER & ARRAS-CAMBRAI ROAD. 'D' Company north of CAMBRAI ROAD. 'B' Company in CAVALRY TRENCH & FARM TRENCH. 'A' Company in CAVALRY TRENCH with right resting on COJEUL RIVER. 'C' Company in support in RAKE TRENCH.	
Trenches N.E. GUEMAPPE	21/5/17		Good deal of work done by Battalion in improving trenches, which had suffered severely from shelling. Supplies, rations & water carried from MARLIER to front line by "C" Company.	
	22/5/17		Enemy artillery very active. 'D' Company Headquarters hit and C.S.M. RICHARDS killed, 2/Lt J.G. WELLER, commanding 'D' Company sent to hospital suffering from shell shock.	
	23/5/17		Position of enemy doubtful and several patrols were sent out to reconnoitre ground and locate enemy positions, for which they were commended by the Brigadier. Enemy snipers became more active and special measures were taken to deal with them. For two hours 10 p.m. to 12 midnight, enemy bombarded our support trenches with gas shells, for which the wind was favourable.	

WAR DIARY
or
INTELLIGENCE SUMMARY

Army Form C. 2118.

(Erase heading not required.)

Place	Date	Hour	Summary of Events and Information	Remarks and references to Appendices
SCHRAMBEE	24/5/17	12 m/d-night	Battalion relieved by Royal 100th Lancs and moved to support lines in HANCOURT- FEUCHY Line, formerly the enemy BROWN LINE.	
N.E GUEMAPPE	25/5/17		Battalion found working parties for the line and for the New Zealand Tunnelling Company.	
	26/5/17		Battalion found working parties and covering parties for front line Battalions, 30 men with Lewis Guns sent from "C" Company to act as close supports in front line for 6th Bedfords, the Left Battalion Brigade.	
	27/5/17		Battalion occupied on working parties and improving HANCOURT - FEUCHY line.	
	28/5/17		Battalion was relieved by 13th K.R.R.C and marched to ACHICOURT, S.W. of ARRAS. Party with Lewis Guns sent from "C" Company to act as close supports in front line for 6th Bedfords on 26/5/17 rejoined Battalion today.	
ACHICOURT	29/5/17		Battalion rested. Lt. Col. H.I. WEBB-BOWEN took over the command of the Battalion.	
	30/5/17		Commanding Officer inspected the Battalion.	
	31/5/17		Battalion marched to DUISANS and was billeted in huts there.	

Llewellin Davis Capt
LT. COLONEL,
COMDG. 11th SERVICE BN. R. WARWICKSHIRE REGT.

Confidential.

SECRET

112/37

Vr 23

War Diary

of

11th (Service) Battalion, Royal Warwickshire Regiment.

From 1st June 1917 to 30th June 1917

(Volume 3, No 6)

Army Form C. 2118.

WAR DIARY
or
INTELLIGENCE SUMMARY.
(Erase heading not required.)

Instructions regarding War Diaries and Intelligence Summaries are contained in F. S. Regs., Part II. and the Staff Manual respectively. Title pages will be prepared in manuscript.

Place	Date	Hour	Summary of Events and Information	Remarks and references to Appendices
DUISANS	1/6/16		Battle in 1st billets in huts. Training was carried out in drill, musketry etc.	
	2/6/17		Battle training.	
	3/6/17		Battle moved to IZEL-LES-HAMEAU by road. The journey was completed in four hours by the route DUISANS - HABARCQ - LE HAMBAU.	
IZEL-LE-HAMEAU	4/6/17		Training carried out under company arrangements, including musketry, bayonet fighting & drill.	
	5/6/17		Battle & company training continued.	
	6/6/17		Battle had practice Brigade Field day on ground between AMBRINES and GIVENCHY-LE-NOBLE. Col. WEBB-BOWEN watched manœuvring of the units of the Battle under the command of MAJOR GROVE-WHITE. He afterwards referred to the destruction in which part did shown mainly of pivoting & wheeling forces. The Divisional Commander also expressed	
	7/6/17		Battle marched to MAREST, where it was billeted. gratification with the turn-out and marching of the Battle.	
	8/6/17		The Battle moved to the Bouly area and marched to COYECQUE, where it was billeted.	

A 5834 Wt. W 4973/M687 750,000 8/16 D. D. & L. Ltd. Forms/C.2118/13

Army Form C. 2118.

WAR DIARY
or
INTELLIGENCE SUMMARY.
(Erase heading not required.)

Place	Date	Hour	Summary of Events and Information	Remarks and references to Appendices
CAYEUX	9/6/17		Battle noted. Reorganisation refitting of companies.	
"	10/6/17		Battle Church parade. Battle orders contained the announcement that in the King's Birthday Dispatch, the names of the following were mentioned by the Commander-in-Chief: MAJOR (A/LT-COL) SAVAGE-ARMSTRONG (killed) T/Lt E.H.DAVIS T/Capt J.R.JONES 10143 Sgt F.V.PELHAM.	
"	11/6/17		Battle Training. BATT'N, Physical + squad drill in the morning. Specialist training & musketry in the afternoon. Lt. G, BROOKE rejoined the Battle from 34th Div. Depot & took over Lt.G. over Lt Gs of D Coy. 2nd Lt W.T.THOROWGOOD rejoined from hospital (VB Coy) 2nd Lt C.E.CARPENTER joined the Battle & was posted to A Coy. CAPT N.W.E.BAZWELL (from 34th Div Depot)	
"	12/6/17		Battle Training with company arrangements.	
"	13/6/17		Battle Training in drill, bayonet fighting, musketry. Lectures to officers on Trench to Trench Attack. Commanding Officer gave a	

Army Form C. 2118.

WAR DIARY
or
INTELLIGENCE SUMMARY.
(Erase heading not required.)

Place	Date	Hour	Summary of Events and Information	Remarks and references to Appendices
COYECQUE	15/6/17		Battn Training in close order drill, musketry and Bayonet fighting. Night operation rehearsed Keuben on COYECQUE - ERNY ST JULIEN rd by every Coy, Coy in turn acting as supporting companies in attack using patrols.	
"	16/6/17		Battle parade when the Commanding Officer congratulated the following recipients of decorations:- CAPT J.W. GRIFFIN M.C. No 9298 L/Sgt YOUNG P. " 10614 L/Cpl LONG A. " 9204 Sgt KEELEY W. " 8130 Sgt HEWITT J. " 8128 Pte HARTLEY G. " 8087 Pte DUNN J. " 265405 " ROGERS H. " 16040 L/Cpl BULL H.L. " 19988 Pte ENGLAND R.T. " 9212 L/Cpl MASON F.H. " 30984 Pte PAPWORTH F.H. " 22406 L/Cpl NANDS P. " 17850 L/Cpl WINFIELD J. Battn Training in musketry & close order drill.	

WAR DIARY or INTELLIGENCE SUMMARY

Army Form C. 2118.

Place	Date	Hour	Summary of Events and Information	Remarks and references to Appendices
COYECQUE	16/6/17	2pm	MAJOR RIGGS R.E. lectured on blocking Posts to Officers, & senior NCOs.	
"	17/6/17		A Brigade Church Parade was held in the Battalion Parade ground. Brigade Sports.	
"	18/6/17		Battalion carried out a scheme of work on the blanket trenches on high ground. A.M. & P.M. in the by. Each man was given a digging task to complete under R.E. & regimental supervision.	
			A field firing musketry competition was carried out by two teams from each company.	
"	19/6/17		Battalion training in drill musketry bomb throwing. Exercise was carried out throughout to put on the tactical handling of platoons.	
"	20/6/17	5am-12 noon	Companies sent on Brigade attack on Range representing short advance & deep.	
		5.30pm	Battalion cross country run & sports.	
"	21/6/17		Battalion parade for musketry out of G.4-4 Army Act. Companies on Range & tactical exercises. Training of specialists in Battalion Range (Lewis Gunners) Bombing Ground.	
"	22/6/17		Companies on Brigade Battalion Ranges. Chaconte drill.	
"	23/6/17		Battalion marched to BOESEGHEM, where it was billeted.	
"	24/6/17		Battalion marched to rest at HONDEGHEM, where it was billeted for the night. Route was via WALLON CAPPEL — CINQ RUES — LES OISEAUX.	

Army Form C. 2118.

WAR DIARY
or
INTELLIGENCE SUMMARY.
(Erase heading not required.)

Instructions regarding War Diaries and Intelligence Summaries are contained in F. S. Regs., Part II. and the Staff Manual respectively. Title pages will be prepared in manuscript.

Place	Date	Hour	Summary of Events and Information	Remarks and references to Appendices
	25/6/17		Battalion marched to LOCRE, by route CAESTRE-METEREN—MONT NOIR—MONT ROUGE. At METEREN the Divisional Commander met a march past.	
LOCRE	26/6/17		At LOCRE the battn was billeted in huts. Battalion trained under company arrangements. Remainder of the day was spent in taking rifle inspection by Armourer Sergt.	
	27/6/17		Battn training under company arrangements. Specialist training under Specialist Officers.	
	28/6/17	11 am	Battn was inspected by the Army Commander (Sir HERBERT PLUMER). Battn was drawn up in mass, each platoon was inspected personally, after which the Battalion marched past in column of route.	
	29/6/17	1.30 pm	Battn relieved the 11th Royal IRISH RIFLES in Divisional Reserve at N.23d 15 8.0. (Map Ref. Sheet 28/40000)	
		5.30 pm	Batt training in Box Respirator Drill etc.	
	30/6/17		Batt training under company arrangements; lectures etc on trench routine by company officers.	

(Sgd) ………………… CAPTAIN.
A/Cd. 11th SERVICE BN. R. WARWICKSHIRE REGT.

Confidential

Vol 24

War Diary

of

11th (Service) Battalion

Royal Warwickshire Regiment.

from 1st July 1917.   to 31st July 1917.

(Volume 3, No 7)

WAR DIARY
or
INTELLIGENCE SUMMARY.
(Erase heading not required.)

Army Form C. 2118.

Place	Date	Hour	Summary of Events and Information	Remarks and references to Appendices
	1/7/17	2.30 P.M.	112th BRIGADE was relieved by 63rd BRIGADE as Brigade in Support & the Battn moved from area in the neighbourhood of IRISH HOUSE & LURGAN LINES and	
DRANOUTRE	2/7/17		LOCREHOF FARM at DRANOUTRE, where it was billeted in huts. BATTLN having in carried out ordinary company arrangements. Lt & 2nd Lt. J. WATKINSON joined the Battn & were posted to D Coy.	
"	3/7/17	4 pm	Working parties were found for the support line. A working party of 100 N.C.O's & men from C Coy under the command of CAPT SHEWRING proceeded to an area near KEMMEL for attachment to the 61 Pl. Field Coy R.E.	
"	4/7/17	4 p.m.	In working parties were found for the front line support. Fatigue parties were employed in cleaning up the Battle line, Specialists were trained under their own Officers; working parties found for salvage work on old British line; Company training. Relieved by Company Officers.	
"	5/7/17		Battle training, training of Specialists. Relieved by Company Officers.	
"	6/7/17		Battle training. Salvage parties were found for the old British front line	
"	7/7/17		Battle training under company arrangements & Specialist Officers.	
"	8/7/17	9.30 am	Battle Church parade. Battn bathed at DRANOUTRE baths.	

Army Form C. 2118.

WAR DIARY
or
INTELLIGENCE SUMMARY.
(Erase heading not required.)

Instructions regarding War Diaries and Intelligence Summaries are contained in F. S. Regs., Part II. and the Staff Manual respectively. Title pages will be prepared in manuscript.

Place	Date	Hour	Summary of Events and Information	Remarks and references to Appendices
DRANOUTRE	9/7/17		Battle training under company arrangements. Training for offensive warfare + trench warfare.	
	10/7/17		Battle training.	
	11/7/17	3.0 p.m.	Battn. relieved the 10TH YORK & LANCS. in tents in the KEMMEL area. 112TH BRIG. MD. reconnoitring down Support.	
			Battn. found working parties for support lines.	
KEMMEL	12/7/17		Battn. found 3 working parties of 300 men. All R.E. for salvage & ammunition work.	
	13/7/17		Training under company arrangements.	
	14/7/17		Church Parade. C.O.'s Coys returned from duties on detachment with R.E's.	
	15/7/17		Battle training in hill musketry, bayonet fighting, bombing & parties found	
	16/7/17		for salvage. Bombing & cleaning up of encampments.	
	17/7/17		Battle training & found working parties for salvage & loading.	
	18/7/17		" "	
	19/7/17	9 A.M.	Bus Parade to Battle + lectures on Trench Routine + Orders	
		11 P.M.	Battn. relieved the 8TH LINCOLNS in the LEFT CENTRE sector of the front line. 2/LT. H.E. HEFFER M.C. assumed the duties of acting A/y Adjut.	

Army Form C. 2118.

WAR DIARY
or
INTELLIGENCE SUMMARY.
(Erase heading not required.)

Instructions regarding War Diaries and Intelligence Summaries are contained in F. S. Regs., Part II. and the Staff Manual respectively. Title pages will be prepared in manuscript.

Place	Date	Hour	Summary of Events and Information	Remarks and references to Appendices
	20/7/17		The front line was held by B Coy (RIGHT) & D Coy (LEFT). C Coy was in support. A Coy in reserve. Enemy aircraft were very active and the Lewis Guns in the front line were got into action. Attacks hostile aircraft driving many inches. Considerable enemy artillery activity during both day & night increasing in intensity during the succeeding days. Our guns replied vigorously. Enemy aircraft caused few very low over our line. Several enemy were hit by our Lewis Gun guards.	
	21/7/17		During the night 21/22nd July, a reconnoitring patrol was sent out under 2/Lt VOSS to locate enemy in positions around BEEK FARM. Enemy artillery very active attacking all roads & buildings during the day and night. During the night 22/23 July, a direct hit on the Battln transport killed the C.Q.M.S. of C Coy (Col Sgt TAYLOR), and the Coy Clerk of A Coy, and wounded the C.Q.M.S. of A Coy & the men of the transport. A direct hit was also obtained on C Coys dug outs near the transport.	
	22/7/17		Near support line. During the night 22/23 July, a patrol was sent out under 2/LT MURCH to reconnoitre the enemy positions in shell holes in front of the outpost line.	

Army Form C. 2118.

WAR DIARY
or
INTELLIGENCE SUMMARY.
(Erase heading not required.)

Instructions regarding War Diaries and Intelligence Summaries are contained in F.S. Regs., Part II. and the Staff Manual respectively. Title pages will be prepared in manuscript.

Place	Date	Hour	Summary of Events and Information	Remarks and references to Appendices
	23/7/17		During the night 23/24th July A & C Companies relieved B & D Companies in the front line. B & D Companies retired to Reserve & Support trenches respectively. The front line was visited by working parties from the Support Companies during the succeeding nights.	
	24/7/17		The Lewis Gun teams of the Companies in the front line were relieved by those from rear and for the purpose each aircraft fire. Aircraft continued to disappear actively, but British aeroplanes were unsuccessful in dealing with the enemy than many of the preceding days. A patrol went out during the night 24/25 July under 2/Lt FULLERLOVE to reconnoitre BEEK WOOD + FARM, and obtained information about the enemy's work in the neighbourhood.	
	25/7/17		Battalion relieved by the 8th LINCOLN REGT & proceeded to camp near KEMMEL. During the Battalion tour in the trenches the following casualties were reported:—	

KILLED & DIED OF WOUNDS
16

WOUNDED
28

MISSING
NIL.

Army Form C. 2118.

WAR DIARY
or
INTELLIGENCE SUMMARY.
(Erase heading not required.)

Instructions regarding War Diaries and Intelligence Summaries are contained in F. S. Regs., Part II. and the Staff Manual respectively. Title pages will be prepared in manuscript.

Place	Date	Hour	Summary of Events and Information	Remarks and references to Appendices
KEMMEL HILL CAMP	26/4/17		Battn. w/O, and billetted at KEMMEL.	
	27/4/17	7 PM	Battn. moved to DRANOUTRE, men billetted in huts in LURGAN LINES & LOCREHOF FARM.	
DRANOUTRE	28/4/17		Bath in the afternoon KEMMEL. Working parties in afternoon for the support line of cable laying. Commanding Officer inspects the Battle. Companies afternoon arrangements.	
"	29/4/17		Church parade established LOCREHOF FARM. Capt. J.A. FISHER took over the command, payment of B. Coy. from Lt. T.D. DIXON. Battle found working w/carrying parties for the support line of supports Batt., musketry + drill.	
"	30/4/17		Battn. training in Coy. Reserve Battn. working railway parties on fronts for destructible R.E. supervision.	
"	31/4/17		Batt. training under Company arrangements.	

J.A. Fisher Capt.
CAPTAIN,
11th SERVICE BN. R. WARWICKSHIRE REGT.

11TH (Service) BATTALION, ROYAL WARWICKSHIRE REGIMENT.

In the Field.   6th July, 1917.

CONCERT - PROGRAMME.
(Subject to alteration).

1. Overture. "Col. Bogey". The Band.
2. Opening Chorus. "Salisbury Plain". Cpl. HANNAN.
3. Song. "Are you from Dixie". L/Cpl. MATHEWS.
4. Song. "Juanita". Sergt. WESTOVER.
5. Humorous Song. "I'll Sing you a song". Dr. MERRITT.
6. Song. Selected. Capt. MAX LEWIS.
7. Humorous Song. Cpl. LAISHLEY.
8. Song. "They called it Dixie-Land". L/Cpl. HANNAN & Pte. JENNINGS.
9. Dr. ARTHUR will amuse with a Black-Board & some chalk.
10. Song. "I think we shall have some rain". Pte. DALTON.
11. Lieut. A.L. AUSTIN will do his best to break the Piano". (Kindly lent by the "BARN OWLS").
12. Song. "A broken Doll." L/Cpl. HILL.
13. Song. "Robinson Crusoe". L/Cpl. HANNAN & Pte. JENNINGS.
14. Sergt. De. St. CROIX, D.C.M. and Sergt. SMITH will show the quickest way of ending the War.
15. Song. "Charlie Chaplin". L/Cpl. MATHEWS.
16. Song. "Blue Eyes". Sgt. WESTOVER.

****

GOD SAVE THE KING.

Nat Diary
11th Warwicks
Aug 1917

Confidential

War Diary
of
11th (Service) Battalion Royal Warwickshire Regt.

from 1st August 1917 to 31st August, 1917

(Volume 3, No. 8.)

Army Form C. 2118.

WAR DIARY
or
INTELLIGENCE SUMMARY.
(Erase heading not required.)

Instructions regarding War Diaries and Intelligence Summaries are contained in F.S. Regs., Part II. and the Staff Manual respectively. Title pages will be prepared in manuscript.

Place	Date	Hour	Summary of Events and Information	Remarks and references to Appendices
DRANOUTRE	1/8/17		Battalion training under company arrangements. Battalion found working parties for the reserve and support lines.	
-	2/8/17		Battalion trained, found working and salvage parties. Lewis Gunners fired on the 111th Brigade School Range.	
BEAVER HALL	3/8/17	4 P.M.	Battalion moved to BEAVER HALL (near KEMMEL HILL) relieving the 4th MIDDLESEX Battalion training in drill, musketry and anti-gas precautions. Companies billeted at KEMMEL CHATEAU and found working parties.	
-	4/8/17		Battalion training.	
-	5/8/17		Church Parade. Battalion found working parties for the line. The following officers joined the Battalion. 2/Lt N Rolles — posted to B Coy. 2/Lt G A Moore — posted to C Coy.	
-	6/8/17		Battalion training. Battalion marched to KEMMEL SHELTERS, where it was billeted in hut shelters.	
-	7/8/17	2 P.M.	Company training and equipment. Reclass in hand sides, enemy gas, and musketry.	
-	Night 7-8/8/17		Battalion relieved the 6TH WILTSHIRES and the 9TH WELCH REGT in the line, taking over a two battalion front.	

Army Form C. 2118.

WAR DIARY
or
INTELLIGENCE SUMMARY.
(Erase heading not required.)

Instructions regarding War Diaries and Intelligence Summaries are contained in F. S. Regs., Part II. and the Staff Manual respectively. Title pages will be prepared in manuscript.

Place	Date	Hour	Summary of Events and Information	Remarks and references to Appendices
	9/8/17		Manoeuvre impossible in the front line by day; although considerable work was done in wiring outposts, improving & building up positions, salvage work, &c.	
	10/8/17		Enemy snipers machine guns were active in the frontline neighbourhood. Back area was heavily shelled, chiefly at 8–10 PM and 1–3 AM. Battn. H.Q. was shelled by H.E. intermittently during the evening & beginning of yrs shells were put over. Counter - measures were taken against enemy snipers and a number of his MGs were cleansed.	
	11/8/17	6.30 AM	Joint post was formed with the 4 th Australian Battalion on our RIGHT. BRIGADIER-GENERAL MacLACHLAN was killed near the RIGHT Company's H.Q., after making a tour of inspection round the outpost line. Improvements were made in the outpost & support trenches & fire positions were made.	
	night 11–12/8/17		Battn changed over with 10 th Loyal NORTH LANCS, and became Battn in support to RIGHT sub sector. During the relief a heavy barrage was put down by the enemy between the front & support lines; a direct hit was obtained on D Coy. H.Q.	

Army Form C. 2118.

WAR DIARY
or
INTELLIGENCE SUMMARY.
(Erase heading not required.)

Place	Date	Hour	Summary of Events and Information	Remarks and references to Appendices
ONRAET WOOD	12/8/17		Battalion was in support line, with C & A Coys on LEFT & RIGHT front companies respectively, move into close support from the front line. Battalion was arranged in depth with B Coy at THE TOWER SOUTH of OOSTTAVERNE WOOD, & D Coy in dug-outs near Batt H.Q. & ON RAET WOOD	
	13/8/17		Battalion was employed in cleaning and improving support position. Reparations were commenced for main offensive operation to be carried out on this front. At night working parties were found for the front & support lines of the new C.T. between H.Q. & front battln aid the front line.	
	14/8/17		Battn. found working parties and carried out salvage work in the support area.	
	Night 15-16/8/17		Battalion was relieved by the YORK & LANCS, (½ 112th BRIGADE) becoming Brigade in support. The Battln marched by companies to camp near KEMMEL at 28.S.W. N 22. c. 5.6.	
	16/8/17		Battalion rested. Re-equipment & re-organisation of Companies.	
	17/8/17		Commanding Officer inspected the Battln. Training of Specialists & companies.	

Army Form C. 2118.

WAR DIARY
or
INTELLIGENCE SUMMARY.
(Erase heading not required.)

Instructions regarding War Diaries and Intelligence Summaries are contained in F. S. Regs., Part II. and the Staff Manual respectively. Title pages will be prepared in manuscript.

Place	Date	Hour	Summary of Events and Information	Remarks and references to Appendices
ROSSIGNOL CAMP.	18/8/17		Battle Training; cleaning of equipment; company drills. BRIGADIER-GENERAL A.E. IRVINE D.S.O. C.M.G. and 2nd in command of the 112th Infantry Brigade.	
"	19/8/17		Church parade was held of all denominations. D Company practises the proposed raid on a model of the ground which has been laid out, and visits the model at LOCRE.	
"	20/8/17		Companies carried out company rifle drill and physical & bayonet fighting training. D Company practises the raiding scheme in the special area.	
"	21/8/17 9 p.m.		Battalion moved to the line, relieving on the same sector (EAST of OOSTTAVERNE) which it had during the previous tour. D Coy held the right, A Coy the centre & B Coy the left of the front line; C Coy was in support. The relief was carried out without incident or casualty.	
"	22/8/17		There was little enemy activity, as enemy sniping was considerably less than during the previous tour. Machine Guns however continued to be active. Enemy shelling was greatly reduced in comparison with the previous tour.	

A3834 Wt. W4973/M687 750,000 8/16 D.D. & L. Ltd. Forms/C.2118/13

WAR DIARY
or
INTELLIGENCE SUMMARY.

Army Form C. 2118.

Place	Date	Hour	Summary of Events and Information	Remarks and references to Appendices
Front Line	23/8/17		As enemy aircraft covered lines flew very low over our lines during the early morning, Lewis Guns were mounted in the support line for anti-aircraft work. Companies carried out a valuable amount of salvage work and improvements were made to Battle Head Quarters near INDER STEENTE FARM road. During the tour, companies in the front line patrolled 100 yards of our wire nightly and set trip wires; relief including nights of relief, the wiring was carried by C Company, which also carried rations. 9 sel nightly during the tour of Trench duty, patrols were sent out from D Coy to reconnoitre the ground around 'BEE' FARM and useful information about enemy dispositions was gained.	
	24/8/17		Battalion changed over with 10th Manchesters, becoming Battalion in support. C Coy became the front support company, with A B & D placed in two rows in depth behind.	
Support Line	25/8/17		Battalion Headquarters were in dugouts near ESTAMINET CORNER, hut had not formerly been used as Batt HQ; the old dugouts were handed over to 150 D Companies. A great deal of improvement work was carried on	

WAR DIARY or INTELLIGENCE SUMMARY

Army Form C. 2118.

Place	Date	Hour	Summary of Events and Information	Remarks and references to Appendices
			where the Spruits, and the whole surrounding were visible. Preparations were to complete for the raid the following night by D company, with two additional officers men from B & C companies.	
	Night 26/27 Aug.		A raid was carried out on BEE FARM, where the enemy had been located by Machine Gun emplacement found. It was carried out from the RIGHT company's outpost line through the N. Lines, and Battle H.Q. to moved Fund & IN DER STERKTE CAB. The raid was carried out by a force of 130 under Lt ROWLEY. The first line was commanded by 2/Lt HALLET & to aus 2/Lt SEAMAN, and the supports were commanded by 2/Lt HARPER. Zero hour was 2.30 A.M. 27th August, as the ground covered a depth of a frontage of 700 yds. Movement was difficult owing to heavy rain + to shell torn ground. The line was gained in Spruit at 2.40 A.M., and at 2.50 A.M. the Spruit was given. Sometime regined in Spruit at 2.40 A.M., and at 2.50 A.M. the Spruit was given. but all the party had returned safely. Three prisoners were captured, belonging	

WAR DIARY or INTELLIGENCE SUMMARY

Army Form C. 2118.

Place	Date	Hour	Summary of Events and Information	Remarks and references to Appendices
			to the 39th (Person) Regt, 24th D.W., while there we were driven by the Plan R. machine gun barrage to provide ten of the Posts on our RIGHT. Our casualties were 2/Lt SEAMAN & four O.R. slightly wounded; there are only one stretcher-case Amongst casualties were inflicted on the enemy with rifles, Lewis rifle periods. A barrage of Machine Gun, Field Artillery, Heavies & Trench Mortars commenced at 2.32 & continued to 3.2 A.M. on the Flanks and enemy support lines. Once the captured Person Slits is in expansion that a company of the enemy Storm-troopers had been brought up that night with the intention of counter-attacking in which the Prussian feelers from fact 274 A.M. The presence of this company was confirmed later. The 76th was relieved by the 73rd K.R.R. and moved to ROSSIGNOL WOOD Camp near KEMMEL. Thereby pass of f n with 9, except for some shelling on our & between RIGHT, which caused no casualties or damage.	
	28/8/17		Battln rested & re-equipped.	
	29/8/17		Company training; cleaning of huts & improvement of camp. Working parties were found for Div. H.Q., the Support lines & the Reserve line.	

WAR DIARY
or
INTELLIGENCE SUMMARY

Army Form C. 2118.

Place	Date	Hour	Summary of Events and Information	Remarks and references to Appendices
ROSSIGNOL WOOD	30/8/17		BRIGADIER GENERAL IRVINE inspected all ranks shortly after BREAKFAST BEE FARM and congratulated them on their work & successful result. Working party of two men in front for making a entrance from IN DER STERNE CAST & ROSE WOOD. Other working parties were found in the evening.	
"	31/8/17		Both fronts working parties & batters. Reorganisation of our paries was completed, so that each company should have two full platoons, a Headquarter platoon if possible the nucleus for a fourth platoon, with reserve Lewis guns.	

signed J. Little
2nd Lieut.
11th SERVICE BN. R. WARWICKSHIRE REGT.

Confidential

War Diary
of

11th (S) Bn. Royal Warwickshire Regiment.

From 1st September 1917 to 30th September 1917.

(Volume 3, No. 9).

Army Form C. 2118.

WAR DIARY
or
INTELLIGENCE SUMMARY.
(Erase heading not required.)

Instructions regarding War Diaries and Intelligence Summaries are contained in F. S. Regs., Part II. and the Staff Manual respectively. Title pages will be prepared in manuscript.

Place	Date	Hour	Summary of Events and Information	Remarks and references to Appendices
ROSSIGNOL WOOD	1.9.17		Battalion Training. Trench order read. Gas drill. Working party of 100 privates for extending French Tramway from DE STEENTJE CROT to ROSE WOOD.	
BOIS CARRÉ	2.9.17	10 a.m.	Battalion moved to BOIS CARRÉ	
	3.9.17		116th Brigade relieved by 112th Brigade in sector YPRES COMINES CANAL (exclusive to J.31 a 75. 75.) Battalion moved to relieve E. Lancs Regt in front line. Disposition — Nucleus system FRONT LINE (right) 1 Platoon B Coy + 2 Lewis guns " " (left) C Coy SUPPORT A Coy and remainder of B Coy. Bn HQ at J.6.a.3.8 RESERVE D Coy.	
	4.9.17		Consolidation of front line, all wire was to be done at night owing to direct observation of enemy.	
	5.9.17		Patrols sent out to enemy's (German) wire. Saps slipped out, wire put out. Enemy average activity. Support and reserve lines. New posts made.	
	6.9.17		Enemy shelled Support & reserve. 2 wounded. Casualties 2 killed	
	7.9.17		M.G. busy all night – 6.7" Gas Shells sent over. Casualties 2 wounded (Gas)	

WAR DIARY
or
INTELLIGENCE SUMMARY.

Army Form C. 2118.

Place	Date	Hour	Summary of Events and Information	Remarks and references to Appendices
	7.9.17	10pm	Battalion relieved by 8th E. Lancs in front line. A + C Companies (more?) to reserve positions at TRIANGUCHE BUFFS and SPOIL BANK. B Coy to BOIS CARRÉ. D Coy remained in trenches to act as carrying party to E. Lancs.	
	8.9.17		B Coy provided working party of 100 men to dig communication trench. Enemy shelling. 1 man wounded.	
	9.9.17		Companies provided working and carrying parties. N. of ST ELOI.	
	10.9.17	4.5pm	B Coy moved to BEAVER CORNER for one night.	
NOIR MONT ROUGE	11.9.17	5pm	Battalion (less D Coy) moved to MONT NOIR - MONT ROUGE area M 20 d 5.6	
	12.9.17		D Coy rejoined battalion at M 20 d 5.5. Inspection of Battalion by Commanding Officer.	
	13.9.17		Medical inspection of all ranks. Parade of battalion in fighting order under Commanding Officer.	

WAR DIARY or INTELLIGENCE SUMMARY

Army Form C. 2118.

Place	Date	Hour	Summary of Events and Information	Remarks and references to Appendices
	14.9.17		A & D Coys supplied working party of 1 officer & 100 men for R.E. The following honours were gained by members of the Battalion for operations E of WYCHAETE on Aug 22/17: Military Medal — T/Lieut E.C.W. ROMNEY, T/2/Lieut H.H.L. HALLETT. D.C.M — Sgt F. Young "B" Coy 9298, Sgt E.H. LONG 4763, A/L/Sgt WYNORTON 7916, Sgt A. DAVIS 1154, Sgt C.H. COOK 18527, Pte E. GREEN 28717. The 37th Divr Congratulatory Card granted to the following by the Battalion for the raid carried out by the Battalion 26/27 August.	
	15.9.17	7 a.m.	C and part D Coy on IX Corps School range. Lewis Gun training. Company wiring parties to be formed. Commanding Officers conference with all officers of Battalion. Baths for B & D Coys. Battalion training.	
	16.9.17	9 a.m.	Church parade.	
	17.9.17	9.30 a.m.	Conference of officers preparatory to Brigade Reserve Practice.	
			Reconnaissance by Company officers of cross country route to SPOIL BANK.	
	18.9.17	9.30 a.m.	Battalion inspected by G.O.C. 112th Infantry Brigade.	
		11.30 a.m.	Demonstration by wounded Gas Officer in Battalion parade ground. Lieut J.D. DIXON takes over temporary command of C Company.	
	19.9.17	5.45	Battalion march to ROSSIGNOL Wood in Bivouacs.	

Army Form C. 2118.

WAR DIARY
or
INTELLIGENCE SUMMARY.
(Erase heading not required.)

Instructions regarding War Diaries and Intelligence Summaries are contained in F.S. Regs., Part II. and the Staff Manual respectively. Title pages will be prepared in manuscript.

Place	Date	Hour	Summary of Events and Information	Remarks and references to Appendices
	20.9.17		Bn at training drill, and inspection. Inspection by Commanding Officer of all ranks who were to take (to proceed) to France in second of taking part in attack.	
	21.9.17		Battalion Training. Bomb throwing instruction.	
MONT NOIR			Battalion moved to near MONT NOIR in tents, in WESTOUTRE.	
Trenches BULGAR WOOD	22.9.17	6.30 pm	39th Division in BULGAR WOOD relieved by Battalion. Reconnaissance by Officers on ground to be held by battalion.	
		12.30 pm	Battalion moved via WESTHOEK SPOILBANK to BULGAR WOOD. Seek to relieve HERTS Regiment on right Battalion front.	
		6.0 pm	Disposition of Battalion. Headquarters in RAVINE J25.c.9.3 B Coy in Reserve. C Coy in Support A & D Front line — Eastern edge of BULGAR WOOD.	
	23.9.17		Owing to ground having only just been gained from enemy a great deal of work was necessary to strengthen the line. Correct and deepening trenches, and place the sector in state of defence. The supposed area shelled intermittently. Machine situation was quiet. Front line consolidated. Shell holes converted into trenches. Strengthening of Support trenches. A good deal of Salvage Work	

A8834 Wt. W4973/M687 750,000 8/16 D.D.& L. Ltd. Forms/C.2118/13.

WAR DIARY or INTELLIGENCE SUMMARY

Army Form C. 2118.

Place	Date	Hour	Summary of Events and Information	Remarks and references to Appendices
Bulgar Wood Trenches			effected, also cleaning out of dugouts in front line. These were in bad condition owing to low wet ground, and recent occupation by the enemy.	
	24.9.17		Enemy observed in line of trenches & dugouts from T.26 a 7.5 to T.32 d 7.2. Shelling of our trenches continued, and owing to our front and support line being under direct view of the enemy, little work could be accomplished during day. Situation quiet.	
	25.9.17		Patrols refind wire in front line, but broken and almost useless. Further reconnaissance revealed this wire all across battalion front. 20 coils of wire were necy. to improve to enemy wire and form obstacle 10 feet wide, three high.	
	26.9.17	11 am	New posts formed in front line. Line consolidated. Movement of enemy and progress of fighting in Lectio de on our left (T.27 &c) during operations observed from our F.O.P. at T.28 d 9.3, and immediately reported to Brigade. Intermittent shelling on our forward track area throughout the day. 1 Officer & 4 N.C.O's A. of the 8th Staffs. Regt. in camp in the trenches previous to relieving the battalion	

Army Form C. 2118.

WAR DIARY
or
INTELLIGENCE SUMMARY.
(Erase heading not required.)

Place	Date	Hour	Summary of Events and Information	Remarks and references to Appendices
ROSIGNOL WOOD	27.9.17		Reports on enemy's movements in Sector of operations on our left.	
		6.30	Battalion relieved by 6th JAGER TRENCH & again send in 27th JAGER SLUSTERS. Arrangements made for our guides to conduct incoming battalion from BRICKSTACK up to their positions in the line. All stores, maps, and intelligence handed over and receipts obtained. Relief completed by 10 p.m. 5 days' rain in trenches! Total casualties 20 other ranks killed or died of wounds 1 Officer and 66 " " wounded 1 " " Battalion marched to ROSIGNOL WOOD N.22, 2cm SPOILBANK BUS HOUSE.	
N.9.6.7.9	28.9.17 1.30pm		Battalion moved to N.9.6.7.9.	
	29.9.17		Battalion engaged in cleaning up after trenches. A Coy baths.	
	30.9.17		Inspection of Battalion by CO. Remainder Corps baths. 4 hr Church Parade.	

Confidential

112/37

War Diary
of
11th (Service) Battalion, Royal Warwickshire Regiment

From 1st October 1917 to 31st October, 1917.

(Volume 3, N° 10).

Army Form C. 2118.

WAR DIARY
or
INTELLIGENCE SUMMARY.
(Erase heading not required.)

1/1th (S) Bn Royal Warwick Shire Regt

Instructions regarding War Diaries and Intelligence Summaries are contained in F.S. Regs., Part II. and the Staff Manual respectively. Title pages will be prepared in manuscript.

Place	Date	Hour	Summary of Events and Information	Remarks and references to Appendices
N9 L 29 SWIN & EOS	1919 Oct 1	7am 10am	Regimental parade under officers & attendance by NCOs. Commanding officers Conference. Company arrangements. Decision being come to under Battalion Commanders of Bttn went into in case of broken releasing 113 Brigde	
		1 pm	Regt'al parade. Junior officers briefed. Battalion having received orders sent to all Companies and HQ. French and Hindustani orders sent. S.O.S. 6 battalion's Demonstration of daylight.	
	3	8 am	Reconnaissance by 6 officers of TOWER HAMLETS Sector, in event of battalion moving into line as support battalion.	
		7 am	Companies parade. Junior officers to attend. Companies organised for full fighting order. Eagles S.S. 135 between 10 to be ready to move into line at 15 minutes notice after 5 am T the 4th.	
	4	10.30 pm	Preparation of battalion in complete fighting order by Company officers. Orders received for battalion to relieve N9 23 in Sector TOWER HAMLETS on the 112th Brigade's sector 63.D - 111th Brigade in TOWER HAMLETS also in SPOIL BANK and attached by	
	5	5 pm	Battalion moved off in buses by Coys. Battalion ready to move in by buses at SWOFORT.	
TOWER HAMLETS			Disposition of Brigade - E LINES { Eyk Bedfords { Cent { Inn E Cent { inniskg A Coy (left) B Coy (centre) D Coy (right) in forward line in contact Coy HQ. in forward line C Coy a carrying Company HQ battalion at POPLAR REDT collated by midnight 5/6	

Signature of Battalion |

Army Form C. 2118.

WAR DIARY
or
INTELLIGENCE SUMMARY.
(Erase heading not required.)

Place	Date 1917	Hour	Summary of Events and Information	Remarks and references to Appendices
	6.		Situation quiet. Artillery very active. Great difficulty with transport and carrying of rations, in spite of careful arrangements beforehand, on account of intense darkness, damage of tracks and heavy shelling. Serving parties delivered and returned, also trench joined up between B and 13 where gap existed. Gets made in trenches as precaution against explosive fire.	
	7.		Occasional shelling throughout day. New support trench dug in front of evening one, to new kennels to front line. Considerable amount of salvage done.	
	8.		Heavy shelling at intervals. Frequent rain. Movement of troops to serve as R.A.P.	
	9.	5.20	Attack by our troops on left of our sector. Simultaneous attack by the 3 bns in front line (112th Bde) now close objective. In event of enemy retaining balloon to more forward (St Quentin) by rockets for about 1500 yards by means of Hopkins patrols (4 patrols) (two troops). No development.	
	10.	5.45	Intense artillery retaliatory bombardment lasting 15 hours. Bombs went shells. Bn. H.Q. R.A.P. Bossenville R to Tomatoes Dump and	
		7 hrs	Artillery very quiet all day. Bn. Commences relief, ready from 11am onwards. 112th Brigade relieved by 63rd Brigade.	

WAR DIARY or INTELLIGENCE SUMMARY.

Army Form C. 2118.

(Erase heading not required.)

Place	Date	Hour	Summary of Events and Information	Remarks and references to Appendices
	Oct 10		Battalion relieved by York and Lancs Regt. All on entraining out by 9.30 pm; but owing to Y & Z being over awkward guides was necessary to lead them to support line. Relief reports complete 9.45 am. Total casualties of 3 days fighting 33 Killed, 75 wounded, 11 missing. Battalion arrives at Caudre midnight 10/11th.	
N9 & 29 (SWAN LODGE) near	11		Day spent in cleaning up and baths	
	12		Cleaning up and baths. Capt Chambers to command Hy C Coy. Inspection of Lewis Guns. Battalion moves to Camp at Mont Noir. Company pay.	
MONT NOIR	13	noon		
	14	10.30 am	Divine Service	
	15		Battalion training continued.	
	16	2 pm	Battalion entrained, proceeding to Camp N.E of YPRES on the ST-JEAN — POTIJZE Road — 250 S.A. of 6th Bedfords attached to Battalion, being absorbed by # 11 R. Warwick R —	
REF YPRES	17		Day spent in cleaning of Camp, making dug outs etc. Battalion administered by II ANZAC Corps.	
	18-21		Work on Front roads of YPRES-NOUGERS & YPRES-ZONNEBEKE roads - 2 pm 6th RAN casualties from aeroplane bomb dropped by day -	
	22		After usual day's work Battalion starts to Mont Noir, entraining at KRUISSTRAAT	

Army Form C. 2118.

WAR DIARY
or
INTELLIGENCE SUMMARY.
(Erase heading not required.)

Instructions regarding War Diaries and Intelligence Summaries are contained in F. S. Regs., Part II. and the Staff Manual respectively. Title pages will be prepared in manuscript.

Place	Date	Hour	Summary of Events and Information	Remarks and references to Appendices
MONT NOIR	Oct 22-25		Battalion training —	
	26		Battalion march to DRAMOUTRE, temp. billets in LUGAN lines & LOCRE & of FARM —	
DRAMOUTRE	26-31		Battalion training	
	31		Brigade Band Competition — 11 R Warwicks won 1st & 2nd Competitions by 135 marks, running back of the 4 units —	

Signed [signature]
CAPTAIN.
ADJT 11th SERVICE BN. R. WARWICKSHIRE REGT.

YM 28

Confidential

War Diary

of

11th (S) Bn. Royal Warwickshire Regiment.

from 1st November 1917 to 30th November, 1917.

(Volume 3, No 11.)

Army Form C. 2118.

WAR DIARY
or
INTELLIGENCE SUMMARY.
(Erase heading not required.)

Place	Date	Hour	Summary of Events and Information	Remarks and references to Appendices
DRANOUTRE	Nov. 1		Coy. Training	
	2		Inter Company Yukon Pack Competition — C Coy wins —	
	3		Working parties under R.E. —	
	4		Brigade Commemoration Service for those who have fallen in the last two months, on Brigade School parade ground —	
	5–7		Company Training —	
	8		Battalion moved to MOATED GRANGE to our right —	
	9		Battalion relieved the 6th Bn Gloucester R. in the line, taking over the section immediately N of YPRES – COMINES canal — Two Companies in the line, one in support, one in Reserve in Spoil Bank —	
	13th		Inter Company reliefs took place without incident.	
	14		Owing to weakness of companies the Coy in SPOIL BANK was brought up to the support area —	
	17		Battalion was relieved by 13th R. Fusiliers — Two men of holding a post were missing on relief — Battalion returned to MOATED GRANGE —	
	18–25		Working Parties were found daily for whole Battalion — On the night of the 24th the camp was bombed & Capt Chambers, 2465 Wilson & Gwynne were killed.	
	26		Battalion marched to CURRAGH CAMP, taking over from 4 Bn Middlesex Regt —	
	28-29		Brigade alleged operations on an extensive scale —	
	30		Company & Recreational Training — Draft of 1 W.O. & 1 O.R. & 10 m[en] on 27th inst.	

CONFIDENTIAL.

WAR DIARY

of

11th (Service) Bn. Royal Warwickshire Regiment.

From 1st December 1917. To 31st December 1917.

W. J. Webb-Bowen Lt.-Colonel
Comdg. 11th Service Bn. R. Warwickshire Regt.

WAR DIARY or INTELLIGENCE SUMMARY

Army Form C. 2118.

Place	Date	Hour	Summary of Events and Information	Remarks and references to Appendices
CURRAGH CAMP	1919 DEC 1		Small working parties supplied. New draft ("trip") inspected by Brigade Commander. Brigade Commander's conference with all Bn Officers, regarding posts being captured by enemy, and posts not to be held by less than 6.	
	2		Bn Church parade at LOCRE. C of E and Non Conformists R.E. at LA CLYTTE	
	3	AM PM	Bn training in P.T. Musketry, Drill. Recreational training.	
	4		Bn training as above. 2 Officers and NCO's to take over (New stores) Sent up in advance of Bn and remain in trenches with order to get to know posts &c.	
Trenches WHITE CHATEAU Sector	5		Bn moved by light railway (entraining at KILMARNOCK) to take over sub sector immediately south of the YPRES-COMINES Canal. O.C. 70-45 — HOLLEBEKE ROAD O.11.90.55. from LINCOLN'S REGT A Company front line " B " " " C " close support " D " 2 Lieutenant at WHITE CHATEAU Bn HQ 2 Officers/Batman sent out	

WAR DIARY
or
INTELLIGENCE SUMMARY.

Army Form C. 2118.

Place	Date	Hour	Summary of Events and Information	Remarks and references to Appendices
Trenches WHITE CHATEAU Sector (Continued)	DEC 6 1916	Dusk	In consequence of terminal orders receiving 24 hour relief — B Coy relieved A Coy in front line, and A Coy went to close support.	
	7	Dusk	2 officers patrols sent out each night during tour. The two Companies in reserve did no carrying parties. Inter-company relief — "A" in front line "B" in close support. Wiring in front of posts and in support line by Pioneer Officer and wiring party.	
	8	Dusk	Liaison with Australians on our right effected by interchange of men & reports. B Company relieves "A" in front line. A Coy going back to close support.	
		Midnight 8/9	At midnight 8/9th our front line was subjected to a heavy bombardment for 45 minutes by Enemy 7 M.G. Rifle Grenades, MG's and small calibre Shells. The enemy made an attempt to raid our posts, but was driven back by rifle and L.G. fire and casualties inflicted. A further search was made though our own lines and no Killed were found. Our casualties close our own lines in the early hours of the 9th. Our Casualties 1 killed 3 wounded.	
			In accordance with terminal order, three officers (in addition to O.C. Coy) were on duty in front line posts, each officers being considerable for his group of 3 posts and visiting them continually throughout the tour. Each Coy was carried out during the whole tour. Etc.	

Army Form C. 2118.

WAR DIARY
or
INTELLIGENCE SUMMARY.
(Erase heading not required.)

Instructions regarding War Diaries and Intelligence Summaries are contained in F. S. Regs., Part II. and the Staff Manual respectively. Title pages will be prepared in manuscript.

Place	Date	Hour	Summary of Events and Information	Remarks and references to Appendices
Trenches, WHITE CHATEAU Sector (Continued)	9 Dec	dusk	A Company relieved B in front line at 3 am of the 10th. 1 Off. and 12 O.R. from A Coy raided an enemy post discovered by our patrols at 0.12.a.58.75. Bombs were thrown by our party and an attempt to enter post made. The Officer and Sgt were wounded (Officer slightly) and the post was discovered to be stronger than expected. The enemy counter-attacked & hung bombs amongst our men and our party withdrew being sniped at in its return. Commanding Officer regarding defence of the Reconnaissance of General line of Flanders. Left flank and A in front line. C Coy moving to C Coy relieved A in front line.	
WHITE CHATEAU	10	dusk	The Enemy artillery more active & the posts shelled being Br HQ, Blore support line, and Lart Aux, near WHITE CHATEAU and AID POST. No S post Snepery M.G. fire became more active in front line. We S post and Coy HQ were fired at at intervals during night. 10/11 C Company det 36 hours in front line being relieved by D Coy etc. before dawn on the morning of the 12th.	
	11	dusk	C Coy in front line. D in close support	

A 5834 Wt. W4973/M1687 750,000 8/16 D. D. & L. Ltd. Forms/C.2118/13.

Army Form C. 2118.

WAR DIARY
or
INTELLIGENCE SUMMARY.
(Erase heading not required.)

Instructions regarding War Diaries and Intelligence Summaries are contained in F.S. Regs., Part II. and the Staff Manual respectively. Title pages will be prepared in manuscript.

Place	Date	Hour	Summary of Events and Information	Remarks and references to Appendices
Trenches WHITE CHATEAU SECTOR	Dec 11		Establishment of Strong point at O5c 25.95 covering left flank up to Canal bank, and liaison with M.G. for strong object	
	12	dawn	C Company relieved by D Coy in front line	
	13		Battalion relieved by 10th Bn R. Fusiliers. Companies moved out as relieved to Spoil Bank, and battalion entrained on light railway here for PARRET CAMP in Support Area.	
	14.	8.45 10.15 am	Battalion was baths at SPICE FARM. Remainder of day was for cleaning up equipments &c	

Army Form C. 2118.

WAR DIARY
or
INTELLIGENCE SUMMARY.
(Erase heading not required.)

Instructions regarding War Diaries and Intelligence Summaries are contained in F. S. Regs., Part II. and the Staff Manual respectively. Title pages will be prepared in manuscript.

Place	Date	Hour	Summary of Events and Information	Remarks and references to Appendices
PERNOT CAMP	15		Battalion supplied small working party. Remainder of battalion inspected by Commanding officer. (Full marching order.) Recreational training carried out in the afternoon	
	16		Battalion supplied large working parties. Divine Service for remainder of battalion. The men who were not on working party on the 15th inst were inspected in full marching order by the Commanding Officer.	
	17.		Battalion supplied large working parties. Bomb throwing etc.	
	18		Ditto	
	19		Blankets fumigated. Large working parties supplied by battalion. Bomb throwing etc.	
	20		Large working parties supplied by battalion	
	21		Ditto	

WAR DIARY
or
INTELLIGENCE SUMMARY.
(Erase heading not required.)

Army Form C. 2118.

Place	Date 1917	Hour	Summary of Events and Information	Remarks and references to Appendices
PARAY CAMP	Dec 22		Large working parties supplied by battalion	
	23		Ditto	
	24		Small working parties supplied. The remainder of battalion went for route march.	
	25		Xmas day. Divine Service for battalion.	
		12.30 pm	Xmas dinner for men. Huts decorated, and men waited on by officers and NCOs. Menu: Turkey, Vegetables, Plum Pudding. Baths at SEIGE FARM. Reconnaissance of Trenches by O.C. Coys.	
	26		Battalion on fatigue clearing away snow from ASQUEUT lorry roads	
	27		Small working parties provided. Lecture to all officers NCOs and men of the battalion on duties &c in trenches by the Commanding Officer.	
	28		Small working parties provided. 2 officers + 3 NCOs sent up to G Trenches in advance of battalion	

WAR DIARY
or
INTELLIGENCE SUMMARY.

Army Form C. 2118.

Place	Date	Hour	Summary of Events and Information	Remarks and references to Appendices
PARRAT CAMP	29		Leaving of Trench orders to all ranks. Anti Gas appliances inspected. "Trench fire precautions" carried out, and new inspection to See if complete for the line.	
BULGAR & BITTER WOOD J 26 b 2.5 to J 32 a 3.3			Battalion moves by train to Trenches taking over left battalion sector of Divisional front from 8th Bn Lincoln Regt. Disposition :- D Company on Right front C " " Left " B " in Support A " Reserve	
	30		Special orders issued to improving the wire defences in front of posts particularly round No 6 Post (O 26 c 93.15) and night posts to be established at J 26 a 96.02 & J 26 c 78.356 to increase the security of No 6 Post. Duly carried out	

WAR DIARY
or
INTELLIGENCE SUMMARY.

(Erase heading not required.)

Army Form C. 2118.

Place	Date	Hour	Summary of Events and Information	Remarks and references to Appendices
Tranchee - BULGAR - BITTER WOOD Sector	Dec 31	Dusk 5 pm 8 pm	D and C relief in front line by A + B Coys. C Coy withdrawing to Supports and D Coy to reserve. Special wiring party of 1 off and 10 OR to improve wire defences	

WAR DIARY
or
INTELLIGENCE SUMMARY.

(Erase heading not required.)

Army Form C. 2118.

Place	Date	Hour	Summary of Events and Information	Remarks and references to Appendices
Trenches BULGAR-	1-1-18 to 4/1/18		The 2 front line Coys. relieved nightly by support & Reserve Coys. The Special wiring party continued to improve the wire defences.	
BITTER WOOD sectr	4/1/18		Total casualties during tour :- One man killed (shot by sniper), 3/1/18	
SPOIL BANK	5-1-18 to 9-1-18		Battalion was relieved in front line by 10th Royal Fusiliers and went into support at SPOIL BANK. Tunnels 5/1/18. On forward large working parties for front line 6th to 9th 1-1-18	
"	10-1-18		Battn. relieved by first of 4th Australian Divn., marched to DICKEBUSCH, proceeded thence by train to EBBLINGHEM & subsequently marched to LYNDE there to be billeted.	
LYNDE	11-1-18 to 14-1-18		Battalion training	
"	15-1-18	9.30am	Battalion inspected by the Divisional Commander. The following message was subsequently received from Headquarters, 112th Infantry Brigade:- "The Brigade Commander desires me to convey his heartiest congratulations to you on the excellent turnout of your Battalion, including transport, when inspected on the 15th inst., by the Divisional Commander. The Brigade Commander considers that the result of the inspection reflects great credit on all concerned".	
"	16-1-18 to 20-1-18		Battalion training	

Army Form C. 2118.

WAR DIARY
or
INTELLIGENCE SUMMARY.
(Erase heading not required.)

Place	Date	Hour	Summary of Events and Information	Remarks and references to Appendices
MICMAC CAMP.	21-1-18		Battalion marched to EBBLINGHEM, proceeded thence by train to DICKEBUSCH, & subsequently marched to MICMAC CAMP. H 31 & 2.4 where it was quartered.	
	22-1-18 to 31-1-18		Battalion employed on Working Parties strengthening the defences of the 'B' Line, etc.	

S.C. [signature]
CAPTAIN,
ADJ. 11th SERVICE BN. R. WARWICKSHIRE REGT.

Confidential

War Diary
of
11th (S) Battalion
Royal Warwickshire Regiment.

From 1st February, 1918 to 21st February, 1918.

(Volume H. No. 2.)

To: D.A.G.
G.H.Q.
3rd Echelon

R.44

Herewith War Diary of the 11th
(S) Bn. Royal Warwickshire Regiment for
period 1st to 21st February 1918.
Kindly acknowledge receipt.

W.I. Webb-Bower
Lieut. Colonel
Commanding "Reinforcement" XXII Corps.

Hist. Sec. C.I.D.

The attached diary sent
to this office in error, is passed
to you.

J. Treloar Capt.
Officer i/c Aust. War Records Section. 26/3/18.

21-3-18.

Army Form C. 2118.

WAR DIARY
or
INTELLIGENCE SUMMARY.
(Erase heading not required.)

Place	Date	Hour	Summary of Events and Information	Remarks and references to Appendices
MICMAC CAMP DICKEBUSCH	1st to 4th		Battalion employed on "B" line, strengthening existing defences, constructing strong points, wiring etc.	
	4th		Battalion entrained at DICKEBUSCH station. Proceeding to EBBLINGHEM.	
	5th		Battalion detrained 3.15 p.m. & marched to the village of LA SABLONNIÈRE, LE RONS & ISLINGEM, where it was billeted. Orders received re the distribution of the battalion, to take place on the 7th inst.	
	7th		The Battalion was detrained(?) except for 14 Officers & 83 O.R. 19 Officers & 350 O.R. under Capt. G. BROOKE entrained at EBBLINGHEM en route for the 10th Bn R. War. R. 15 Officers & 300 O.R. under Capt. J.H. SIMMS entrained en route for the 1st Bn R.War.R.	
	10th		Remainder of 11th Bn proceeded to the Divisional Wing of Corps Reinforcement Camp — Lt Col W.T.BB BOWEN D.S.O appointed o.c. reinforcements i.e. details of Battalion — Lt. Col. WEBB-BOWEN posted to command 8th Bn Lincolnshire Regiment — Capt. A.H. HEFFER posted to 4th Bn Middlesex Regiment —	
	21st		Remainder of Bn proceeds to join No 15 Entraining Bn at WIPPENHOEK, & all W.O.'s & N.C.O.'s were sent to the Base ——	
			J.H.Brooke Lt for Lt Col	
			17/5/16 O.C. 11 War R	

NOT FOR VISITORS.

Extracts from the Diary of Brevet-Colonel
C. S. Collison, D.S.O., 11th Royal
Warwickshire Regiment.

Col Collison DSO.

11 R Warwicks

112/37

1915

NOT FOR VISITORS

Extracts from the Diary of Brevet-Colonel C.S.Collison, D.S.O.,
11th Royal Warwickshire Regiment, 112th Infantry Brigade,
37th Division.

WITH THE ELEVENTH ROYAL WARWICKS IN FRANCE.

Duty at Rochester.   I take over command of 11th Battalion, Royal Warwickshire Regiment at Shoreham. Strength of Battalion, March 1915. Its want of elementary training. Move to Ludgershall, Salisbury Plain. The Battalion forms part of the 112th Brigade, 37th Division, 2nd (New) Army.

The Great War was seven months old, when I received telegraphic orders to take over the command of the 11th(Service) Battalion, Royal Warwickshire Regiment. I was then at Rochester with my Reserve Battalion of the Middlesex Regiment, officially known as the 5th Special Reserve Battalion, agreeably to the pre-war commercial custom of labelling as "Special" all commodities, including cigars and toothpaste, designed to attract home markets.

The despatch of reinforcements, with which Reserve Battalions were principally, but by no means entirely, concerned, had by this date assumed some method. The wild enthusiasm that marked the departure of drafts in the early days of the war, with its senseless screams of "Are we downhearted?", had given way to a more orderly and soldierlike attitude, in keeping with the great task that confronted the nation, but an attitude, nevertheless, no wit less determined, because it was, in comparison, a quiet one.

Having elected to join a Reserve unit on my retirement from the Army, I might very well have remained with it for the duration of the war, but for the kind offices of the Inspector of Infantry (Major-General L.G.Drummond [late Scots Guards]), in whose Brigade I had formerly served as a company commander. It was solely at his instance that I received the call to a more active service.

Of Rochester, itself, I shall always have pleasant

memories. Chatham encompassed her on the East, whilst Strood would have crushed her on the North (if the Medway had not intervened) and trams from both places clanged and rumbled through her streets; and yet like a mid-Victorian Mother, surrounded by the pushing, bob-haired, half-men, half-women, girls of to-day, she retained in a wonderful manner an atmosphere of dignity and repose, worthy of her historic past.

We reached the large and gloomy terminus at Brighton on a murky day in March, and following a drive through rather a mean looking neighbourhood arrived at "the most respectable hotel" in the town; for so it was called by the Dean, on whose selection we had relied. It was on the sea-front, of course, and could not have been more respectable, especially in the matter of its charges.

At this time the 11th Royal Warwickshire was stationed at the large camp at Shoreham, near Brighton, and formed part of the "Army Troops" of the 3rd (New) Army, attached to the 24th Division under Sir John Ramsay. The Battalion was raised in October 1914, so that on my arrival it was about 5 months old. The Adjutant, Captain J.Falvey-Beyts, met me at the hotel, and it was from him that I learnt these details. It had a strength of about 1000, with a formidable corps of nearly 100 officers. A few of these had previous service in the Regular Army, or had served in the late South African War with irregular troops; but as a whole both officers and other ranks were fresh from civil life. I found that the Battalion had taken part in either Brigade or Divisional tactical exercises(!), that all ranks were exceptionally keen, and that the physique of the rank and file was generally excellent.*

---

* The fact that the Battalion had taken part in Divisional exercises before my arrival, and was at the same time so ignorant of both sectional and company training that I had no alternative but to start elementary instruction from the very beginning, is an instance of the entire want of method that obtained in the training of some units of the New Army.

Officers without the faintest idea of how to train men, and often as ignorant of their work as the people they were supposed to teach, were occasionally put in command of these battalions and the results were deplorable.

On the principle of teaching a child to walk before he can run, I started training from the very beginning, i.e., "First position of a soldier", "Right-hand salute", etc. The months during which the Battalion had been under arms, combined with the keenness and aptitude of the officers and men, enabled this ground work of their training to be pushed forward with unusual rapidity. It is not actually correct to say that the Battalion had been previously 'under arms' at all, as very few men had rifles, they were mostly dressed in blue and had hardly any equipment; but with all these drawbacks, not the least of which was the presence of 100 officers, nearly ninety per cent. of whom had not the foggiest idea what to do, or how to do it, the universal desire to learn was so noticeable and enthusiastic that the tasks and responsibilities of my instructorship were immensely lessened.

Training had lasted about a month when the Battalion was ordered to Ludgershall, Salisbury Plain. There the 37th Division under Major-General Lord Edward Gleichen, was in progress of formation as part of the 2nd (New) Army, and the 11th Royal Warwickshire joined the 112th Brigade, under Brigadier-General J.Marriott, D.S.O., M.V.O., the other battalions being the 6th Battalion Bedfordshire Regiment, 8th Battalion East Lancashire Regiment and 10th Battalion Loyal North Lancashire Regiment. As regards clothing, equipment and rifles we were still in a noticeably backward condition in comparison to the remainder of the Infantry of the Division; but these matters were now pushed on energetically, and by the end of May/we were practically complete. Tactical instruction in the field, concluding with Divisional Operations, put the finishing touch to the training, and on the 25th June 1915 the Division was reviewed by the King preparatory to embarkation for the seat of war. *

---
* At this review mounted officers were directed to be dressed like the men and to carry full packs. The disorderly appearance of a mounted officer on a mettlesome steed barging about the country with a heavy load bumping about on his back was not to be contemplated, so my servant (Bowden), an old soldier, overcame the difficulty by packing mine with straw and a few copies of the "Northcliffe Press", and it was greatly admired for its symmetry and attractive appearance.

The four months' training that the Battalion had had was all too short. About a month after its arrival at Ludgershall, when it had not completed its instruction under the company commanders, or had even started battalion training, it was called upon to take part in brigade exercises. That it acquitted itself so well at this and at divisional training was due both to the efficient work of the company officers, and to the great keenness and determination to make good of the N.C.Os. and men.

* * * * *

CHAPTER V (Extract) Hannescamps Sector - 1915.

I was then, and am still, convinced that the British system of defence, as then adopted, was most unsuitable. Instead of the front line being lightly held, and formations distributed in depth, the exact reverse was the case, and the supporting portions of front-line battalions were so close to the troops that they supported, that in case of attack both must inevitably have been overwhelmed, or at least committed to action, at the same time; in either case a most undesirable result. Under this system, once battle was joined, it was impossible for either the battalion or brigade commander to influence it effectively; their main forces, instead of being held in hand, would have been automatically involved in the action from the outset. It was, in short, the negation of all offensive action. "No line whatever lends itself for defence, unless it also possesses capabilities for offence", said Napoleon; but arguments in favour of "defence in depth", as it was called, were usually met by remarks, such as "My dear fellow, British troops always hold their trenches to the last", or, "It did very well at Ypres!" with other equally futile and irrelevant observations; and it was not until long afterwards that the British and German armies were forced to adopt more elastic and up-to-date methods.*

---

* In a "Secret" Memorandum, issued by German Army Headquarters, dated 1st August 1915, and entitled "Essential principles for the defence of positions, etc.", paragraph 1 states:-"The fundamental principle is that the first line must be held at all costs". However, as a result of the British gun fire in the Battles of the Somme the Germans were quickly compelled to abolish this "fundamental principle".

The plan (Sketch 5) shows the general lie of the trenches at Hannescamps. The front of the Battalion was roughly 1,200 yards. At night-fall the Reserve Company reinforced the front by sending a platoon each to the Lille Road and Lens Road support trenches; this left half a company at my disposal to meet eventualities!

It will be seen that the village of Hannescamps lay in rear of the right of the Battalion, consequently had the Hannescamp Sector been the objective of a hostile attack from the East, the movements of reinforcements from the Battalion Reserve to any portion of the support line would have been exposed at once to flank attack. Battalion Headquarters was still further echeloned to the right rear though its 'Battle Centre' was at the Northern outskirts of the village, where the main communication trench (Lulu Lane) joined the Hannescamps - Monchy road. The French had made this communication trench, in the stress of battle, alongside the road, and so it remained. There was an alternative one, called Left Avenue, on the North side of the road, but it was not possible to maintain it in repair, and it eventually fell upon evil days. For the time, then, that the Battalion occupied this front, its communications were of a decidedly unpleasant and lopsided character. Nevertheless the advent of rainy weather and the snows of winter caused such havoc in the long front line that neither men nor material were available for other work than its bare upkeep and for the provision and maintenance of dug-outs in it, so the best had to be made of the communications as they already existed.

The right and left sections of the line were held alternately by A and B Companies, and C and D Companies, respectively; the extreme right being as far as 600 yards from the enemy's front trench, whereas this distance was lessened to about 200 yards in the section held by the left-half battalion; sap-heads thrust out as listening posts further reduced it, here and there, to 150 yards. The proximity of this flank to the enemy caused it to experience the frequent attentions of his trench-mortars and minenwerfer, whereas on the right our men were, by comparison, little disturbed in that way. The wide expanse of no-man's land was extensively used by our patrols, which soon gained a reputation for daring and successful reconnaissance; the 'osarie' bed, in particular, being a great rendezvous for these enterprises.

* * * * * * * *

CHAPTER VI. (Extract) Anémente. Our patrols dominate no-man's land. Review by the King and the President.

A few days later the Division on our right reported that the enemy was in "unusual strength" in front of them, and that airplane reconnaissance had located gas-cylinders in his trenches. In conformity with this news we took some additional precautions, but nothing unusual occurred. The enemy was at the same time rather active with his rifle grenades on the left of the Battalion front, causing us a few casualties. At this period we had no means of replying to these attentions; our only possible reprisals being in the form of close attacks made by Thain's grenadiers under cover of night. There was never the least difficulty in getting volunteers for enterprises of this description; on the contrary it required some care to prevent the overlapping of the different reconnoitring and fighting patrols that wished to make no-man's land their happy hunting ground. The Hun, on the other hand, never an individualist (except in such matters as murder or rape), usually only scoured the country in comparatively large parties of 50 or so, and judging by what we heard, and subsequently proved for ourselves, made a special study of the ground about the Hannescamps ravine, where organizing and moving his strong patrols with his usual thoroughness he soon obtained a fair measure of success, though, owing to this same lack of individuality and want of initiative, his activities were always liable to be brought to an untimely end, as the sequel will show. As previously explained the area of no-man's land became much restricted in front of the centre and left of the Battalion, and here the movements of large patrols were practically impossible; it became consequently the domain of small parties, of the individual as opposed to the organized mass, in other words it was the domain of the 11th Royal Warwicks, and their control of it was never seriously disputed.

Our 'out-of-trench' resort, from now on and for many months, was St.Amand, and here we arrived on the 21st October after relief by the 13th Royal Fusiliers.

On the 25th we marched via Coigneux and Bus-les-Artois to Acheux to represent the 37th Division at a review by the King and the President of the French Republic. The weather was cold, misty and unpleasant. The chateau at Acheux was the headquarters of the 4th Division, and the review was held in the fine grounds surrounding it. Here I was hospitably entertained to luncheon, the remainder of the Battalion being provided for in the adjoining park. The 4th Division was represented by the 1st Royal Warwick Regiment, 2nd Seaforth Highlanders, 1st Royal Irish Fusiliers, 2nd Royal Dublin Fusiliers, and 7th Argyll and Sutherland Highlanders, with some artillery elements; and the 48th Division by the 1st/4th Oxfordshire and Buckinghamshire Light Infantry. The parade was under the command of Major-General Lord E.Gleichen, Commanding, 37th Division.

His Majesty and the President arrived at 3 p.m., and were received with the usual honours. After this, they walked along the fronts of the different battalions, being received on the flank by the battalion commanders. The King after explaining to the President that ours was "Le régiment de Warwick", at which M.Poincaré politely bowed and raised his hat, asked several questions about the Battalion, and about our march from St.Amand. A 'march past' was on the programme, but was cancelled owing to the rain; and after tea in the wood that surrounded the chateau, we returned to St.Amand, which was reached at 9 p.m., after a wild wet march.

CHAPTER VII (Extract). Hannescamps, Nov. 7th 1915.

Unhappily this was not the only regrettable occurrence of that night. Hearing of Thain's wound, and being asked for permission to allow L/Sergt. Gilbert to take out the party of 10 raiders, now without a leader, I readily gave my consent <u>over the</u> telephone. Sergt. Gilbert had distinguished himself on several occasions when in command of small patrols; he had a great eye for country, and was a fearless and enthusiastic soldier in whom I had complete confidence. In the small hours of the morning of the 7th November the party left our trenches. They never returned! Months later a letter was received from one of the men, then a prisoner in Germany; in it he described a football match of 10 men under Sergt. Gilbert in which Sergt. Gilbert's team got 11 goals and their opponents six. He described the game in such a way that it was evident that his patrol had been engaged with a strong hostile patrol, of which it had accounted for 11, with a loss of 6 of its own men. All that we knew at the time was that, shortly after leaving our lines, a white mist fell like a mantle over the country, lying with special density in the Hannescamps ravine, and it was concluded that the patrol had either lost its way and had mistaken the enemy's line for its own, or that it had come up against one of the strong hostile patrols that operated in that neighbourhood. It was ascertained that Sergt. Gilbert usually went without a compass, relying upon his intimate knowledge of the ground, gained during his many reconnaissances over it. The fact that he and all the men of his party were essentially fighters made it obvious that they would not have been taken without a severe struggle, and the complete disappearance of such fine fellows was much deplored.

Now the frequency with which we heard of encounters between the patrols of other units and the enemy's patrols, and the fact that in spite of the great activity of our own people they had hitherto experienced no opposition of this nature, led us to conclude that the Hun had some means of knowing when patrols were leaving the line and laid plans to capture or destroy them.

Suspecting that the use of the telephone, in the movements and arranging of our patrols, might have something to do with it, the strictest orders were in force that this method of communication was not to be used under any circumstances. As explained above, Sergt. Gilbert's operation was, unfortunately mentioned on the telephone, and his was the only patrol of ours that ever came to grief. This may have been only a coincidence, on the other hand it is now well known that the enemy possessed means of tapping into our wires, or at least of listening to our talk over telephones, and something of the sort may have happened on this occasion.

It was on the same night that 2/Lieut. A.E. Boucher performed the remarkably rash and daring feat of entering alone the German front line trenches. This Officer was with a witing party in front of our lines, but depressed by the (to him) unexciting nature of the work, he took advantage of the same mist, that had engulfed Sergt. Gilbert's patrol, to walk towards the enemy's trenches. Finding himself up against their wire and meeting with no opposition, he proceeded to cross it, though with some difficulty and damage to his clothing. Having surmounted this obstacle he lay for some time on the parapet, but hearing nothing and seeing a ladder leading into the trench, he descended it and walked along, meeting no one until he came to a dug out. Standing near its entrance he heard voices, but not being conversant with the language, there was nothing to be gained by listening. He thereupon returned by the way that he had come, narrowly escaping an encounter en route, and regained his working party without incident. Absolutely fearless, he considered that his action was nothing worth mentioning, and as officers were not allowed to make reconnaissances unless accompanied by another officer or man, there was an additional reason for his not reporting it, and it only came to my notice some days later, when I got from him a very exact and detailed explanation of all that he had seen and noted.

There may have been other equally daring enterprises of

this nature, but I have not heard of one on the Western Front.

CHAPTER IX. (Extract) February 1916.

Three Companies now held the front line, with one in reserve. The Hannescamps ravine, and the line for about 500 yards south of it, was also included in our front system, and a great extent of no-man's land was brought within reach of the activities of our reconnoitring and offensive patrols. Our left was, approximately, in its former position; but on the right we now extended beyond the northern outskirts of Fonquevillers, which lay just north-west of the wood and village of Gommecourt, a heavily fortified salient in the enemy's line, and, later the scene of some bitter fighting.

At 2.30 a.m. on the 4th May the enemy opened a sudden and intense bombardment on the divisional front. His barrage extended from the Berles Sector, on the north, to the right of the 6th Bedfordshire, where the latter touched our left Company at the Hannescamps Salient. The southern limit of this storm was, in fact, clearly marked by the communication trench, Lula Lane. The bombardment lasted with sustained fury for three quarters of an hour, and was replied to by all the guns on the divisional front. Throughout it was steadily punctuated by the ear-splitting explosions of the minenwerfer, which appeared to be particularly directed against the line held by the 6th Bedfordshire. It ended just as dawn was breaking, and almost as suddenly as it had begun. In the weird silence that followed, was heard the singing of countless larks welcoming the coming day, and the effect of this outburst of music after the infernal clamour of the night was distinctly impressive. The Infantry casualties on the front attacked were about 130 killed and wounded. The front line of the 6th Bedfordshire, where the full fury of the storm had burst, was obliterated, and a party of Huns entered the devastated area, when the barrage had temporarily lifted on to the support lines. It was not definitely established whether this party had taken any prisoners, as only one or two of our badly wounded men survived the ordeal, and they were unable to give a coherent account of what had happened. A few hours before the commencement of the raid, our left Company had handed over a portion of its front to the 6th Bedfordshire, and so escaped being seriously involved in the action. The Battalion stood to arms, and Brocksopp's Company pushed out a platoon into no-man's land, with the object of engaging any hostile elements that might be advancing against the Bedfordshire. But his timely action was not able to affect the issue.

Courtney, of the Bedfordshire - the man-of-all work and fidus Achates at brigade headquarters - visited the trenches after dawn and described the scene as a "Shambles". He said that identification of the dead was very difficult, as their remains had to be collected in sandbags.

This was the first raid made against the 37th Division. In spite of the meticulous care that they devoted to all operations of the sort, the Germans seldom attained the success that we did in similar enterprises. The last word in all raids rested with the actual raiders themselves, i.e. the Infantry; and the training of the latter in the German Army, together with the whole character of the nation itself, was opposed to anything except organized action, and consequently to the qualities of initiative that this sort of action required.

On the night 10th/11th May, Captain E.L.Routh, with 2/Lts.Jenkins & Stalker, and 53 N.C.Os and men, finally disposed of the pretensions of a strong hostile patrol to dominate no-man's land in the region of the Hannescamps Ravine. As previously recorded, our front now embraced this area, and it was quite unthinkable that it should be controlled by anyone except ourselves. The enemy's movements had been carefully watched by Routh, who laid his plans accordingly.

It was his (the enemy's) custom to advance in a fan-shaped formation towards the British line and to then assemble in a cutting, about 200 yards from our trenches, before either continuing his advance northwards, or returning to his own lines. Routh's plan was framed to meet either eventuality. In effect when his patrol had left our trenches, the enemy, in about equal strength, was found concentrating in the cutting at the conclusion of his first movement. The subalterns, with 30 men were at once directed to attack from the north; at the moment that Routh, with the remainder of the patrol, after a détour to the west, came into the fight against his right flank. The manoeuvre was quite successful. Both attacks were made simultaneously and with great dash. The party under Jenkins was received with a sharp fire, but Routh's men had little opposition and got to work with bayonet and bomb, and the surviving Buns scattered in every direction. No prisoners were taken; but a dead N.C.O. was brought back for identification purposes.

Our losses wre 1 killed (Private Rickarby) and 9 slightly wounded. A conservative estimate of the German loss was 24 killed and wounded, mostly by the bombs of the flank attack, which came upon them when massed in the cutting and whilst engaged with the frontal attack from the north.

As showing the excellence of the German intelligence system - for it must be remembered that the Battalion had only recently come into this part of the line - as showing, also, the linguistic abilities of their rank and file, the opening of our attack was received with shouts of "Here are the bloody Warwicks again!" and other familiar expressions of the sort.

For his initiative and leading, on this occasion, Routh received the "immediate" award of the Military Cross, and Sergt. Yates was selected from amongst several non-commissioned officers and private soldiers for that of the Military Medal.

The whole affair well merited the appreciation that it received from the Army, Corps and Divisional Commanders.

CHAPTER XI. (Extract) The Battle of the Somme.

"At 6.30 a.m. our artillery opened an intense bombard-
"ment of the German positions about Gommecourt. At 7.25 a.m.
"smoke was discharged along the fronts of the 37th, 46th and 56th
"Divisions, and at 7.30 a.m. (zero hour) the two latter Divisions
"attacked from the N.and S. Up to midnight no really accurate
"record of the results of these actions is obtainable; but the
"advance of a Brigade of the 46th Division was stopped, and re-
"newed at 3.30 p.m. I watched this phase from the Divisional
"line, but was unable to see any progress, though there was
"some apparently. The attack of the 56th Division (hidden from
"us by the bend of Gommecourt Wood) is reported to have been
"satisfactory - also unsatisfactory. Very heavy fighting was
"going on here at about 10 p.m. At 1 a.m. (2nd July) information
"was received that the 46th Division was to be withdrawn to its
"original line, after attempting to extricate two battalions,
"which had not been located since the commencement of the attack."

The above account is taken from my diary, under date 1st July, and I only record it as an example of the confused and scanty nature of the information that reaches those whose knowledge of battles is usually confined to what takes place in their immediate neighbourhood. In this case the event in our immediate neighbourhood was the *advance* of the left brigade of the 46th Division, but the clouds of smoke from our own trenches and from those of the attacking troops, combined with the vapour and dust from the bursting shells, made even this movement very hard to follow. It was, however, apparent to us that the smoke cloud put up at 3.30 p.m., to cover a renewal of the attack on the left, was ineffective. Probably it was found impossible to arrange it effectively in the stress of battle; moreover what wind there was, was not then in the right direction. It had been a day of intense heat and of strenuous fighting against a resolute resistance, and in this part of the field, at any rate, the action seemed to die out during the afternoon.

Our own part in this first phase of the historic battle was naturally a minor one. The German defensive fire was directed almost entirely upon the fronts of the attacking divisions, and our loss was only one killed (Private Wilson) and 2/Lt.Denley and 6 men wounded. At night-fall a strong patrol, under Brocksopp, attacked the ground between the opposing lines, bombed a listening post opposite our front, and returned without encountering any opposition.

Unusual quiet marked the 2nd July in this Sector, and only the thunderous rumblings and mutterings to the South indicated that the struggle was still in progress in the region of Albert, and on the French front. The 46th and 56th Divisions had now withdrawn to the positions they occupied before their advance, and an uncanny silence succeeded to the noise and turmoil of the last week.

CHAPTER XII.

<u>The Combat at Pozières (15th August 1916).</u>
<u>On the Tara-Usna Ridge</u>: <u>We become supporting battalion to the Brigade</u>: <u>Orders for the attack on Pozières</u>: <u>The advance is stopped by heavy fire</u>: <u>A Company loses all its officers</u>: <u>Millard withdrawn and sent to the exposed flank</u>: <u>The attack is renewed at 6 p.m., but without success</u>: <u>Hostile attempt at counter-attack is crushed</u>: <u>The fight is broken off</u>: <u>Gallantry of Private Ward</u>: <u>Heavy Casualties</u>: <u>Comparisons with former losses</u>:

The Battalion now bivouacked on the reverse slope of the Tara-Usna Ridge, but during the afternoon it was driven to take cover in trenches, as the enemy shelled the position with 5.9" guns, blowing up a Company's cooker with 4 of the men employed there, and rendering the neighbourhood 'unhealthy' as a resort. Headquarters went through a modified version of this experience during the night, which was also marked by intense artillery activity in the region of Thièpval.

In the late evening of the 13th July we relieved the 8th East Lancashire as the supporting battalion, and occupied the German trenches, adjacent to, and in rear of, those that we had recently vacated. At 3.a.m. on the 14th, an intense bombardment heralded the attack of the 15th and 13th Corps on the line Longueval - Bazentin - le Petit, forming a wonderful picture of the might and destructive power of modern war. From our position we were able to see much of the artillery action; besides, it was quite feasible to walk about above ground in a way strange to people accustomed to long months of trench warfare. I think this feeling of freedom was the most pleasant of any that we experienced in the battle!

For the most part, officers and men lived in recesses dug out of the sides of the communication trenches that they now occupied. There were only a few dug-outs available, and of these, Hart, Russell and I had one about 15 ft. by 5 ft.

Later in the morning our guns turned their attention to Pozières, which lay a mile north of us, and when visiting McKay (8th East Lancashire) he told me that during the night his patrols had succeeded in reaching the south-west outskirts of the village. Probably they mistook the trenches, some distance this side of the lisière for the actual village line, as subsequent events showed that it required something like a Division to get into the place, and that the vigilance of the enemy would hardly have tolerated the presence of a patrol there.

In the small hours of the morning of the 15th July, we were told that the Brigade would attack Pozières at 9.20 a.m. After repeating the 'glad tidings' to the company commanders, I went to McKay's dug-out, where the arrangements were further discussed by the Battalion Commanders at a Brigade Conference. The dispositions made were as follows:-

The 8th East Lancashire was to lead, and was to clear that part of the village south of the Albert - Pozières road. It was to be followed by the 6th Bedfordshire, which was to account for the area north of the road. The 11th Royal Warwickshire was to carry tools, and assist the Lancashire Battalions to consolidate and hold the ground gained. It followed the 6th Bedfordshire. The 10th Loyal North Lancashire was to carry bombs, stores, etc., for the three leading battalions. All battalions were to enter the village by the trench marked T (see sketch). Each battalion having two companies in front line, followed by two in support. The flanks of battalions, during the advance, were to be marked by the Contalmaison - Pozières and Bailiff Wood - Pozières roads, on the right and left respectively. The attack was to be preceded by a heavy artillery bombardment of the objective. It was also notified that the 1st Division would co-operate, by engaging the enemy to the east of the village, whilst the 23rd Division would develop a bombing attack against its W.defences.

After receiving these instructions I rejoined the battalion which began at once to move forward, keeping under cover of the communication trenches till the open ground was reached, north-west of Bailiff Wood. As it emerged into the open, the tail of the battalion in front was seen just ahead of it; there was thus ample time for deployment, the function of the battalion being to hold and consolidate the ground gained by the two attacking battalions.

The advance up to this point had not been opposed; but as the troops came over the crest above the Chalk Pit, they were met by heavy and sustained machine-gun fire at decisive ranges. So fierce and accurate was this fire that the Brigade became immobilized on its narrow frontage, and the three leading battalions, which had pressed forward with great boldness, became to a great extent intermixed. Nevertheless they staunchly held their ground, and, although suffering appreciable losses from artillery and machine-gun fire, showed no signs of wavering and maintained a firm front.

Brocksopp's Company moving by the E.edge of Contalmaison Wood was at once involved in the fight, and, in its determined advance, soon lost both its officers and many of its men. Brocksopp was severely wounded whilst leading a rush, and French, his 2nd in command, was hit at about the same time. The command then devolved upon Sergt. W.J. Moon,* a very young but able soldier, as the Company Sergeant-Major (Freeman) had closely followed his captain and now lay with him well in front of the line, and in a position from which any movement during daylight was impossible.

On the left, Stalker and Bowen were wounded within the first few minutes. Half the company officers were thus early out of action, and only one captain (Millard) remained. In his position on the left, the congestion of units was very marked, as it was here that the bulk of the attacking troops had massed on the restricted front of their advance.

During these happenings, battalion headquarters, whilst crossing the open south of the Chalk Pit, had been driven to the cover of a shell hole by flanking machine-gun fire from the direction of Villers-la-Boisselle, and by artillery fire from the north. Vacating this shelter it again established itself successively in other shell holes, before finally coming to rest in a disused trench wast of Contalmaison Wood† Here Harrison's signallers quickly put us in touch with Brigade Headquarters; communication with the companies being maintained by orderlies.

It was soon apparent that the right flank of the attack was very much in the air; nothing having been seen, or heard, of the 1st Division, whose action on that side had been promised. At 2.30 p.m. I accordingly sent the following message to Millard:-
"If you can evacuate your present position behind the 8th N.L. and 6th Bedford without observation from the enemy, do so, and move via valley which runs round south edge of Contalmaison Wood where my headquarters are (X.16.a.9.7)". Millard effected this change of position successfully, and was then told to move up the valley to Brocksopp's exposed flank. During his withdrawal an agitated voice was heard through our telephone complaining to "Brigade" that '"Warwicks" are retiring' and that their action had a depressing effect upon the spectators. I called through, in

---

* For his services in the field he was promoted to commissioned rank in the Regiment on the 31st October 1917.

† Contalmaison Wood was a wood only in name. It was a small and much battered spinney, and I saw few trees or remnants of trees over 6 ft. in height.

interruption of this conversation, to calm the speaker and explain the situation. He was in the Chalk Pit with most of the other battalion commanders and it appeared that Millard's progress past their fastness had caused germs of "gloom and despondency" to pervade the assemblage.

Later on, Hart and I walked over to this Chalk Pit, and found there a great gathering. A steady stream of wounded was constantly arriving, and either receiving attention or being directed further to the rear; in addition, the bulk of the 10th Loyal North Lancashire was stationed here, ready to move forward with the tools and other accessories, as they might be required by the leading battalions.

Information now arrived that the heavy artillery would renew the bombardment at 5 p.m., and that the Infantry (i.e. 119th Brigade and 10th Royal Fusiliers) were to attack again at 6 p.m. The signal for the advance was to be the firing of a red rocket.

As the hour approached the antics of a man on the ridge about 300 yards away were eagerly watched from the Chalk Pit. Punctually at 6 p.m. this individual apparently fired the signal, as a puff of smoke about 2 ft. high ran along the ground for a few yards and then disappeared. As this performance was repeated the spectators became greatly excited; every second's delay was of value to the enemy in enabling him to man his machine guns, for, in accordance with the custom then prevailing, the bombardment of the front line ceased at the hour arranged for the infantry advance. As quickly as possible a rocket was obtained in the Chalk Pit and fired from there, but valuable time had been lost, and the rising of our men was met by a devastating fire at the closest ranges, and in spite of the most determined efforts, all attempts to force the defences of the village failed once more.

In this assault all units behaved with a gallantry, of which many instances are on record. 2/Lt. Onslow forced his way to within a short distance of the German wire, but, with the few men that were able to follow him, and in face of the deadly machine-gun fire that met him was unable to penetrate the line.

On the right, Millard at the head of D Company led his men with equal dash and determination, and, charging over the advanced hostile trenches, fell severely wounded at their head. But all attempts to storm the village were without avail, and the Brigade became again immobilized on the ground it had won at such cost.

Emboldened, probably, by his success, the enemy now pushed troops from the north-east outskirts, in an attempt to turn our right/flank. The movement was promptly met by A Company, and crushed at its birth, a result largely due to the bold and accurate handling of his Lewis Gun by Lance-Corporal Hitchman, who was unfortunately shot through the head and killed at the moment of his success.

It was now obvious that a spear-head attack, on such a narrow frontage, with both flanks in the air, was bound to fail in the face of the unshaken fire of massed machine guns, orders were accordingly given to the 10th Loyal North Lancashire to take over the ground gained, whilst the remainder of the Brigade returned to the positions held prior to the attack. These movements were carried out after nightfall, and without interference from the enemy. Well into the small hours of the morning (night 15th/16th July) the stretcher-bearers were busy evacuating the severely wounded, and removing them to the comparative shelter of the cross roads, north of Bailiff Wood. Here at 1.a.m. we found Russell attending to cases by the fitful light of a candle, whilst around him lay the wounded and dying. Occasionally the scene would be lit up by the flashes of exploding shells as they fell in the vicinity of this temporary hospital, but the work went on quietly and expeditiously, and when Hart and I left at 2.a.m., most of the casualties had been evacuated to the rear.

Conspicious, among many brave deeds, was the work of Private Ward, a regimental stretcher-bearer. To places far in advance of the general line of battle and marked only by the bodies of the very foremost stormers; places, too, where all ordinary movement would have been impossible, this intrepid man penetrated, crawling on his hands and knees or at full length. Possessed of immense strength, he was able to carry or drag many

of his comrades to a more sheltered position, and thus saved many
lives. He witnessed, so he told me, several acts of Hun brutality,
such as the shooting of our wounded at close quarters, and being
himself but a rough man, with the rude sense of justice of the
ancients, it was doubtless unfortunate for their wounded, who lay
about amongst our own, that this powerful and relentless soldier
should have been an eye-witness of the treacherous conduct of
their fellow-countrymen! Recommended for the "immediate award" of
the Distinguished Conduct Medal, Ward never lived to receive it.
Nearly a month later, and before the intricate and involved
machinery that surrounded the grant of "immediate" awards had had
time to operate, he was killed in the act of removing a badly
wounded man to the shelter of the dressing station; thus dying, as
he had lived, a fine example of the fearless band of regimental
stretcher-bearers, who were always to be found where the greatest
danger lay.

In this engagement the casualties in the battalion
amounted to 5 officers* and 270 other ranks, percentages of 41.6 &
46.5 respectively. I have no record of the losses in the 6th Bedfordshire, 8th E.Lancashire and 10th Royal Fusiliers; but as they
opened the attack, their losses were probably heavier, whereas those
of the 10th Loyal N.Lancashire, which was not heavily engaged,
would be lighter. A conservative estimate of the total losses would,
then, be about 1,200 or say 40 per cent. for the 5 battalions.

In comparing losses it is interesting to note that
students of military history, and soldiers themselves, generally
regarded the seriousness, or otherwise, of the losses sustained,
from the standpoint of contemporary fighting only. Thus Sir John
Adye, in his "Recollections of a Military Life", talks of the losses
of the British Army at the storming of the Heights of the Alma (20th
September 1854) as "very severe", although, according to his estimates,
they only amounted to just over 7 per cent. of the forces engaged,
and in no regiment, he says, did they exceed 239 in killed and
wounded. In the Battle of Inkerman, where, he says, "the English
losses were very serious", the percentage was much higher, amounting

* Only 12 officers were engaged.

to about 29. He gives the casualties for this action as 2,614, and included in them are no less than 8 generals!

It must be remembered that the British Army in the Crimea had not been seriously engaged since the Napoleonic wars, and forty years of comparative peace had dulled the recollection of the fierce fights and heavy casualties of former days. The Colonial wars that followed the Crimea had a similar effect, so that when, after the lapse of another forty years, the Army became involved, on a large scale, in S.Africa, we find a British General breaking off an action (Colenso 1899) after a loss of less than 1,200 of all ranks, or something under 8 per cent. of his total strength.

Writing on this subject a German authority says:- "Good troops which unexpectedly get into a difficult situation (as for example the British Brigade of Highlanders at Mägersfontein) and which have been trained to look upon heavy losses as unavoidable will be capable of enduring a loss of 25 per cent. in the course of a battle without going to pieces, and without discontinuing the attack". But the lessons of the Russo-Japanese War warned all thinking soldiers to be prepared to accept losses far in excess of that estimate, and the Great War has shown that good troops will endure the heaviest losses without becoming disorganized.

However, in spite of its losses the fighting round the Chalk Pit was but an incident in the far-flung battle that raged along the Franco-British front, and the official communiqué only recorded of it that "East of Ovillers a further advance has been made and our troops have fought their way to the outskirts of Pozières.

CHAPTER XIII. (Extract). The Battle of the Somme.

The British troops were now approaching the summit of the great ridge, whose southern slopes are marked by the villages of Bazentin-le-Petit, Pozières and Thiépval. To the east of this ridge and acting as a bastion to it, stands a conspicuous feature, its western crest crowned by the Bois des Fourreaux, called by the English, High Wood. Fierce fighting still raged for the possession of this obstacle, whose skeleton trees could be plainly seen dominating for miles the southern approaches to the ridge. From here, the German line ran westward, at an average distance of two or three hundred yards from our own. Just north of Bazentin, a curious position ensued, for the enemy now held, for a matter of 500 yards, a line in prolongation, and west of the British front line trenches. This hostile stretch was known as the "Intermediate Line", and was connected with his main defences, called the "Switch Line", by a communication trench at its western limit. The 10th Loyal N.Lancashire held the front to the east of the "Intermediate Line", i.e., in touch with the German left, whilst the Royal Warwickshire faced it, at distances varying from 150 yards to 230 yards, being connected with Cobbold's battalion by a communication trench. On our left was a battalion of Scottish Rifles.

The trenches were not of a permanent character, such as existed in the old front lines, but were deep enough for all purposes. The weather, for some time, had been very hot and rainless, and though this resulted in an increase of smells, especially in the vicinity of the "Intermediate Line", where the dead lay thickly in the neutral ground, it was of benefit in the upkeep of the parapets and fire-steps, which would have easily have succumbed to moisture.

CHAPTER XIV. (Extract). ("Attack on the Intermediate Trench").

Having had an order to attack the remaining portion of the German "Intermediate Line" on the following night, I called a meeting of the company commanders and discussed with them my plans for the operation. It had been suggested that we should imitate Cobbold's successful manoeuvre, and attack from the flank, but for several reasons I considered a direct attack preferable and arranged accordingly.

The British troops holding this section had already made two attempts to effect a lodgment in the line opposite; but, with the exception of that just mentioned, without success. The objective was roughly 250 yards in width, and varied in distances from our line, from 150 yards on our left to about 200 yards on our right. The intervening ground rose slightly, in parts, especially about the right centre, and prevented the opposing lines from having a direct view throughout their length, and it was much cut up by shell fire.

The remainder of the day passed without incident, but at night the artillery on both sides displayed their customary activity.

On the 12th there was a final conference with the officers making the attack, the dispositions for which were shortly as follows:-

(a) The attack was to be delivered by A & C Companies, each with 2 platoons in front line, followed, at a distance of 25 yards, by their remaining two platoons, A Company (Captain Chambers) directing. The 2 Companies, in their extension, would cover the space between the Crucifix - Martinpuich, and Bazentin-Martinpuich roads, which, it was hoped, would provide an additional safeguard against a possible loss of direction.

(b) Graham's (B) Company was to hold the front vacated by Little's men, and was to be prepared to advance in support of the attack if required. In addition, it was to detail 4 sections to follow the attacking companies, for purposes of connection between them and our front line, and for the supply of bombs and wire for the protection of the captured trench.

(c) Barwell's (D) Company was to take over the front vacated by A Company.

(d) The artillery support, which was arranged for by higher authority, and by which our movements were to be controlled was as follows:-

    (i) At 10.30 p.m. (Zero hour) light artillery was to shrapnel 'no-man's land' (50 yards S. of the objective) for 30 seconds.

    (ii) At 10.30½ p.m., it would lift on to the enemy's trench till 10.33 p.m., when

    (iii) It would again lift and put down a barrage about 150 yards N. of the trench. This barrage to last about 1 hour.

(e) In conformity with this action, the attacking companies were directed to be outside their trenches by 10.30 p.m. (Zero hour). They were to move forward as close to the barrage as possible, and when it lifted to the N. side of the trench, the assault was to be delivered.

(f) Bombing groups were formed on the right and left flanks of the attack. The principal one, that on the left, under the Grenadier Officer, 2/Lieut. Onslow, M.C., had for its special mission the blocking of the enemy's trench communicating with his main (Switch) line. There were other bombing groups about the centres of companies and every soldier carried a bomb in each of his two hip-pockets.

(g) Every man carried 170 rounds of ammunition, with the exception of the men composing the bombing groups, who only carried 50.

(h) The supporting platoons also carried tools, and every man carried two empty sandbags.

(i) The Loyal North Lancashire promised to co-operate by engaging the enemy's attention at the point where their line joined his, and by the fire of Lewis guns against a possible attempt at reinforcement from the north, whilst the Scottish Rifle Battalion, of the 15th Division, brought his main communication trench under fire from a sap-head that commanded it.

These comprised the general arrangements for the attack. There were, of course, others, connected with the employment of the Lewis guns, signals, etc., etc., but it is unnecessary to mention them here.

In order to connect our line with the captured trench an Engineer Officer with a party of his men arrived on the 12th, for the purpose of constructing a "Russian Sap"; I am unable to remember the details of this construction; but, shortly, it consisted in blowing up with one bang, so-to-speak, a length of straight trench from our line to that of the enemy. I remember that water formed an essential part of the working requirements, as several requests for its supply were received; but a battalion in battle does not specialize in this liquid, so we could not be of much assistance. In the event, our friends were unable to make much headway, and later in the evening, the officer departed for further assistance. He never returned, and it was rumoured that he had stumbled upon an artillery barrage and got hurt, but I hope it was only a rumour.

To facilitate and improve the communications from battalion headquarters, slits or feathers were cut in the main communication trench to accomodate the 2nd in Command (Rooke), two headquarters orderlies, and 2 signallers with a telephone. These slits, which constituted an advanced battle centre, were placed about 100 yards from the trench occupied by Little's Company. In addition Milne's signallers had done all that was possible to perfect and ensure the maintenance of telephonic communication by the use of the "ladder" system on all the lines.

In the late afternoon the objective was severely shelled by our heavy guns. I at once asked the Brigade to

26

stop this bombardment. Not only would it render the trench uninhabitable to our men, should they succeed in taking it, but it was a plain intimation to the Hun that we contemplated some action against him in the near future. In fact it clearly eliminated the factor of surprise which is of vital importance in night operations. The Brigade were, however, unable to do anything. The bombardment, they said, was arranged by people above them, and was part of a plan in the operations that were to be carried out by the 15th and an Anzac Division, that night.

It was at 9.p.m., and so an hour and a half before "Zero" hour, that the enemy started a systematic and accurate shelling of our position, directing his fire particularly on our front line and trenches of communication. Rooke, who had left to take up his position in the advanced battle-centre (previously mentioned), was forced back by the accurate fire of shrapnel, that swept the ground and trench between it and battalion headquarters. Graham's Company, from support, was fast approaching its assembly point in Little's line, when it was overtaken by the same storm; but, although he was himself more than once blown off his feet, he succeeded with great gallantry and perseverance in getting his men into their positions. Once there, they escaped the full force of the fire, which continued to be chiefly directed against the ground behind, and in a lesser degree against the front occupied by the right (A) Company.

This state of things continued till 10.30 p.m., at which hour the prevailing clamour was increased by the rolling drum-fire of the British guns heralding the infantry advance.

It is difficult to present a clear and accurate picture of all that followed, even on this small corner of the battlefield. For one thing, the night was exceedingly dark, and for another, of the 5 officers, that actually formed the storming party, only one now survives. It is to him (Captain Wilfred Little) that I owe the story of what the left company did that night; but even that story is incomplete, as he was himself severely wounded at a critical stage of the operations

It is not to be denied that the hostile bombardment to which the assaulting companies had been subjected for more than an hour previous to the advance, had somewhat shaken their composure. It was to many of the men their first experience of the kind, and at least half of them had not been three weeks in the country. The delivery of an assault under such conditions was a test that would have tried veteran troops; but the bravery and devotion of the officers, and the steady valour and example of the old remnants of the original battalion provided the necessary impetus, and punctually to time the leading line of stormers left the trenches and advanced against the enemy.

At the outset of their forward movement they suffered little loss, and as the first wave of the right company approached the slight rise of ground, that intervened between them and the hostile trench, a red rocket was seen to soar in the air. An eye-witness of this incident told me that he and those of his comrades who were able to notice it amid the turmoil of surrounding events were puzzled at its appearance, for it seemed to rise but a few yards from them, though at the moment they were, to the best of their belief, still some distance from the German line. And this was actually the case. When returning, later, over the same ground, my informant, who had marked the spot, found a deep pit-like excavation, partly open at the top. The time was not then suitable for loitering and he did not examine it carefully; but it was undoubtedly the temporary home of the rocket man, and lay midway between the opposing lines, being so sited that whilst its occupant could observe our trench, he was himself unseen, and because of his central position, reasonably clear of our own and the hostile artillery barrages. Nevertheless, he was certainly a stout and determined soldier, for he dared much and ran great risks.

Coming now within the zone of the hostile artillery and machine-gun fire, which swept across the front of the objective, men began to fall fast. The gallant Chambers was one of the first to be hit, and fell severely wounded at the head of his company. Vigors, a brave and dashing young officer, whose first battle it was, was wounded in the hand, but scorning to relinquish the fight, continued to press forward, and was last seen, at the head of a small and devoted band, leading a charge against the enemy. He fell almost upon the parapet of the enemy's trench, and, in the words of Napier "no man died that night with more glory - yet many died, and there was much glory".

Some of the right company undoubtedly succeeded in forcing their way into the German line; but the weight and impetus of their attack had broken under the severity of the hostile barrage fire, and the failure of C Company to engage his right enabled the enemy to concentrate his energies at the point of greatest danger, and it is certain that these bold spirits were all either killed or captured.

On the left, Little's first line had advanced with equal steadiness and devotion. It was ably led by Lieutenant Roberts, who was on the extreme right in order to keep up the connection with A Company which was directing. In view of the fact that a road and a communication trench ran northwards, and on the left flank of Little's advance, he had asked whether he could move by this flank, instead of entirely by his right in touch with A. As his extension on the left of A Company would in any case have placed his outer flank on the road and communication trench in question, and further, as the darkness of the night and the confusion due to the enemy's curtain-fire might accentuate the difficulty of inter-company connection, I readily assented to his proposal. The group of bombers, under Onslow, were accordingly made responsible for direction on this flank.

The advance continued with great regularity till it occurred to Little, who was in the rear of the centre, that his Company should now be coming to grips with the enemy; but as this did not happen, he passed along the line of men towards the left. Here he found that Onslow's group of bombers had <u>crossed</u> the communication trench, marking the left flank, and were consequently heading north-west across the front of the battalion of Scottish Rifles, and away from the objective. Conforming to this movement, the bulk of the company had trended, also, in that direction. The hostile artillery and machine-gun fire had by this time assumed great intensity; but, making the men lie down, Little was in the **act** of rectifying the direction by compass, when a shell burst above him, mortally wounding Onslow. This very gallant young officer only survived his wound for a short time. He had proved his worth at Pozières, and it is only justice to him to say that the road and trench, by which he was to advance, and over which he had unfortunately passed, were by no manner of means easy of location in the darkness and confusion of the assault. On the other hand, had he been able to maintain the right direction, it is more than probable that the objective would have been carried, and that he himself, by his well-known courage and resolution, would have largely contributed to the success.

Collecting what men he could, and intensely anxious to rectify the mistake, Little now led them afresh against the enemy. The hostile fire was at the time at the height of its fury, but, in spite of it, the forward movement appeared to make progress. But his gallant attempt to put matters right was without success, for he was himself severely wounded shortly afterwards.

Meanwhile, Roberts on the right had kept in close touch with A Company, but word being passed along for the men to march by the <u>left</u>, all except a few of those in his immediate neighbourhood gradually edged away towards the outer flank. He was killed at a short distance from the German line. He, too, had only lately joined the battalion, and those who knew him spoke in high terms of his courage and resolution.

The telephone wires connecting battalion headquarters with the advanced battle-centre and with the front line had been cut early in the operation, some of them before the commencement of the attack. The site of the advanced battle-centre was partially demolished; several signallers were wounded and their instrument smashed. Privates Hunt & Saunders (Headquarters orderlies) who occupied an adjacent slit, were both hit, the latter being killed. He had enlisted with his Father, a steady good soldier, who had fallen in a recent engagement, after doing duty for several months as a regimental barber. It was one of many occasions, where Father and Son served together, and the country can never do too much for the dependents of such true patriots. Neither, may it be added, can it better encourage Bolshevism, anarchy and the like, than by spending thousands of pounds upon Dutch pictures, young Chancellor's bath-rooms, and so on, whilst the families of its saviours want for anything that may make life happier for them - including baths. *

With considerable difficulty, and at great risk, Hunt managed to get to Battalion Headquarters. He brought the information, which he said he obtained from Graham, that the attacking companies were in no need of support or assistance. This was very welcome news, as it was naturally inferred that the attack had succeeded. These hopes, however, were soon dashed by the coming of other messengers with more exact information as to the real course of events; and Rooke's arrival on the scene confirmed the story as I have just related it.

The casualties in this affair were unfortunately heavy. Of the 5 officers that actually led the attack, three were killed and two severely wounded, and Graham, who commanded the supporting company had to be evacuated owing to shock.

The other casualties amounted to about 150, principally from amongst the two assaulting companies.

During the evening, a company of the 9th (Pioneer) Battalion, N.Staffordshire Regiment, had come up to assist in

* Written in 1919.

the consolidation of the captured trench. Its services were, however, not required, but it had the disagreeable experience of being heavily pounded by hostile artillery, as it lay in the support line awaiting the course of events.

If the story has taken rather long in the telling, the whole affair (from 10.30 p.m.) only lasted a few minutes. The enemy was well prepared and had been sufficiently warned; in spite of which had Forthne been a little more friendly, those few minutes would have seen us in possession of his line. But one must allow him the credit of a very stout defence.

CHAPTER XV. (Extracts).

With its departure from Fréchincourt the battalion left the zone of the Somme Battles. Since its entry into the region about Albert, its casualties had amounted to (i) Officer - Killed 7, Wounded 24, Total 31. (ii) Other Ranks - Killed 87 Wounded 524, Missing 61 (mostly killed), Sick 55 (largely shell shock), Total 727. In the assault made by the right company at Bazentin-le-Petit, it is probable that a few men succeeded in entering the German line, where they would have been out-numbered and taken. This handful would not likely have exceeded 10 in number. Of the 61 men reported missing, 50 must thus be accounted killed. As usual, we had very little sickness, so that of the "sick" cases, two-thirds, or say 35, should be added to the numbers shown as wounded. The number of killed to wounded is, roughly, in the proportion of 1 to 4, which approximates the general normal of battles; but it is a ratio that rises and falls considerably with the intensity or otherwise of the fighting. The proportion of officer casualties (31) to that of the other ranks (727) will appear small in the light of the early actions of the war and former wars. But this is not actually the case. The Battalion never went into battle with its full complement of officers and Hart and myself were the only two that escaped being hit among those that were in action throughout this period.

James Thain, my incomparable Bombing Officer, rejoined at this time. When recovered from his wound he had been seized upon by the Home Authorities, and made Chief Instructor of a Grenade School in the New Forest. Soon after his arrival, he was again abducted, this time by the Division, and made Commandant of their School. The cult of the bomb was now at the height of its fame. First extensively used in trench raids, its importance had not diminished as a result of the recent fighting on the Somme, where tactics were reduced to Artillery bombardments, followed by an Infantry rush (like a Trafalgar Square riot) into the smashed and obliterated position. I dont suppose that my battalion fired more than 5 rounds per rifle during the whole time that it was in action in that region; for the simple reason that there was hardly anything, or anybody, at which to aim. On the other hand the stacks of bombs that covered the battlefield were prodigious. The result was, that the stream of bomb-enthusiasts had assumed the proportions of a flood, which, joined by the lesser stream of Lewis and Machine gun enthusiasts, actually threatened to engulf the formidable body of musketry enthusiasts (or "ffiends", as they were commonly called) that had long been paramount in the Army. Fortunately for everyone, the musketry fiends were able to keep their noses above the current, and backed by the powerful influence, due to the traditional success that the rifle had always had when in the hands of the British Infantry, and by the support of the calmer and older heads of the Army, they were <u>eventually</u> successful in damming the flood to their entire satisfaction. So much so, that about a year later, when I was at home, all the old Hythe "stunts" were in full swing again, and recruits were being told to "Assume the prone position", <u>not</u> to "lie down", and if asked at what part of a man they should aim, were to reply "At the lowest part of the central portion of his figure"; any other reply such as "at his feet", or "just below his ankles", or "at his left nostril" (if only his face was visible) being anathema, and a certain indication that the whole system of training in that regiment was bad, and that the complete defeat of the Allies on the battlefield was imminent.

CHAPTER XVI. (Extract)

On the 15th, Rooke, the Regimental Sergeant-Major (Shear), and a Private Soldier, went on 10 days leave. To account for this exodus, it should be explained that 3 "leaves" had been granted to the Battalion - the usual number. For Battalion Commanders, and occasionally for other Field Officers, going on leave was made very comfortable. A car, from somewhere or other, could generally be got to take one either to Boulogne (as an exceptional case) or to some important railway junction, such as Doullens or Amiens, whence the rest of the journey was easy enough. On the other hand, junior officers and the rank and file were carried away in a large 'bus, which appeared to start, for choice, in the middle of the night. This conveyance, after cruising about through the various villages, picking up its quota of passengers, and waking up, at the same time, everyone within a mile of it, transferred its freight at some wayside station to a long heavily-laden train. The latter, which maintained an average speed of about a mile an hour, varied by long halts and much whistling, was calculated to reach its destination in sufficient time to allow passengers to be marched to some camp there to wait for another boat than the one just missed! Havre was the embarkation port for our people (except for Lieutenant-Colonels, who travelled by Boulogne) and the journey from Havre to Southampton was a long, uncomfortable and crowded one. Not that I ever heard any grumbling about it. It was obvious that leave was a great privilege, and much greater inconveniences would have been cheerfully borne by those who took it.

APPENDICES.

CONTINUATION OF NOTES ON TRENCH WARFARE.

(1) Company Commanders will arrange for collecting boxes for holding rubbish, tins, etc., to be placed on the flank of each Platoon. Rubbish from these boxes must be emptied daily in a deep pit which Company Commanders will provide for that purpose.

(2) SUMP PITS.
Sump Pits in the Fire Trenches should be dug to a depth of at least 4 feet 6 inches and stakes should be at the four corners to support the wooden grating.

(3) Company Commanders are reminded that Sentries on duty must always have their rifles in their hands.

(4) Many men do not seem to realise the importance of keeping their rifles clean. Rifles should be cleaned and oiled every morning at daylight.
In connection with this cleaning no N.C.O. or man is to clean his rifle until the bolt has been removed.
Neglect of this order will be severely dealt with.

(Signed) C.S.Collison,
Lieut.-Colonel,
Commanding 11th (Service) Bn.
Royal Warwickshire Regiment.

16th September 1915.

TRENCH NOTES. (PART III).

1. **PATROLS.**
Until Officers and others are accustomed to find their way easily and to move quietly they should not carry out patrolling work to any distance. Officers Commanding Companies should arrange that their scouts go out for a distance of not more than one or two hundred yards at a time (i.e. if the enemy's line is some distance away) in the first instance. This distance can be gradually increased on subsequent occasions until the patrols are accustomed to their work.

2. **AMMUNITION, BOMBS.**
Boxes of ammunition must be kept in secure places and not in places where the rain can fall or drain into them. Bombs are not to be carried by Grenadiers in the Fire Trench unless they are required for immediate, or a probably immediate use. They must be kept in bomb-proof shelters BEHIND and adjacent to the bay occupied by the Grenadier Group concerned.

3. **MACHINE GUNS** must be kept in such a position and in such order that they can be brought into action in less than a minute.

4. **VERMORAL SPRAYERS** should be kept in a proportion of two per Company.

5. **PERISCOPES** not in use should be kept clean and stored. The box periscope is to be used as a rule by officers and intelligence scouts only; they should rarely be placed on the parapet of a Fire Trench. Single glass periscopes have been provided for sentries in a sufficient proportion for all purposes.

6. **GRASS** should be thinned where it interferes with the view in front of the parapet.

7. Company Commanders will as far as possible let their men know the names of important places, hills, woods, villages, houses, etc., and the general lie of the hostile trenches.

        (Signed) C.S.Collison,
           Lieut.-Colonel,
     Commanding, 11th (Service) Bn.
     Royal Warwickshire Regiment.

18th September 1915.

ORDERS IN THE EVENT OF AN ADVANCE.

The advance may be any one of the following:-

(a)   Normal advance in column of route without opposition,

(b)   Advance in preparatory formations for attack in rear of a Brigade.

(c)   Advance to the assault of trenches.

- - - - - - - - - - - - -

ON RECEIPT OF AN ORDER TO ADVANCE.

1. AMMUNITION.
Companies in the trenches will complete their ammunition to 120 rounds per man from trench stores. Ammunition marked K., KL or KN should always be taken in preference to any marked otherwise.

2. RATIONS.
Company ration parties to be sent to Battalion Headquarters to draw two days rations per man in addition to the iron ration already in the man's possession.

3. KIT.
(a) The following will be carried in the pack:- 1 pair socks. 1 pair drawers. 1 Housewife. Soap. Towel. Razor. Shaving Brush. Cardigan. Cap Comforter. Face Mask. Knife, fork & spoon. Hair brush & waterproof sheet, under flap of pack. The iron ration will be carried at the bottom of the pack.
(b) Each man will carry one tube helmet and one smoke helmet.
(c) All articles of clothing other than the above will be taken by the Company Salvage Party, hereinafter referred to, to the dumping place.

4. COMPANY SALVAGE PARTIES.
(a) The N.C.O. & 3 men (called "the Company Salvage Party") who have already been detailed by companies to collect trench stores, spare ammunition, etc., will, on orders being received of an advance, immediately start the work of taking them to the dumping place, the ammunition being left until the last.
(b) On the conclusion of their work these parties will remain at the dumping station until the whole of the stores, ammunition, etc. of the 4 Companies had been placed there, when they will report to Sergeant Mason who will apply to Captain Lowe for instructions as to the quickest way of re-joining the Battalion should the latter have advanced.
(c) The two companies in Reserve will each detail one N.C.O. & 3 men to assist the Company Salvage Parties of their sister-Company in the collection of trench stores, i.e., A assisting B and D assisting C, or vice versa.

5. GRENADIERS.   the Platoon
(1) In the event of an advance under paras.(a) or (b) 4 Grenadiers will march in rear of their respective Platoons.
(2) In the event of an advance under (a) or (b) 4 Grenadiers per Platoon of the Companies in the fire trenches after arranging with the remaining Grenadiers of the Platoons as to the disposal and packing of their kits will take, in boxes, the Platoon and Company Bombs at once to Battalion Headquarters. They will report to 2nd Lieut.Thain, the Grenadier Officer, when this duty is completed.

(2)

(3) The Grenadiers of the Companies not in the fire trenches, in the proportion of 2 (trained) per Platoon, will report to 2nd Lieut. Thain at the Dumping Station for the purpose of undetonating bombs not required.
(4) In advances under (a) & (b) the bags for carrying grenades will be packed with the bombs in the limbered wagon set aside for this purpose.
(5) The Grenade Officer will detail 4 men from D Company as escort to the Grenade Section wagon.
(6) In the event of an advance under (c) the Platoon Grenadiers will carry 12 bombs in the carriers. They will carry a bandolier and rifle but will not carry packs or equipment. Details as to their equipment will be arranged for by the Grenade Officer.

6. SANITARY SQUAD.
The Sanitary Squad will parade with their Companies.

7. SIGNALLERS.
The following Signallers will parade and move with the Battalion Headquarters:-
Sgt.Yeomans, Cpl.Daffy, L/C.Grainger, L/C.Searles, L/C.Smith, Pte.Setchell, Pte.Jennings, Pte.Jacobs.
The following with A Company:-
L/C.Kirby, Pte.Smith, Pte.Wilson, Pte.Reader.
The following with B Company:-
Pte.Spooner, Pte.Billingham, Pte.Ryman, Pte.Sandles.
The following with C Company:-
Pte.Rally, Pte.Bull, Pte.Stevens, Pte.Hooper.
The following with D Company:-
L/C.Gardner, Pte.Waters, Pte.Barrington, Pte.Jinks.
The following will remain with Brigade Headquarters:-
Pte.Dainter, Pte.Jerram.

8. STRETCHER BEARERS.
(1) In the event of an advance under (a) or (b) the 20 stretcher bearers will march in rear of the Battalion under the Medical Officer.
(2) In the event of an attack under (c) they will remain in their present positions until required.

9. WATER MEN.
The water cart men will be with the water carts in any event.

10. MEDICAL OFFICER's ORDERLIES.
The Medical Officer's Orderlies will report to the Medical Officer.

11. ORDERLY ROOM STAFF.
In the event of an advance under (a) or (b) Sergeant Pelham will accompany the Battalion with first line transport.

12. REGIMENTAL SERGEANT-MAJOR.
The Regimental Sergeant-Major will accompany the Battalion Ammunition Reserve.

13. COMPANY SERGEANT-MAJOR.
In an advance under (a) or (b) Company Sergeant-Majors will be with the Company pack animals. In an advance under (c) they will be at the disposal of Company Commanders.

14. COMPANY QUARTERMASTER-SERGEANTS.
Company Quartermaster-Sergeants will parade with their Companies.

15. OFFICERS' SERVANTS.
The servants of company officers will under (a) and (b) be with their Platoons.
and under (c) with the Company Sergeant-Major for employment as ammunition carriers as may be required.

16. OFFICERS' KITS.
Officers kits (except what they take on an advance, which will be as little as possible) will be packed (<u>ready</u> for returning to baggage wagons at St.Amand) at once.

17. SHOEMAKERS.
The shoemakers will be with the first line transport.

18. COOKS.
Four Company Cooks under Sergeant Beddows will accompany each cooker, the remainder will parade with their companies.

19. TAILORS.
All tailors will parade with their companies and move with them.

20. MACHINE GUN TEAMS.
The second machine gun team, less a reserve of 12 men who will accompany the first team, will parade with their companies till required.

21. QUARTERMASTER'S DEPARTMENT.
Sergeant Heritage will accompany the Battalion under (a) or (b).

22. HEADQUARTER ORDERLIES.
The Commanding Officer's Orderly will accompany the Commanding Officer.
Two orderlies from each Company will be with Battalion Headquarters in any event.

APPENDIX IV.

NORMAL FORM OF ATTACK OF THE DIVISION ON THE ENEMY TRENCHES ON A FRONT OF 1,200 YARDS.

1. Two Brigades will attack each on a front of 600 yards. One Brigade in Divisional Reserve.
2. Each Brigade will attack with three battalions. Each battalion on a front of 200 yards and one battalion in Brigade Reserve.
3. Each battalion will attack with two companies in front and two in support each company on a front of 100 yards.
Each company has two platoons in 1st Line and two platoons in 2nd Line.
Formation:- line of Sections in file - each platoon on a front of 50 yards.
Distance between 1st and 2nd Line - 20 yards,
    "   " and and 3rd Line - 30 yards by night and
                                30 to 50 yards by day.
R.E.(about 25 per battalion) between 2nd and 3rd Lines.
Pioneers and machine guns in rear of 4th Line, advancing from our front trench as soon as the enemy's first trench is taken.
4. One Company(100) R.E., and one Company (200) Pioneers will be allotted to each Brigade carrying out the attack. The remaining two companies Pioneers will be with the Reserve Brigade.
5. The Grenadiers (6 per platoon) of the platoons in the leading two lines will move in front of the 1st Line to cover the Company wire-cutters (who will move with them) when cutting the wire obstacle and, secondly to clear the first trench (enemy) of Germans when taken.

6. The most careful preparations will be made by the Divisional Staff for ensuring complete co-operation between the assaulting columns and the artillery.
The detail cannot be laid down in advance, but the principles will consist, broadly, in the artillery bombarding the enemy's lines of trenches and engaging the hostile artillery and then, at a given signal, when our columns have nearly reached their first objective, increasing their range so as to enable our troops to advance further, under cover of a curtain of our own shells ahead.
7. An objective for the assaulting columns will be given in rear of all the enemy's lines.
8. During the night previous to the assault, all our own wire entanglements will be cleared away or numerous openings prepared in it.
9. If feasible, a starting trench should be dug in front of our own entanglements from which the assaulting parties should start. This trench shoud, of course, be connected by numerous trenches, passing under the parapet, with our front line trenches. It should be asy to get out of.
10. Asembly trenches will be dug, laterally, from the communication trenches, sufficient to hold all the troops required.
11. Large supplies of ammunition and especially of bombs, as well as R.E.stores, will be stored at convenient points in or near our own firing trenches, and their exact location will be explained to the troops.
12. 4 hurdles per front line platoon will be carried for getting over wire entanglements.
13.. Unless the weather is very inclement, men will leave their packs behind.
14. Men will carry their entrenching implements in their belts, and every third man will carry a pick or shovel on his back, through his braces.
15. Every man will carry 200 rounds of ammunition and 2 empty sandbags stuck through his belt.
16. The 1st line when it reaches the enemy's/trench will pass over it and proceed to attack the trenches in rear of it, leaving only some grenadiers (who will be told off beforehand)

to clear the enemy out of it.

17. The 2nd, 3rd & 4th Lines will act in a similar manner. No one in these lines will enter the enemy's first trenches. They will pass over the trench and on to the objective, taking their grenadiers with them. The immediate object of the latter will be to clear the enemy's communication trenches.

18. Machine guns will be pushed forward boldly and act according to circumstances - mainly in making ground good and supporting against counter-attack.

19. the outer flanks of the assaulting battalions will in the first instance be covered by scouts, who will be pushed out a few yards from the flank for the purpose of keeping a sharp lookout and locating danger points between the opposing lines.

20. Whilst the attack is in progress the troops in the front trenches on either falnk of the assaulting parties will keep up an incessant fire to protect their flanks outside the line of scouts.

21. The enemy's first trench will be occupied and prepared for defence by the R.E. and Pioneers; the former will also search at once for mine and connecting wires and will cut them.

22. R.E. and Pioneers will also arrange defences for the protecting of the flanks and begin to prepare communicating trenches connecting the captured trench with our firts line trench.

22. When the first trench has been captured, detachments from the flank battalions, previously told off, will face outwards and working in conjunction with the R.E. and Pioneers, will enfilade, if possible, the hostile trenches on their flanks and prevent their own trench from being enfiladed or bombed. One or two machine guns will be attached to these detachments.

23. Parties will be organized and provided by the Brigade Reserve Battalion for the purpose of bringing up the ammunition, grenades and R.E.Stores, already referred to, to the captured trench as soon as possible.

24. A communication trench, for the purpose of evacuating casualties only, should be dug from front to rear behind each Brigade.

www.ingramcontent.com/pod-product-compliance
Lightning Source LLC
Chambersburg PA
CBHW080925230426
43668CB00014B/2199